day trips® from
phoenix, tucson
& flagstaff

eleventh edition

getaway ideas for the local traveler

pam hait

gpp®
travel

Guilford, Connecticut

To buy books in quantity for corporate use or incentives, call **(800) 962-0973** or e-mail **premiums@GlobePequot.com.**

Editor: Amy Lyons
Project Editor: Meredith Dias
Layout: Mary Ballachino
Text Design: Linda R. Loiewski
Maps: Trailhead Graphics Inc. © Morris Book Publishing, LLC.
Spot photography throughout © David M. Schrader/Shutterstock

Section on Arizona Climate is reprinted with permission from the 1984 *KOY Almanac*, by Pam Hait for KOY radio.

ISSN 1543-0499
ISBN 978-0-7627-6461-7

Printed in the United States of America
10 9 8 7 6 5 4 3 2 1

contents

east

day trip 01

day trip 02

day trip 03

southeast

day trip 01

day trip 02

day trip 03

southwest

day trip 01

west

day trip 01

northwest

day trip 01

part ii: tucson

northeast

day trip 01

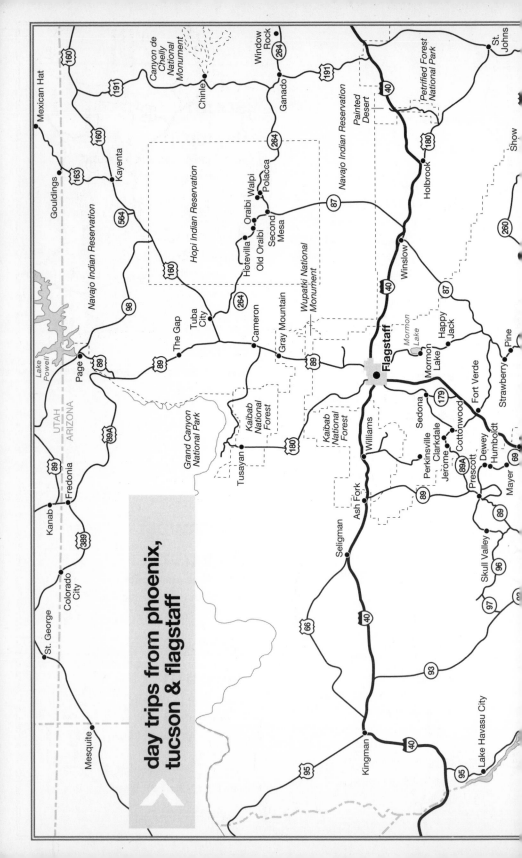

day trips from phoenix, tucson & flagstaff

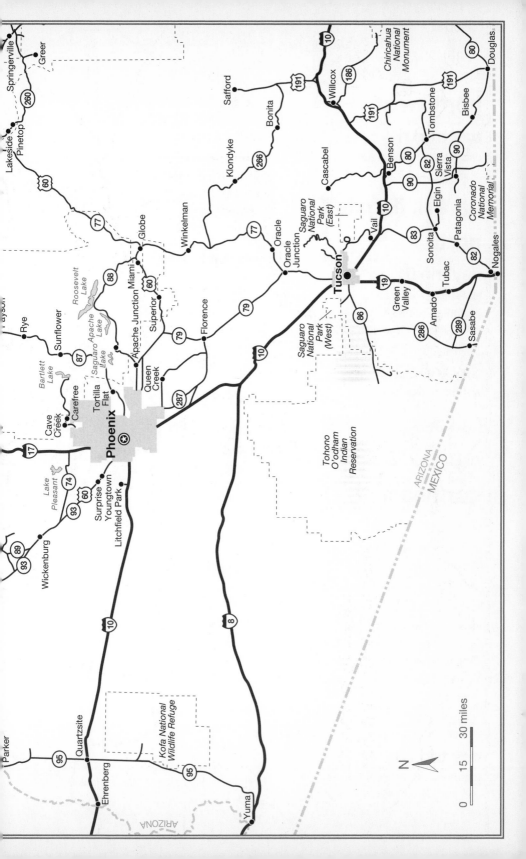

about the author

Pam Hait is a freelance writer and award-winning author of thirteen books. A member of the American Society of Journalists and Authors, she is a graduate of Northwestern University Medill School of Journalism. Pam was a contributing editor to *Metropolitan Home*, covered Arizona for *Sunset* and *Travel & Leisure*, and has written for many national publications. She is a longtime contributor to *Arizona Highways*. Pam and her partner own Strategies, a media relations and marketing firm that focuses on tourism and has special expertise in eco and heritage tourism. Pam and her husband, Dr. Glen Hait, live in Paradise Valley and continue to explore and discover more treasures in Arizona.

introduction

Arizona. The name sings with romance. This is the landscape celebrated in western films where rugged cowboys still ride a vast, rolling range. This is a countryside blessed with sunsets that burst upon the horizon spilling apricot and purple hues as far as you can see. This is a land of immense physical size and unparalleled variety. Mountains and desert, cities and wilderness—Arizona has all of them.

While directions are as clear and exact as possible, you should refer to an Arizona road map as you travel. Write to the Arizona Office of Tourism, 1110 West Washington, Suite 155, Phoenix 85007, or call (866) 275-5816 or visit www.azot.com to request a map. You may also write or call the communities or regional tourism information offices of the specific areas you plan to visit and ask for city maps. Read these and refer to them as you travel. Always note the scale of the map. If you are accustomed to eastern maps, you're in for a shock. With 113,956 square miles of land, Arizona is the 6th largest state in the nation. Only 17 percent of the state is private land. In these wide open spaces, 1 inch on the state road map equals approximately 16 miles!

In addition to its sheer physical size, Arizona is dazzling in its infinite sights, sounds, and moods. In a short 2-hour trip from the urban centers of Phoenix, Tucson, or Flagstaff, you can drive from the floor of the desert to a rocky red precipice and travel in time from prehistoric to frontier days.

There's variety in the climate, too. Travelers should consider both the season and their destinations when they plan day trips in and around the three metropolitan areas. Plan summer trips in the Phoenix area with special caution. Because of its low elevation and irrigated Sonoran Desert location, the capital city can sizzle under extremely hot daytime temperatures from late May through mid-September. Getting in and out of a hot car saps the enthusiasm of even the most dedicated tourist. In contrast, the fall, winter, and early months of spring offer warm days and cool evenings that guarantee almost ideal conditions for driving and sightseeing.

Although Tucson and Phoenix have similar desert climates, because Tucson is about 1,200 feet higher than Phoenix, Tucson's summer temperatures generally are about 10 degrees cooler than those in Phoenix. Tucson is less humid as well, making summer sightseeing more comfortable there than in Phoenix. Winter temperatures in both cities, however, are comparable. If you are visiting there in the hot summer months, don't be surprised if you hear Tucsonians ask, "Have you come to Tucson to cool off?" They are proud of those few degrees!

Flagstaff and northern Arizona offer travelers a radically different experience. Perched at an elevation of more than a mile high, Flagstaff's climate is similar to that of Michigan or Wisconsin. The cold winters can come complete with deep snows, making winter day trips around Flagstaff risky. However, a delightful climate with warm, sunny days and cool evenings makes northern Arizona a perfect vacationland during spring, summer, and fall.

Be prepared for some local idiosyncrasies. For instance, if you ask a direction, you'll generally hear, "It's just 20 minutes down the road," or "That's only a couple hours away." Arizonans measure distance in time more frequently than in miles. And they think nothing of driving 2 hours to a destination—that's hardly even a jaunt—which is why many of the day trips included in this book stretch the 2-hour getaway time to 3 hours and sometimes more.

Once you venture even a few miles outside of the three major cities, you can still encounter open, empty country. This is a treat for people who love the wild, untamed outdoors, but it can pose challenges for those who prefer urban conveniences. One delightful way to handle the great distances when planning day trips is to carry a picnic lunch. Frequently you will find good restaurants few and far between, so you can eat at any of the scenic roadside rest stops. You bring the food; the state provides the ambience, with shaded ramadas and sweeping vistas.

One concern must be mentioned. As of this writing (2010), Arizona, like other states, is undergoing severe budget issues that are expected to continue for several years. Many of the rest stops along the interstate highways that were always available to travelers are closed. Rumor has it they will reopen, but pay attention as you drive and don't assume that they are available to you. If you need to stop, get off the highway when you can drive into a town. Several state parks have also been closed. I will note these in the appropriate day trips but urge you to visit the website and call should you decide to include a park in your itinerary as park closures may change.

Heed the road signs at all times of the year. If you see a warning, NOT RECOMMENDED FOR SEDAN TRAVEL, believe it! Arizona back roads can be rugged and extremely rough on automobiles. When driving through country marked "open range," be alert. Although a rare occurrence, you could encounter loose cows, sheep, or other livestock wandering across the road. Obey both flash-flood warnings and dust-storm warnings. That dry wash may appear harmless, but a wash can quickly turn into a deadly torrent.

Safe driving in the desert demands that travelers take certain precautions. Arid lands can be unforgiving, especially during the hot summer months. During the hot months it's a good idea to carry water in your car for emergencies. You may need it for drinking during the early morning hours or after the sun sets. Always tell someone where you are going and when you expect to return. If you are overdue, somebody will know when to start worrying and can alert the authorities. If you have car problems, stay with your vehicle. Don't wander off for help; let help find you.

Finally, don't hike into the wilderness alone. Even experienced hikers get lost, and GPS may not work in a very remote area.

Despite these precautions, know that every day trip and casual hike in this book is planned so you can enjoy Arizona without running into any of the aforementioned emergency situations. Arizona is not hazardous to your health. If you treat this unique and often untamed landscape with the respect it deserves, you can have safe and exhilarating experiences. What's more, you will be free to appreciate its magnificence and learn to love it as I do.

using this guide

highway designations

Federal highways are designated I or US. State roads use AZ or SR. Forest roads use FR. County roads, truck routes, and Indian routes are identified as such.

hours of operation

In most cases, hours are omitted in the listings because they are subject to frequent changes. Instead, phone numbers and websites are provided for checking up-to-date information.

credit cards

Most of the restaurants and accommodations in this book accept credit cards, unless otherwise noted.

pricing key

Rate for Accommodations

This price code reflects the per-night average cost of a double-occupancy guest room during a peak-price period (not including hotel tax or fees). Always ask if any special packages or discounts are available during your preferred dates. Rates often change seasonally, so be sure to call first for prices.

$ Less than $100

$$ $100 to $200

$$$ More than $200

Rates for Restaurants

This price code reflects the average price of an entree per person (generally dinner unless only breakfast or lunch is served) and does not include wine, beer, cocktails, appetizers, desserts, tax, or tips.

$ Less than $15

$$ $15 to $25

$$$ More than $25

»» part i: phoenix

Welcome to Phoenix, capital city of the state of Arizona and hub of "The Valley of the Sun." The valley is surrounded by mountain ranges, clear cool lakes, and a plethora of four- and five-star resorts. It is a veritable paradise for tourists. Because visitors have such a choice of accommodations, it is suggested that you write to the Arizona Hotel & Lodging Association, 1240 East Missouri Ave, Phoenix 85014-2912, and request a brochure describing the hotels, motels, dude ranches, and cabins in the state. Or you may call (800) 707-3921 or visit www.azhla.com for information.

Because of the way this book is organized, some of the best Phoenix attractions are listed in the section Day Trip 01 Northwest from Tucson. With Phoenix as your starting point, you'll be amazed to discover how much variety awaits you even in a 2-hour drive. Some easy day trips can take you to urban areas, such as Scottsdale, Mesa, Tempe, or even Tucson. On other trips, you can climb quickly from the desert floor to mountainous pine forests, or you can enter a time warp that takes you back to pioneer and ancient Native American eras.

Ideally, visitors to Arizona should plan to spend some vacation time in Phoenix, Tucson, and Flagstaff, taking day trips from each. In this way, you'll get a true flavor of the state. A second plan could include Phoenix as your hub, because it is centrally located and is the largest metropolitan area in the state. As you journey around the Phoenix environs, you'll soon discover that many of the Phoenix-based trips easily fall within the 2-hour limitation. In some cases, you'll need to drive longer than 2 hours; however, each trip is worth it.

If you use Flagstaff as your starting point for several of the Phoenix-based day trips, you can cut your travel time by an hour or even more. As you read along, you'll note that many of the itineraries described can be done as an overnight instead of a single day's journey. If you have the time, it's always nice to stay over in a destination town. That way you can spend more hours seeing the sights and exploring the area, and proportionately less time on the road.

One last piece of advice: As you peruse the Phoenix section of this book, you'll read about sights to see, canyons to explore, side roads to wander along, shops not to miss, and special trips to take. In your enthusiasm to do it all, don't overload yourself. This is especially true when traveling during the summer, because the high desert temperatures can be extremely tiring. If you decide to visit a museum or Native American ruin, allow enough time

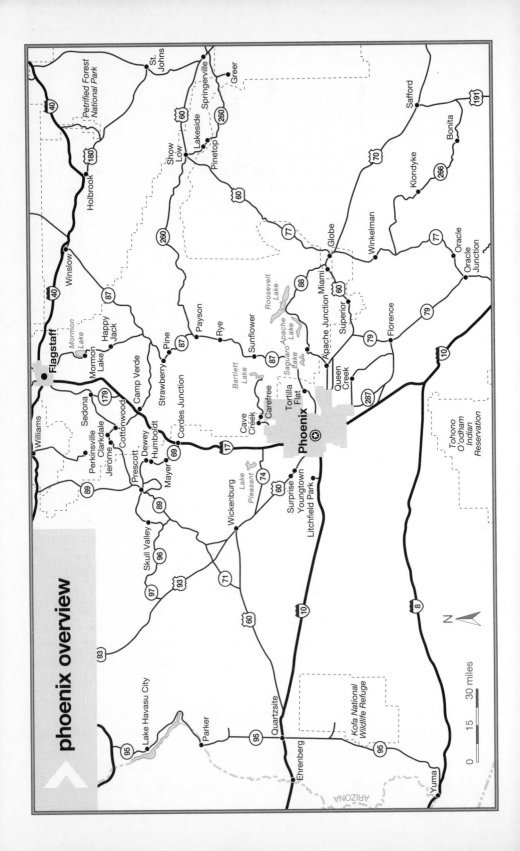

phoenix overview

to study the exhibits or soak up the atmosphere of a few selected attractions rather than rushing from point to point. The essential Arizona experience is a casual, laid-back lifestyle. Whether sitting at a sidewalk cafe in Scottsdale or standing silently before Montezuma Castle, don't push yourself to cover too much too fast.

Visitors always want to know how to pack for a destination. You are right in style if you dress casually in Arizona. Very few restaurants require men to wear a tie and jacket. During the winter months, evenings are cool, so women should bring a wrap. You need to know that one of the defining characteristics of a desert is the temperature change from day to night, so expect cool winter nights even if daytime desert temperatures are warm enough that you can go swimming.

For brochures, maps, and specific information on the fascinating Phoenix metropolitan area, contact the Phoenix & Valley of the Sun Convention & Visitors Bureau, 1 Arizona Center, 400 East Van Buren St., Suite 600, Phoenix 85004; call (602) 254-6500 or (877) Call-PHX; or log on to www.visitphoenix.com. The Downtown Phoenix Visitor Information Center is located at 125 North 2nd St., Suite 120. Open daily.

north >>>

day trip 01

north

the victorian heart of arizona:
prescott
worth more time: prescott to
ash fork to seligman (and on to
kingman) via historic route 66

prescott

This trip covers some of the same territory found in Day Trip 02 North from Phoenix. However, in this itinerary, Prescott is your destination. Prescott calls itself "Everybody's Home Town," which is more a statement about its style and ambience than its population. If you've never been to Prescott, or if it's been a few years, be ready for a surprise. This town has grown in size and sophistication, making if a "must" for visitors and Arizona residents.

A pine-studded jewel of a town 2 hours north of Phoenix and once the capital of the Territory of Arizona, it is the seat of Yavapai County. Since there are so many scenic drives in the Prescott area, and so many good restaurants and shops, along with art shows, festivals, and hiking, you may want to plan an overnight here. But you can also cover much of this in a day trip.

The town of Prescott was founded not too long after gold was discovered in nearby hills in 1863—the same year that Abraham Lincoln signed an act to create the Arizona Territory. Prescott has approximately 525 buildings on the National Register of Historic Places and is a favorite destination for Phoenix residents who enjoy the cool summer days, when Prescott's high temperatures average in the '80s. Visitors will especially enjoy the Fourth of July weekend, when Prescott's rodeo is held. This is billed as the "World's Oldest Rodeo" parade and festivities.

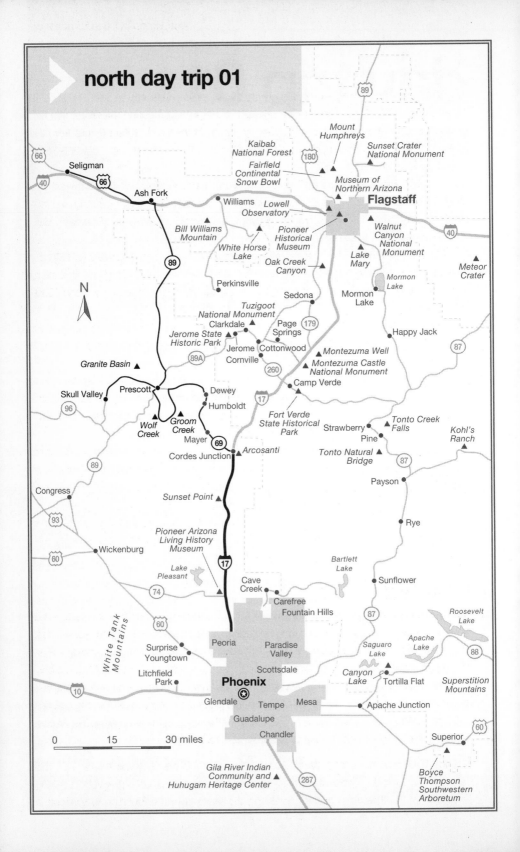

N

The temperature in Prescott is generally about 20 degrees cooler than Phoenix, so it's always safe to take a sweater or lightweight jacket with you during the winter months. Festivals and celebrations occur during every month of the year. Obtain details from the Prescott Chamber of Commerce at 117 West Goodwin St., Prescott; call (800) 266-7534; or visit www.prescott.org.

To reach Prescott, follow I-17 north to Cordes Junction. Take AZ 69 northwest and meander past the small towns of Mayer, Humboldt, Dewey, and the fast-growing community of Prescott Valley. Don't be dismayed by the sprawling development in Prescott Valley. In a few more miles you'll see the charming town of Prescott.

Mayer is located in the foothills of the Bradshaw Mountains. Founded in 1881 by Joseph Mayer, it was established as a store, saloon, and Wells Fargo Stagecoach station, a stop along the stage line between Phoenix and Prescott. Today, it is a stop along AZ 69 for motorists.

Enter Prescott on AZ 69 west until it meets Gurley Street. Travel left on Gurley past Marina Street, and you're in the heart of town. Park anywhere between Cortez and Montezuma Streets for your tour of this historic area.

As you gaze at the gingerbread homes and tall brick buildings, you may think that Prescott is an unlikely Arizona town. Remember that the desert, with its low-slung adobe structures, is only one Arizona image. In the more northern parts of the state, two-story brick and wood buildings are just as appropriately an "Arizona" style.

Here territorial Arizona springs to life. Prescott flourished when the area was a wild and untamed place. As military personnel and miners moved in, no doubt they were anxious to make it seem like home, so they built what they knew: "back-East" buildings, proper brick and two-story structures reminiscent of Ohio or Pennsylvania.

The first capital of the Arizona Territory, Prescott ultimately lost its bid to become the permanent state capital; the honor went to Phoenix instead. Still, much Arizona history was made here and, fortunately for visitors, remains well preserved.

where to go

Courthouse Plaza. This is the area bounded by Cortez and Montezuma, Gurley and Goodwin Streets. It's a real town square that functions much as it did during territorial times. During festivals, the grassy square is lined with booths, and people sprawl on the lawns. In more quiet times, you can soak up the serenity that the solid courthouse building exudes. The statue is of Bucky O'Neil, a newspaper publisher who became mayor and led the volunteer cavalry up San Juan Hill in 1898. Wander through the streets to explore the galleries and stores. Although Prescott is a tourist mecca, it has resisted ticky-tacky tourist shops. You'll find a real community here, not cardboard storefront images.

Sharlot Hall Museum. 415 West Gurley St.; (928) 445-3122; www.sharlot.org. This museum is actually a number of separate buildings grouped together to give visitors a living panorama of Southwestern history. Spanning the years from the founding of Prescott in

1864 to the present, the buildings appear to be in architectural sequence. You can tour the Governor's Mansion, which was built on this site in 1864 from local ponderosa pine. Several territorial officials, including Governor John Goodwin, lived in this mansion.

The John C. Fremont House. Built in 1875, it is constructed of wood and reflects the rapid growth Prescott experienced during its first 10 years. Fremont, known as "the Pathfinder," served as the 5th territorial governor of Arizona from 1878 to 1881.

Arizona became a state on February 14, 1912. The **William C. Bashford House** represents the type of architecture common to the area during the 2 decades before statehood. Complete with a solarium, this house was built in another location and moved to the museum grounds in 1974.

The **Sharlot Hall** building, completed in 1934, is the primary exhibit hall and includes the Museum Shop and display rooms for pre-Columbian artifacts, historic Southwestern items, and old photographs. These pictures capture the essence of what it was like for white and red men to live in this territory more than 100 years ago. This exhibit is all the more remarkable when you realize that Native Americans feared—and some still do fear—the camera, believing that it takes away a person's soul.

Who was Sharlot Hall that an entire enclave of a museum is devoted to her? She was an outstanding woman—a writer, poet, collector of Arizona artifacts, and territorial historian—who moved to Arizona from Kansas in 1882. She remained fascinated with Arizona until her death in 1943.

As you stroll along the sidewalks, which circle and connect the museum's major buildings, you can visit other memorials and exhibits, including the Blacksmith Shop; one of the town's first boardinghouses, which the frontiersmen called "Fort Misery"; a replica

arizona at its historic best

On a recent trip to Prescott, I was impressed by the number and variety of fun restaurants and boutiques that line the square, and the absence of the usual chain retailers. My husband and I discovered some terrific new art galleries, a shop devoted to gourmet balsamic vinegars and olive oil, and an array of antiques stores definitely worth your attention. The art galleries are now so numerous that, during the spring and summer, Prescott has art walks on the fourth Friday of the month. But none of the new, upscale businesses detract from the old Prescott charm, which is still the heart of the experience. One happy surprise was learning that the historic Hotel Vendome has been updated by a young couple who are bringing the property back to its former glory, replete with a color palette that is on the National Historic Registry list. Our day exploring Prescott inspired us to plan an overnight trip there soon.

of Prescott's first public school; and the Pioneer Herb and Memorial Rose garden. The museum is open daily. Fee.

Smoki Museum. 147 North Arizona St.; (928) 445-1230; www.smokimuseum.org. Designed to resemble a Native American pueblo, this museum opened to the public in 1935. It houses collections of pre-Columbian and contemporary pottery; pre-Columbian jewelry of shell, stone, and turquoise; and an outstanding collection of basketry, kachinas, stone artifacts, and textiles from the Southwest. A collection of war bonnets, costumes, and beadwork is from the Plains Indians. Open daily. Tour groups are welcome. Visitors can also arrange tours by appointment. Fee.

Phippen Museum of Western Art. 4701 AZ 89 North; (928) 778-1385; www.phippen artmuseum.org. George Phippen was one of the founders of Cowboy Artists of America. Western-art buffs will enjoy the collection of works by Phippen and other Cowboy Artists, including Joe Beeler and Frank Polk. Bronzes, paintings, and Native American arts and crafts are on display, and special exhibitions are mounted. A major art show and sale on Courthouse Plaza are held every Memorial Day. Closed Mon. Tours available by appointment. Fee; children under 12 free.

Whiskey Row. Montezuma between Goodwin and Aubrey Streets. This is Prescott's famous "wicked" street—the name says it all. Everyone needs to walk up Whiskey Row, even if he or she isn't thirsty. Today it is more sedate, except during festivals and celebrations. Then the Old West springs to life again as cowboys belly up to the crowded bars.

Prescott Historical Tours. Prescott and the Bradshaw Mountains. In 1981 Melissa Ruffner, dressed in authentic period costumes, began giving tours of Arizona's first territorial capitol. Since then, she has offered walking tours of the 4-block historical district. Call ahead to find out more about this trip. Wear comfortable shoes. Ask about the couples tour. Fee. Contact Melissa Ruffner, (928) 445-4567.

where to stay

Hassayampa Inn. 122 East Gurley St.; (928) 778-9434 or (800) 322-1927; www.hassa yampainn.com. Established in 1927, this is Prescott's historic grand hotel. It is centrally located in the heart of town and offers a step back in time to the West of 1927. Rooms are spacious and accented with lace curtains, comforters, and period furniture. Charming and comfortable, the inn provides complimentary breakfast in the graceful Peacock Dining Room. $$–$$$.

Hotel Vendome. 230 South Cortez St.; (928) 776-0900 or (888) 468-3583; www.vendome hotel.com. Built in 1917, this historic hotel with 20 guest rooms is being carefully restored by its owners. All rooms offer either king- or queen-size beds, and guests may choose rooms with garden tub/shower, which are updated bathrooms, or rooms with original claw-foot tubs and showers. The property has original, working transom windows, paneled wainscoting, and the original second-story veranda with seating. Continental breakfast includes homemade butters prepared by the young owners. It's served in the lobby where an original "enunciator" still works to buzz rooms. They will tell you how the cowboy silent-film star Tom Mix stayed here years ago when he was making movies at Granite Dells. $$.

where to shop

Downtown Prescott. Prescott is a great place to hunt for antiques and "treasures." In addition, Prescott has attracted many boutiques along with fine-art and craft galleries. Here are just a few favorites close to Courthouse Square.

Antique and collectibles district. Antiquers will want to walk along North Cortez where many antique and collectible shops are clustered. Pick up a free guide and map at any of the shops. Quality is high, and prices are reasonable.

Arts Prescott Cooperative Gallery. 134 South Montezuma St.; (928) 776-7717; www.artsprescott.com. Founded in 1994 by a group of local artists and craftspeople, this is member owned and operated. The quality of the work is outstanding and includes jewelry, clothing, paintings, pottery, photography, and decorative treasures.

Ian Russell Gallery of Fine Art. Old Firehouse Plaza, 220 West Goodwin; (928) 445-7009; www.ianrussellart.com. Showing original art and prints by artist Ian Russell and others, this gallery is Prescott's only fine-art *giclée* reproduction shop. You can bring in your own art or photos, and they will reproduce it on art tiles, plaques, and cutting boards as well as on photography and watercolor papers and canvas.

The Llama House. 108 South Montezuma; (928) 445-9689. This is a lovely women's shop that has clothing and accessories.

Olive U Naturally. Bashford Court, 130 West Gurley, Unit 203; (928) 778-2337; www .oliveunaturally.com. Opened in November 2009, this shop sells balsamic vinegars and extra-virgin olive oils. The owners are enthusiastic and knowledgeable and suggest pairings that will bring out the best in meats, fish, and pasta as well as salads. Olive oils and vinegars are imported from Tunisia, France, Italy, Spain, and California. Tastings are complementary, and once you sample the offerings, it is difficult not to bring them all home!

Van Gogh's Ear. 156 South Montezuma; (928) 776-1080; http://vgegallery.com. A fine-art gallery featuring many local as well as international artists, Van Gogh's Ear presents an outstanding collection of contemporary art. Jewelry and one-of-a-kind art clothing are also exhibited.

scenic drive

Granite Dells. Drive east on Gurley Street and north on AZ 89 for about 4 miles. Just north of Prescott, nature has carved a sculpture garden of ancient rock formations. As you approach, you'll notice that the rocks appear to have human or animal forms. That's Mother

Nature, the artist, at work. Centuries of wind, rain, snow, and sun worked on these granite cliffs to form eerie figures. Formerly known as the "Point of Rocks," the Granite Dells is set off by Watson Lake, a clear blue pool that contrasts vividly with the subtle colors of the smooth, round boulders.

Granite Mountain and Granite Basin. This trip will take about 20 minutes each way. Drive west on Gurley Street to Grove Avenue. Turn right on Grove and continue out Miller Valley Road. Bear left at the junction of Iron Springs and Willow Creek Roads onto Iron Springs and continue to the Prescott National Forest sign on the right side of the road. Turn right and continue to Granite Basin Recreation Area, a unique geological and historical wilderness area. Long before Congress declared the Granite Mountain Trail a National Recreation Area in 1979, hikers and rock climbers were well acquainted with its spectacular scenery. If you are in good shape and dressed for outdoor action, you can hike to the overlook. Otherwise, walk along the trails and marvel at the sheer, smooth cliffs.

Lynx Lake. Fifty-five acres of lake just 15 minutes away! Follow AZ 69 east for 4 miles to Walker Road. Turn right for approximately 3 miles. Lynx Lake, which is fed by nearby Lynx Creek, has a rich history. Gold was discovered at the creek during territorial days, giving the men and women of the frontier even more reason to make the trip to Prescott. Fishing is good year-round, and during the summer, you can rent a boat from the lakefront conces-sion. Take your sweetheart on a moonlight cruise across the smooth, clear waters.

Senator Highway Drive. This is an hour's round-trip that's well worth it, especially if you like to relive history. Drive east on Gurley Street to South Mount Vernon/Senator Highway. Along the way, you'll pass by Groom Creek, which was a Mormon settlement. Turn right on South Mount Vernon/Senator Highway and head south to Wolf Creek picnic grounds. If you are so inclined, head for either Wolf Creek or Lower Wolf Creek campgrounds, where you can hike, picnic, or do some four-wheeling on all-terrain vehicles (ATVs) if you trailer them in with you. Continue following this road to the right as it goes down the pine-studded mountain to the Indian Creek picnic grounds. Join AZ 89 6 miles from Prescott. Turn right and continue back to town. This used to be an old stage route that connected Prescott with Crown Point. As you make this drive, you can imagine how the pioneers felt as they bounced along on rutted roads shaded by these tall ponderosas.

Skyline Drive (also called Thumb Butte Loop). Plan on 45 minutes to cover this truly spectacular drive. Head south on Montezuma Street (AZ 89) to Copper Basin Road. Turn right on Copper Basin Road, make a circle, and return to Thumb Butte Road. Along the way, you will see the Sierra Prieta Mountain range, which overlooks Skull Valley. As you approach Thumb Butte, you'll have a panoramic view of the San Francisco Peaks. These mountains are sacred to the Hopis, who believe that these peaks are home to their kachina gods. During this drive, you'll ascend some 1,500 to 1,700 vertical feet. If you think this is a steep drive, imagine what it's like to run up this road. The Whiskey Row Marathon Society uses it as its course.

Along the way, you'll see a number of places to pull off to drink in the views. Be sure to do so when you see a viewpoint for Skull Valley. The name, Skull Valley, came from a group of cavalrymen who discovered mounds of sun-bleached skulls there in 1884. Later it was decided that these were the skulls of Apache and Maricopa Indians who clashed over stolen horses.

If you're dressed properly and not bothered by the altitude, take advantage of the hiking trails. These are well marked. A 2⅓-mile trail leads to Thumb Butte. It begins easily. For almost a mile you can stroll along shaded ponderosa pines and three kinds of oak trees. Gradually, the vegetation changes . . . the pines recede, and junipers, prickly pears, piñons, and other scrub vegetation gain on you as the trail approaches the exposed ridge. You'll come to a junction at 1¹⁄₁₀ miles. To the left, the trail rises to the base of the butte. This climb involves 200 feet of steep cliff and is not recommended for nonclimbers. Instead, hikers should follow the right fork and continue about 150 yards to a vista point. When you reach it, you'll understand why you've made this trip.

The city of Prescott is virtually surrounded by the Prescott National Forest. Just a few minutes outside of town are campgrounds, picnic sites, lakes, and areas for nearly every kind of outdoor activity, including exploring, prospecting, rockhounding, backpacking, horseback riding, and fishing. If you do any of these drives, wear comfortable shoes so you can get out of the car and walk around.

where to eat

Dinner Bell. 321 West Gurley St.; (928) 445-9888. Locals know this is one of the best places in town to enjoy breakfast and lunch. It's tucked beside the creek just a block or so off the square. Food is home cooked and healthy, and an inviting outdoor patio makes it hard to leave. Chef/owner is Ben Alvarez. No credit cards. $.

Murphy's. 201 North Cortez St.; (928) 445-4044. www.murphysrestaurant.com. In this general-store setting, you can munch on mesquite-broiled seafood or chow down on a variety of entrees, including excellent prime rib. $$.

Palace Saloon. 120 South Montezuma St.; (928) 541-1996. www.historicpalace.com. Go through the swinging doors into Arizona's most historic saloon. First opened in September 1877, the Palace Saloon set a new standard for Prescott's Whiskey Row. When most of Prescott burned on July 14, 1900, the Palace was reduced to ashes. Rebuilt in 1901, it reopened on June 2, and today it continues to welcome visitors to the oldest frontier bar in the state. $–$$

Raven Café. 142 North Cortez; (928) 717-0009. www.ravenscafe.com. An excellent organic cafe with art-lined walls, the Raven offers inside dining and an upstairs, open-air patio. Board games are available for customers to play while waiting for their made-to-order food. A long bar occupies the center of the restaurant, which features 35 beers on tap and 350 brands in bottles, a selection of international brews that wows even the most sophisticated beer lover. Open daily for breakfast, lunch, and dinner. $–$$.

The Rose Restaurant. 234 South Cortez; (928) 777-8308. www.theroserestaurant.com. Serving continental cuisine with an excellent wine list. Have a delightful romantic dinner and choose to eat on the Victorian porch, outdoor patio, or in the main house. $$$.

worth more time:

Granite Creek Vineyards. 2515 Road 1 East, Chino Valley; (928) 636-2003; http://myweb .cableone.net/gcvineyard. From Prescott, follow AZ 89 north to Chino Valley. Turn right at the stoplight to Road 3 North and follow to the end, approximately 2 miles to Road 1 East. The entrance is ½ mile on the right-hand side of the road. This award-winning vineyard and winery is family owned and, like many of Arizona's small wineries, is gaining a good reputation. There's a lovely place to picnic. Tastings are held Fri, Sat, and Sun from 1–5 p.m.

prescott to ash fork to seligman (and on to kingman) via historic route 66

Arizona has the longest stretch, 158 miles, of unbroken Route 66 in existence in the country. You can take the old Route 66 all the way to California. From Prescott, follow AZ 89 toward Ash Fork, which bills itself as the "Flagstone Capital" of the United States. Pick up I-40 west and continue to exit 139, Crookton Road. Turn onto the highway that was known as"America's Main Street." You'll know you are on the right road when you see re-created Burma Shave signs.

Continue to Seligman, which was a railroad town for the Santa Fe Railroad. In the 1920s it flourished as a stop along Route 66. When the interstate bypassed Seligman, it refused to die and reinvented itself as a Route 66 experience. One favorite stop is the Snow Cap with its quirky menu. Built out of scrap lumber by Angelo Delgadillo, this drive-in has an international reputation, mostly thanks to the friendly antics of Delgadillo. Another stop should be the Route 66 Gift Shop and Visitors Bureau. From Seligman, you can continue west through the Aubrey Valley and on to Kingman where you can overnight. Along the way, you may visit Grand Canyon Caverns and the Haulapai Reservation. Kingman has a Route 66 Museum and the Historic Route 66 Association of Arizona. Or, return to Prescott.

day trip 02

north

time travel from an ancient site to a new city:
pioneer arizona living history museum, cordes junction, camp verde, montezuma castle national monument, montezuma well, Jerome

pioneer arizona living history museum

Prepare to move through time from a prehistoric era to the future. The drive begins in rolling desert but climbs into steep mountain terrain in Jerome. You'll begin with endless vistas, and, as the mountains close in around you, saguaros give way to scrub and ultimately to sycamores. This landscape is filled with silent memories of the Sinaguas, an ancient Native American tribe who lived here hundreds of years ago. During the late 1800s, this country-side was alive with the ring of picks and shovels and the shouts of prospectors who worked in Rawhide Jimmy Douglas's silver mines.

Although the driving time from Phoenix to Jerome is 3 hours, this is considered a full-day trip in this land of wide-open spaces. Should you choose to hike and sightsee, you'll arrive home in the evening tired but happy.

Start off early and take I-17 north toward Camp Verde to the Pioneer Arizona Living History Museum. Plan to arrive around 9 a.m. to do this trip easily in a day.

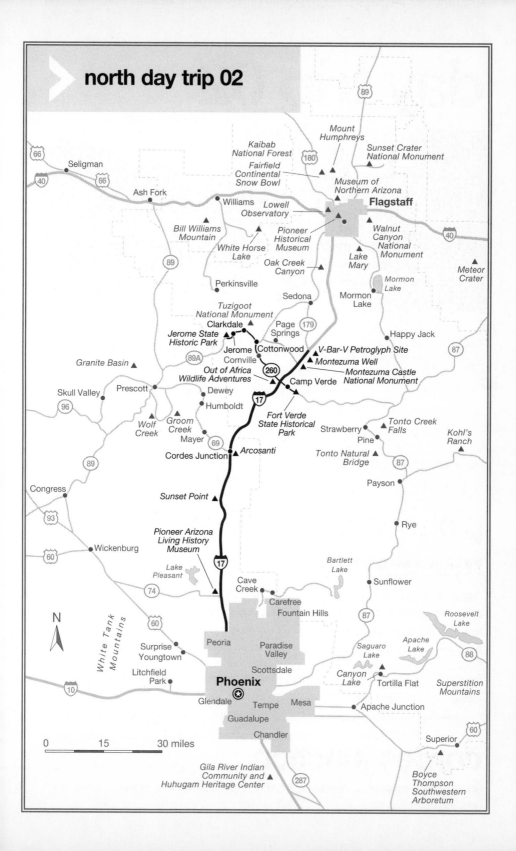

north day trip 02

arcosanti architecture

I have always been a fan of Paolo Soleri, who has devoted much of his life to creating an alternative way to live in cities. Paolo, as of late 2010, is 91 years old and refuses to call himself either a philosopher or a futurist. He describes himself "an earthling." Much better known and respected in Europe and Asia than in the United States., his long-held view that we can live well by conserving our resources and living together more densely has long been seen as an idealistic vision rather than a mainstream concept. Yet the dream has persisted and you can experience it at Arcosanti. A believer in the power of cities to serve humanity, Soleri and his students are still building their view of a better way to live on this planet in Cordes Junction. Part medieval, part futuristic, it's the perfect comple-ment to Montezuma Castle, the multistoried Indian ruin built by the pre-Colum-bian Sinaguan Indians that is nearby. One word of warning: if you expect to see a "city," you'll be disappointed. Arcosanti is just a fraction of what Soleri envisioned, but even this piece is fascinating. Paolo once told me that he might not have per-severed if he knew at the beginning that he would depend upon the sale of Soleri wind bells to finance the construction of Arcosanti. Happily for those of us who enjoy architecture and design, it continues to be built mostly by young volunteers. While you are in this "neighorobood," don't miss the mining town of Jerome. The drive up the mountain to town alone is worth the trip.

where to go

Pioneer Arizona Living History Museum. 3901 West Pioneer Rd., Black Canyon Free-way and Pioneer Road; (623) 465-1052; www.pioneer-arizona.com. On I-17, 12 miles north of Bell Road, take exit 225 and follow signs to the museum. You'll spend a good hour tour-ing the many authentic and replicated buildings on the grounds of this privately supported museum. Although a restaurant exists here, it's closed Tues. A shaded picnic area is always open. Open Wed to Sun. Call for hours. Fee.

Sunset Point. Follow the signs back to I-17 north. You may want to stop for a breathtaking view at this unique roadside rest stop, winner of an architectural award for excellence. Along with a sweeping panorama, you'll find a map, clean restrooms, and picnic tables.

cordes junction

On I-17 north, continue to the Cordes Junction exit and Arcosanti, where you can visit a unique construction site.

where to go

Arcosanti. I-17 at Cordes Junction, Mayer; (928) 632-7135; www.arcosanti.org. Turn right at Cordes Junction Road and left at the stop sign. Follow a dirt road about 3 miles to Arcosanti—architect Paolo Soleri's vision of an alternative future. Called the boldest experiment in urban living in the country, this energy-efficient town, which integrates architecture and ecology, has been under construction since 1970.

Soleri coined the word *arcology* to express his vision of a community in which people can live and work in harmony with the environment. In designing this prototype "city" under a single roof, Soleri combines an urban environment with a natural setting all within one structure. Ultimately, Soleri's plan utilizes space both above and under ground to concentrate human activity into an energy-efficient environment while carefully leaving the vast surrounding acreage natural and undisturbed. The idea was revolutionary when it was first published. But as we are learning more about the interdependency of mankind and our environment, Soleri's concept of how to best integrate human acitivty into the natural world seems more realistic every day. Arcosanti is being built by students and professionals who work and attend seminars on the site. Workshops are open to the general public. Festivals and performances by visiting artists are scheduled during the year. Stop at the bakery and buy some of the excellent homemade breads and baked goods. Fee for guided tours only, which are on the hour, daily.

where to eat

The Cafe. (928) 632–7135. The Cafe at Arcosanti serves breakfast, lunch, and dinner buffets featuring homemade foods prepared without preservatives or additives. The cafe is not fancy, but the food is hearty and healthful. $–$$.

camp verde

As you follow I-17 north, it plunges into a long downgrade that reveals the Verde Valley in all its splendor. Camp Verde (www.pr.state.az.us) is located near the geographical center of the state. Settled in 1864, it is the oldest town in the Verde Valley, literally growing up around what is now Fort Verde State Historical Park. If you've not been this way before, pull off at the marked scenic viewpoints and enjoy grand vistas along the way to this historic area.

where to go

Alcantara Vineyards. 7500 Alcantara Way, Verde Valley; (928) 649-8463 or (888) 569-0756; www.alcantaravineyard.com. From I-17, follow AZ 260 to Thousand Trails Road. Jog onto East Alcantara Way, which is a dirt road leading to the winery. Alcantara Winery is surrounded by 87 acres of property at the confluence of the Verde River and Oak Creek and is the vision of its owner and proprietor, Barbara Predmore. She and her husband,

Bob, started the winery with a vision to make serious wines. The winery offers 12 different varietal's handcrafted from wine grapes grown here. Wine tours are scheduled Fri and Sat at 11:30 a.m. The tasting room is open daily. Fee.

Fort Verde State Historical Park. 125 East Hollamon St.; (928) 567-3275; http://azstate parks.com/Parks/FOVE/index.html. Take the first Camp Verde exit 287; follow that road into Camp Verde; and turn right at AZ 260. Turn left at the light at Main Street and go approximately 1 mile to Hollamon Street; turn right and follow the signs approximately 1 block to the entrance on the right. Visit the ten-acre Fort Verde Historical Park and see where Gen. George Crook accepted the surrender of Apache Chief Chalipun and 300 of his warriors in 1873. Crook left a distinctive mark on Arizona. In addition to his meeting with the Apache chief, the general had a rough wagon road cut up along the Mogollon rim in 1884 to shorten the distance between Fort Apache and Fort Verde. Even today, that area is referred to as Crook's Trail.

Fort Verde was a major base for General Crook's scouts, soldiers, and pack mules during the Native American campaigns of the 1870s. As you walk along the dusty street of Officers' Row, you'll return to territorial days and better understand what it was like for the officers and their families who lived at Fort Verde during this period in history.

Self-guided tours of the officers' quarters overlooking the parade ground, which are furnished in authentic 1880s military style, are available. Open Thur to Mon, except Christmas. At the time of this writing, many Arizona state parks have been closed or operate with reduced hours because of budget issues. Please visit the Arizona State Park website (http://azstateparks.com) for hours of operation. Fee.

Out of Africa Wildlife Adventures. 3505 Camp Verde Bridgeport Hwy.; (928) 567-2840; www.outofafricapark.com. Approximately one-and-a-half hours north of Phoenix, take I-17 north to exit 287 (AZ 260 toward Cottonwood). Turn left (west) over the freeway. Go west 3 miles on AZ 260. Turn left on Cherry Road and take an immediate right on Commonwealth Drive. Follow signs to the park entrance. Visitors can walk or ride through this wild-animal park and enjoy daily shows. You will see animals from around the world living in natural, spacious (but caged) habitats. An adventure experience for children and adults alike, the park bills itself as "Just Like Africa in the Heart of Arizona." Open daily except Thanksgiving and Christmas Days. Fee.

San Dominique Winery. Located off I-17 north and AZ 169, Cherry Road exit; (602) 549-9787; www.garlicparadise.com Established in 1978, this Verde Valley winery is equally well-known for its garlic and garlic products. There's even a "Fiesta Garlica" to celebrate the humble bulb. The vineyard is located about 11 miles south of Camp Verde and is a fun place to stop and shop for San Dominique wines and more than 65 garlic-related items. Open daily.

montezuma castle national monument

To travel further back in time, take exit 289 (Middle Verde Road) off I-17 and follow Montezuma Castle Road 5 miles north from Camp Verde to Montezuma Castle National Monument. The ancient, five-story Native American dwelling is carved out of a great limestone cliff. Although Native Americans lived in the valley as early as AD 600, it's believed that Sinagua farmers began building this dwelling sometime during the 12th century AD. When it was completed about 3 centuries later, the dwelling contained 19 rooms, many of them suitable for living space.

The name Montezuma Castle is a misnomer. Montezuma, the Aztec king, never slept here. In fact, he was never here at all. When pioneers discovered the cliff dwelling, they mistook it for an ancient Aztec settlement and named it Montezuma Castle.

Stop at the visitor center first before taking the self-guided tour. Take time to view the hand-fitted stone walls and foot-thick sycamore ceiling beams; let your imagination fly.

The grounds offer shady picnic spots. Open daily. Fee. (928) 567-3322; www.nps.gov /moca.

montezuma well

Back on I-17 north, continue a few miles to the McGuireville exit. Follow the side road to Montezuma Well, but be ready for a bumpy, rough ride. This limestone sink was formed centuries ago by a collapsed cavern. Springs feed it continuously, and both the Hohokam Indians (who settled the Phoenix area in pre-Columbian times) and the Sinagua used the well for crop irrigation.

Just below the well are cliff dwellings built by the Sinagua Indians, the northern neighbors of the Hohokam Indians who once inhabited the Salt River Valley. The Sinaguans left no written records, so their culture is interpreted only from archaeological evidence and the study of the Hopi, who are believed to be their descendants. A hiking trail follows the rim of the sinkhole and then descends to the water's edge, where more Sinaguan ruins can be seen. The rim trail is well marked with informational markers that describe native plants. The trail ultimately leads to the creek, where the water from the well emerges through an underground passageway.

This area contains a Hohokam pit house, built around AD 1100, and Sinaguan dwellings. It's estimated that around 150 to 200 Sinaguans lived here between AD 1125 and AD 1400, when apparently they were forced out by a drought. Montezuma Well is free. Open daily. (928) 567-3322; www.nps.gov/moca.

where to go

V-Bar-V Ranch Petroglyph Site. Located 2⁸/₁₀ miles east of I-17 and AZ 179, the entrance is on your right less than a half mile past the Beaver Creek Campgound. (928) 282-4119; www.redrockcountry.org/recreation/cultural/v-bar-v.shtml. This is a wonderful prehistoric rock art site with hundreds of drawings on the side of a rock cliff. Access is easy, just a short walk from the parking area. A visitor center and bookstore are about 100 yards from the parking area. Open Fri through Mon. Fee. You can buy a $5 Red Rock Pass, which is available on-site, or show your National Park pass.

jerome

This area is as rich in lore as it was in ore. Although the steep ascent into Jerome is not for the faint of heart, the climb is replete with expansive views of the broad Verde Valley. In the distance you can see the Red Rocks of Sedona and even the far-off San Francisco Peaks in Flagstaff.

This is an unforgettable "living" ghost town that is perched atop Mingus Mountain (7,743 feet). Jerome was established in 1883 as a mining camp on the side of Cleopatra Hill and, over the next 70 years, its mines produced over $1 billion in copper, gold, and silver. Like Tombstone, Jerome was a "Wild West" town. Men came to find gold; women came to find men.

Underneath the town, more than 100 miles of subterranean tunnels and shafts honeycomb the mountain where miners tore out copper, gold, and silver. As mining boomed, people poured in and built glorious residences fit for an eastern city. In 1903 the *New York Sun* proclaimed Jerome "the wickedest town in the West." By 1935, however, the price of copper had tumbled to 5 cents per pound, and the United Verde mine closed. The town's modern history began in 1967 when Jerome was designated as a Historic District, and in 1976 it became a National Historic Landmark.

Today the twisted, narrow streets, reminiscent of Europe, inspire even the most unimaginative photographer, so bring your camera.

To get to Jerome from Montezuma Well or Montezuma Castle, backtrack to I-17 south. Pick up AZ 260 at I-17 and head northwest for 12 to 15 miles toward Jerome. Just north of Cottonwood, AZ 260 joins AZ 89A; follow AZ 89A into Jerome.

where to go

Gold King Mine and Museum. Located 1 mile northwest of Jerome on Perkinsville Road; (928) 634-0053; www.goldkingmineghosttown.com. See miners' cages and artifacts displayed, as well as an outdoor exhibit of a turn-of-the-20th-century mining camp. Open daily Apr to Nov. Fee.

Jerome State Historic Park. Douglas Road; (928) 634-5381; http://azstateparks.com /Parks/JERO/index.html. Originally the home of mining pioneer James S. Douglas, this state park features an extensive display of mining equipment. Follow UVX Road to the park, where exhibits recounting the story of this once-flourishing copper-mining community are displayed. As you browse through the mansion of "Rawhide" Jimmy, you'll gain a sense of the personalities, places, and technology that forged this period of Arizona history. Retrace your steps to AZ 89A when you leave. As of this writing, due to budget problems, the park is closed Tues and Wed. Fee; children under 6 free.

Jerome Winery. 403 Clark St.; (928)639-0067; www.jeromewinery.com. Located within walking distance of all the action in Jerome, the Jerome Winery features more than 30 boutique wines made from grapes the vintner grows in Willcox, Arizona. Family owned and operated, the winery also has a sister gallery and winery, Bitter Creek Winery, located at 240 Hull St. Open daily.

Main Street. AZ 89A becomes Main Street as it continues into Jerome. Park anywhere and walk around to get a sense of this special community. Now a popular tourist stop, Jerome almost became a ghost town; however, it's safe to assume that the ghosts now have left for quieter spots. Revived during the 1960s when hippies discovered it was both cheap and charming, Jerome today is a haven for people who eschew the urban scene.

Enjoy the quaint shops, many galleries, and restaurants that flourish in this area. It's worth your time to spend a few minutes in the Jerome Historical Society on the corner of Main and Jerome Streets to learn more about the town. You may write the Jerome Historical Society at P.O. Box 156, Jerome 86331, or call (928) 634-5477 in advance to request a town map and more information. Additional information is available at www.jeromehistorical society.org. If you're a history buff, pick up a Jerome tour guide, which outlines a complete historical walking tour. While you are at the historical society, visit the Mine Museum in the building to see artifacts and exhibits illustrating Jerome's past glory.

Since 1991 this town has become a center for arts and crafts, especially pottery and jewelry. Items are fairly priced, and help is routinely friendly. You'll discover good bargains— especially during the annual arts and crafts show, held over the Fourth of July weekend. The Old Jerome High School is home to many artists' studios.

Other shops to see include the Mining Museum Gift Shop as well as Made in Jerome, which specializes in pottery, and Nellie Bly's, a jewelry shop that features a wonderful variety of kaleidoscopes.

Stop in at the chamber of commerce and ask for a copy of the art registry, which describes the many art galleries in town. Pick up a directory to lodging and eating and the self-guided walking tour brochure. www.jeromechamber.com.

where to stay

Connor Hotel of Jerome. 164 Main St.; (800) 523-3554; www.connorhotel.com. The Connor Hotel is a funky but fun renovated historic hotel. $$. Call for reservations.

Jerome Grand Hotel. 200 Hill St.; (928) 634-8200 or (888) 817-6788; www.jeromegrand hotel.com. This 23-room hotel was once a hospital and today welcomes guests. Every room is different, whether standard, deluxe, or the hotel's fine 2-room suite. Furnishings are contemporary Southwest. The fine-dining restaurant, which serves lunch and dinner, is called The Asylum because it is, they say, "a restaurant on the fringe." The chef-prepared original dishes are intriguing and delicious. The wine list is extensive. Reservations are recommended, especially on the weekends. Ask about senior and AAA discounts at the hotel. $$–$$$.

The Surgeon's House Bed & Breakfast. On Hill Street, next to the Jerome Grand Hotel; (800) 639-1452; www.surgeonshouse.com. This lovely, small property was the home of George W. Hull, whose original tract of land became the town of Jerome. A hospital was built on the site, and this mansion was constructed for the head physician. It's been beautifully restored and offers the most elegant overnight experience in Jerome. A full breakfast served buffet-style is included. $$.

day trip 03

north

>>> **from indians to eagles:**
cottonwood, clarkdale, Cornville

Begin the day with a visit to a prehistoric Native American ruin, complete it with a breathtakingly scenic ride through the Verde Valley, and, along the way, enjoy some excellent Arizona wines. Arizona is proud to have several excursion trains running in the state. What's special about the Verde Valley train is that it traverses an area that is not accessible to vehicular traffic. The cars are modern, but the scenery is ageless. For maximum beauty, take this trip during the spring or autumn, when the verdant valley is dressed in its seasonal finest.

cottonwood

From Phoenix, head north on I-17 to the Camp Verde Junction. Follow A-279 northwest to Cottonwood.

According to legend, Cottonwood is named for the cottonwood trees that grew in a circle near what is now the center of town. However Arizona historian Marshall Trimble disagrees. He says it was named for the large stands of cottonwoods that grew along the Verde River. In addition to trees, today Cottonwood is gaining new fame for grapes since it is becoming a center for small boutique wineries. Get ready for a surprise: Vintners have long said that the soil in Arizona is conducive to growing great grapes, and many small wineries are now winning awards to prove it. To get a complete list of Arizona wineries, visit www.arizonavinesandwines.com.

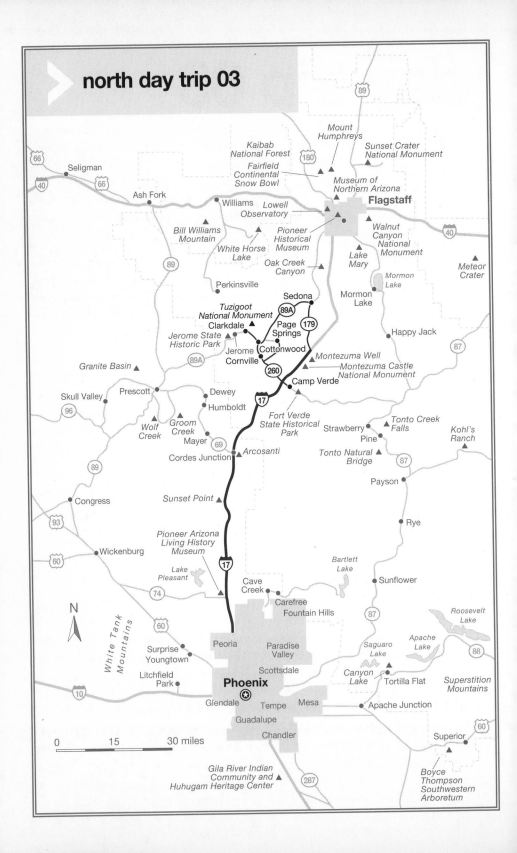

north day trip 03

where to go

Blazin' M Ranch. On 10th Street, just 5 minutes from the Verde Canyon Railroad; (800) 937-8643; www.blazinm.com. The Blazin' M Ranch offers a complete family Western experience with a chuckwagon dinner show that features the Blazin' M Cowboys. Explore a variety of shops, a shooting gallery, and horseshoe pits, and visit the Olde Tyme photo studio for a memory to take home. You can easily combine a ride on the Verde Valley Railroad with an evening of fun at the Blazin' M Ranch. This is a family-run operation that has been delighting guests since 1994. Open Wed to Sat. Closed Jan and Aug. Fee.

Freitas Vineyard. 1575 Paradise Dr.; (928) 639-2149; www.freitasvineyard.com. In Cottonwood, follow AZ 260 to Camp Verde Bridgeport Highway. Turn left onto Fir Street and left onto Paradise Drive. This small micro winery produces handcrafted estate wines in the European tradition. The second-oldest winery in the Verde Valley, it currently does not offer tastings on site but can arrange for tastings at affiliated venues. You can buy their wines on the premises. Open daily.

Pillsbury Wine Company Tasting Room. 1012 North Main; (928) 639-0646; www .pillsburywine.com. Located in the heart of town, Pillsbury Wine Company offers a selection of handcrafted, fine Arizona wines. According to Sam Pillsbury, wine maker, the soil and altitude in this part of Arizona are almost identical to the Rhône Valley. Among them are WildChild White and WildChild Red, as well as other fine reds, whites, and blends. The Tasting Room is open daily.

Verde Valley Olive Traders. 1014 North Main St.; (928) 301-0180; www.vvoliveoil.com. The shop features 32 flavors of olive oil and balsamic vinegars—even dark chocolate vinegar if that's your pleasure. The owners fell in love with Cottonwood's historic atmosphere and stayed to open the shop. They offer recipes and pairing advice. Open Thurs to Sun.

clarkdale

From Phoenix, head north on I-17 to the Camp Verde junction. Follow A-179 northwest to Clarkdale, which was once the smelting town for the mines in Jerome. Today Clarkdale is the departure point for Tuzigoot National Monument, the wilderness of Sycamore Canyon, and the Verde River Canyon Railroad.

where to go

Tuzigoot National Monument. (928) 634-5564; www.nps.gov/tuzi. If you are up for more Native American ruins, don't veer onto AZ 89A, but continue west to AZ 260 to see another Sinaguan village. In Cottonwood, take Main Street north toward Clarkdale to Tuzigoot National Monument. This ancient ruin is located between Cottonwood and Clarkdale and was forgotten until the 1930s, when a team of archaeologists from the University of Arizona

tuzigoot tour

The first time I saw Tuzigoot National Monument, I sandwiched the visit into an extremely busy day. We climbed the hill to enjoy the view, popped into the small museum, and quickly got the lay of this ancient land. This speedy experience created what has lived on in my family as the "Tuzigoot tour," a term referring to a fast and speedy visit, but it proves how easily Tuzigoot National Monument lets you connect with the culture of the Sinaguan people to understand its story.

began excavating and exploring it. Their work was amply rewarded. They deduced that the original pueblo was 2 stories high and had 77 ground-floor rooms. Built between AD 1125 and AD 1400, this ruin offers yet another intimate view of the ancient people who hunted and farmed here. The pueblo is situated on a 120-foot-high ridge that presents a panoramic view of the Jerome-Clarkdale area. No doubt the Sinaguas stood there, centuries ago, and marveled at the undisturbed view.

Take some time to walk along the trail at Tuzigoot. If you are fascinated by these people, don't leave without visiting the museum. Open daily. Fee.

The museum displays rare turquoise mosaics, beads and bracelets made of shells, painted pottery, and a variety of grave offerings, items the native people left in graves to carry into the afterlife.

The Verde Canyon Railroad. (800) 293-7245 (reservation line); www.verdecanyonrr.com. The Verde Canyon Railroad travels through the extraordinary scenery of the Verde River Canyon, one of the richest riparian habitats in the Southwest. The train started service in November 1990 and is powered by a modern diesel engine. Sharp-eyed travelers, at appropriate times of the year, can spot eagles soaring, and everyone can enjoy whitewater rapids and the majesty of the Promethean cliffs.

Trains have been running in this area since well before World War I. This particular train was called the "Verde Mix" because it carried people and coal and was bankrolled originally by Senator William Clark who ran his own 73-foot Pullman Palace luxury car on the tracks. Clarkdale was named for his family. Today, it's possible to duplicate Senator Clark's extravagance as railroad cars can be rented for private parties. Wildflowers may be viewed from mid-March through May, and there are open-air gondola cars for outdoor viewing and photography.

The train leaves from 300 North Broadway, which is about 16 miles west of I-17, via exit 287. The 40-mile round-trip operates year-round, but the schedule changes with the seasons. Summer starlight rides and grape escape (wine and dinner) trips are also offered. The train winds through Verde Canyon adjacent to the Sycamore Wilderness Area and passes a continuously changing landscape—from prickly pear in the desert to hardwood trees. A naturalist onboard provides narration. The trip follows the river past red sandstone formations reminiscent of those seen in nearby Sedona. As Sinagua Indians once lived in this area, the thousand-year-old Sinagua ruins can be seen in the cliffs high above the water. At one point the train slows to go over S.O.B. Trestle, named for the foreman who ordered his crew to build this edifice. First-class passengers receive hors d'oeuvres and cocktail service; coach passengers can purchase drinks and snacks. Overnight packages are available. Along the way, it passes a bald eagle nest, Native American ruins, and sandstone cliffs, and goes through a 680-foot tunnel. Call or visit the website for information on schedules, fares, and tour packages.

cornville

This tiny town is nestled in the Verde Valley very near Sedona and is home to several artists who enjoy the quiet of small town living. If you enjoy wines and picnics, there's one very good reason to get off I-17 and head toward town.

where to go

Page Springs Cellars. 1500 North Page Springs Rd.; (928) 639-3004; www.pagesprings cellars.com. From I-17 north, pass the Cottonwood exit and take a right exit at McGuireville #293. Go left over the highway onto Cornville Road. Travel 9 miles and turn right on Page Springs Road. Travel 3⁷⁄₁₀ miles and see the winery on your left. This family-owned vineyard is 15 minutes south of Sedona and offers a tasting room as well as beautiful grounds where you can bird watch, picnic, or relax. According to the owner, the winery has a "serious relationship with varietals from the southern Rhône." Available wine varietals include Syrah, Petite Sirah, Grenache, and Mouvedre along with red grapes including Cabernet Pfeffer, Counoise, and Cinsault. To really relax, book a chair or table massage in the vineyard. Open daily.

day trip 04

north

>>>

red rocks to crystals and all spirits in between:
sedona, oak creek canyon

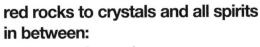

sedona

This is one of the most popular Arizona day trips for visitors and residents alike. Desert dwellers love the lush green of Oak Creek Canyon, and one never tires of the Red Rocks or the startling view as the highway plunges into the heart of this magnificent country. Dedicated shoppers enjoy poking around the intriguing boutiques and art galleries in Sedona and in the village of Oak Creek. Outdoors buffs have a veritable banquet to choose from— everything from water sports, Native American ruins, and hiking to running or jogging up Schnebley Hill for the more hardy.

Although you can approach Sedona in a couple of ways, I-17 north to AZ 179 is a popular route. At the junction of AZ 179 and AZ 89A, head north on AZ 179 and continue toward Sedona. The trip is an easy, nonstop, 2-hour drive from Phoenix. Along the way, you get a full dose of Sedona's famous Red Rocks. While humans have made their mark here with condominiums, shopping centers, and elegant homes, the natural beauty of the Red Rocks still dominates the landscape. At an elevation of 4,300 feet, Sedona's weather is usually delightful. Although snow occasionally falls in winter and summer temperatures can peak from warm to hot, the climate generally is ideal. You can easily spend a day (not to mention money) exploring indoors as Sedona offers a full complement of culture and recreation. Outdoor enthusiasts will find plenty to do as well. The area is rich with campgrounds and Native American ruins. Between the glorious apricot-to-peach-to-purple sunsets and the burnished Red Rocks, Sedona is awash with color.

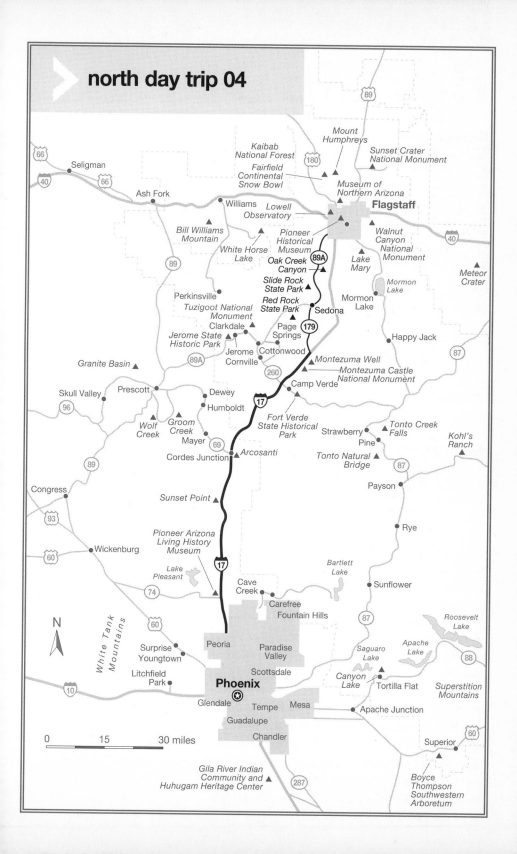

north day trip 04

Seligman

Ash Fork

Williams

Kaibab
National Forest

Mount
Humphreys

Sunset Crater
National Monument

Fairfield
Continental
Snow Bowl

Museum of
Northern Arizona

Flagstaff

Bill Williams
Mountain

Lowell
Observatory

Pioneer
Historical
Museum

Walnut
Canyon
National
Monument

White Horse
Lake

Oak Creek
Canyon

89A

Lake
Mary

Meteor
Crater

Perkinsville

Slide Rock
State Park

Red Rock
State Park

Sedona

Mormon
Lake

Mormon
Lake

Tuzigoot National
Monument

Clarkdale

Page
Springs

179

Happy Jack

Jerome State
Historic Park

Jerome

Cottonwood

Cornville

Granite Basin

89A

260

Montezuma Well

Montezuma Castle
National Monument

Skull Valley

Prescott

Dewey

Camp Verde

96

Humboldt

17

Fort Verde
State Historical
Park

Strawberry

Tonto Creek
Falls

Kohl's
Ranch

Wolf
Creek

Groom
Creek

Pine

Congress

89

Mayer

69

Cordes Junction

Arcosanti

Tonto Natural
Bridge

87

Payson

Sunset Point

Rye

93

Wickenburg

60

Pioneer Arizona
Living History
Museum

17

Lake
Pleasant

Bartlett
Lake

Sunflower

Cave
Creek

Roosevelt
Lake

74

Carefree
Fountain Hills

87

60

Peoria

Paradise
Valley

Apache
Lake

Saguaro
Lake

88

Surprise
Youngtown

Scottsdale

Canyon
Lake

Tortilla Flat

Superstition
Mountains

Litchfield
Park

Phoenix

Apache Junction

10

Glendale

Tempe

Mesa

Guadalupe

Chandler

Superior

60

0   15   30 miles

Gila River Indian
Community and
Huhugam Heritage Center

287

Boyce
Thompson
Southwestern
Arboretum

N

White Tank Mountains

In 2000 Sedona initiated a new policy designed to help pay for the cost of wear and tear on its landscape. Many popular hiking areas now require a $5 parking (or hiking) fee. Be prepared to pay the fee, and enjoy the magnificent scenery knowing you are also helping to ensure that future generations will enjoy the beauty. Contact the Sedona Chamber of Commerce at (800) 288-7336; www.visitsedona.com or www.sedonachamber.com.

where to go

Chapel of the Holy Cross. 780 Chapel Rd.; (928) 282-4069; www.chapeloftheholycross .com. Heading toward Sedona on AZ 179, you pass the village of Oak Creek. Continue on AZ 179 for approximately 5 miles. In the distance, on your right, you will see the Chapel of the Holy Cross against the Red Rocks. Turn right on Chapel Road, which leads to the church. The road is well marked with 3 signs announcing the turnoff. This is an inspirational and architectural treat. Be sure to read the plaque on the exterior of the building that describes the history of this unusual place of worship. Although often busy with tourists, the chapel nevertheless remains a very sacred and inspiring place that should not be missed. It is open daily to the public free of charge.

Tlaquepaque. P.O. Box 1868, Sedona 86339; (928) 282-4838; www.tlaq.com. Continue north on AZ 179. As it bends right before crossing Oak Creek, make a sharp left turn. The entrances are immediately on your left. The cobblestone driveways are marked by rustic-looking stone gates that are almost hidden beneath the tall trees.

Tlaquepaque (Ta-la-kee-pah-kee) is a shopping center worth your time. Named for a suburb of Guadalajara, Mexico, this is a favorite gathering place for locals and tourists. Indulge yourself in the boutiques that feature everything from superb pottery, elegant glass, clothing, and gifts to art and sculpture. You can also feed your body as well as your soul at a number of excellent dining establishments.

As you walk through Tlaquepaque, notice the bell tower, which is a Sedona landmark. Peek inside the tiny chapel near the central plaza. Just as each Spanish and Mexican village has a church, Tlaquepaque has its chapel, which holds approximately 20 people and is used for private weddings and other ceremonies. Open daily.

The Red Rocks. There's no better way to see the Red Rocks of Sedona than by going off-road. Sedona's famous Jeep tours offer adventure for everyone who is daring enough to ride off the road and up the hills and over the creeks to gain this special view of the majestic Sedona landscape. There are about a half-dozen companies in Sedona that provide escorted tours. Here are recommended favorites:

Honantki Ruins Tours. Run by Pink Jeep Tours, these tours give you a chance to be escorted on an archaeological expedition of Native American ruins. Travel by Jeep to backcountry, unexcavated, unreconstructed cliff dwellings, which you'll explore room by room. For more information on these tours, call (928) 282-500 or (800) 873-3662, or visit www.pinkjeep.com.

Sedona Red Rock Jeep Tours. Another great way to see the Red Rocks is through this excellent Jeep-tour company. The guides are informative, and the Jeeps provide exciting transportation over the backcountry. This company also offers horseback rides through backcountry trails. All horseback rides are walking rides, and age and weight restrictions do apply to protect riders and horses. Experienced wranglers and gentle horses make this an unforgettable way to experience Sedona for those who like the view on horseback. Sedona Red Rock Jeep Tours also offers archaeological tours. Prices quoted include transportation to and from guests' hotels. For reservations call (928) 282-6667 or (800) 848-7728, or visit www.redrockjeep.com.

Red Rock State Park. (928) 282-6907; www.azstateparks.com. Follow AZ 89A for 3 miles. Turn off onto Lower Red Rock Loop Road. Nestled on lower Oak Creek near Sedona, this 286-acre park was planned as an environmental center. A naturalist program offers tours that introduce you to the plants and animals in this special riparian setting. Approximately 11⁴⁄₁₀ miles of Oak Creek wind through the park, and more than 135 species of birds and 450 species of plants and grasses have been identified here. First stop should be the visitor center, then take any of several trails. If you visit in winter, carry a jacket or sweater. As of this writing, this park is open daily. Due to budget issues, some Arizona state parks have been closed or are now operating with reduced hours, so visit the website. Fee.

Sedona Arts Center. AZ 89A to 15 Art Barn Rd.; (928) 282-3809; www.sedonaartscenter .com. This center offers theater productions, visual arts exhibitions, and other art exhibits as well as concerts and festivals. Free entrance to the Exhibition Hall; art themes change monthly.

Slide Rock State Park. On AZ 89A about 4 or 5 miles past uptown Sedona; (928) 282-3034; http://azstateparks.com. Developed around a natural water slide that has been smoothed over by centuries of water (not to mention blue-jeaned derrieres), this park is a favorite spot for kids of all ages. Years ago, this was a casual experience. Today the park is well maintained and organized. There's a fee for parking, but sliding in Oak Creek is still free. The less adventurous will enjoy the verdant scene and the grassy picnic grounds. Due to budget issues, some Arizona state parks have been closed or are now operating with reduced schedules, so please visit the website to check for hours. Open daily as of this writing.

Red Rock Crossing. (928) 204-1398; www.fs.fed.us, www.azstateparks.com. Touted as the best all-around hiking trail in the Sedona–Oak Creek area, this trail is good for adults of all ages and fitness levels, kids, and pets. To reach this hiking area, take AZ 89A west from Sedona to Upper Red Rock Loop Road. Go south on Red Rock Loop and look for signs to direct you to Red Rock Crossing. Parking costs $3. The hike begins by walking on a sidewalk that goes through a meadow surrounded by cottonwood trees. The sidewalk ends at Oak Creek. From there the hike continues along a gravel trail for approximately 20 minutes to the base of Cathedral Rock. The tricky part of this hike involves walking across some logs at the deeper parts of the creek.

Due to budget issues, some Arizona state parks have been closed or are now operating with reduced hours, so visit the website to verify days and times. Open daily as of this writing.

Schnebley Hill. One of the most well-known hiking and mountain biking routes in Sedona, this is a 23-mile round-trip through mind-boggling Sedona scenery. The road begins ½ mile south of the intersection of AZ 89A and AZ 179 in town. The dirt road leads west from AZ 179. Hikers and cyclists will see the ruins of the old Foxboro Lake Resort about halfway through the trip. The old carriage house stands on the left side of the road, with the main building and swimming pool at the meadow's edge to the right. This is not a good ride after rain or snow, so I recommend that you check with the Coconino National Forest Office (1824 South Thompson St., Flagstaff; 928-527-3600) for road conditions.

where to eat

Cowboy Club Restaurant. 241 North AZ 89A; (928) 282-4200; www.cowboyclub.com. The Cowboy Club Restaurant serves terrific prickly pear margaritas and an appetizer sampler that includes ostrich, buffalo, rattlesnake, and curly prickly pear fries, all with gourmet dipping sauces. $$–$$$.

Elote Cafe. 771 AZ 179; (928) 203-0105; www.elotecafe.com. Owner and chef Jeff Smedstad came to Sedona from Scottsdsale's Los Sombreros restaurant. His cuisine is sophisticated Mexican prepared with his own flair. He always cooks with local, seasonal ingredients. (*FYI: Elote* is a wonderful corn dish that's served in Mexico as a street treat.) Open Tues through Sat for dinner. Reservations accepted for groups of 5 or more. $$.

Enchantment Resort. Boynton Canyon, 525 Boynton Canyon Rd.; for reservations call (928) 282-2900 or (800) 826-4180; www.enchantmentresort.com. For heavenly ambience, ask to be seated on the patio to enjoy the sunset. Sip a margarita and admire the view of Boynton Canyon $$–$$$.

where to stay

Amara Hotel, Restaurant & Spa. 100 Amara Lane; (928) 282-4828 or (800) 815-62153; www.amararesort.com. In uptown Sedona, turn right after the second traffic light and travel down the hill to the resort. Amara is nestled beside Oak Creek and offers a hip alternative to Sedona's luxury lineup. Contemporary casual is the theme throughout with spacious rooms, and an attentive staff is available for your every request. Breakfast buffet is included, and yoga class is complimentary for guests. Serenity Spa features massage therapies, facials, body treatments, and "foot and hand rituals." $$–$$$.

Enchantment Resort. Boynton Canyon, 525 Boynton Canyon Rd.; for reservations call (928) 282-2900 or (800) 826-4180; www.enchantmentresort.com. Heading west on AZ 89A, turn right on Dry Creek Road and continue approximately 3 miles. Here you'll come to a T in the road. Turn left where you see the sign for Boynton Canyon. Go 2 miles farther. You'll come to a second T in the road. Turn right and follow the signs toward Boynton Canyon. This resort is set in one of the most gorgeous locations in Sedona. The guard will direct you to the clubhouse, high in Boynton Canyon. Enjoy tennis, swimming, golf, and hiking or indulge in treatments in the 24,000-square-foot Mii Amo spa. $$$.

L'Auberge de Sedona. 301 L'Auberge Lane; reservations (800) 272-6777; www.lauberge .com. On AZ 89A, 1 block north of A-179, this informal yet elegant French-style country inn is fast becoming well known throughout the country. The grounds alone are worth a visit. Its rosemary-scented pathways, shade trees, picnic tables, and stepping stones create a magical ambience for the various pine cottages nestled among the cottonwood trees. Beds are handcrafted and canopied. Love seats are overstuffed. Televisions and telephones are nowhere to be seen. $$$.

bed-and-breakfasts

Sedona is awash in upscale bed-and-breakfasts and charming inns that provide the perfect "home" for travelers who want to discover Red Rock country. Day-trippers who decide to stay overnight (or longer) in Sedona have their choice of romantic properties, western-style

something for everyone

I consider myself a spiritual person, so I was excited to go on a vortex tour in Sedona a few years ago. Vortexes are places where you can supposedly feel subtle energy emanating from the earth. Since Sedona is known to have many vortexes, several companies offer tours, which is not a surprise considering that Sedona is a center for metaphysical sensations. So I took one. Except like the song says, when I sat quietly in a vortex field, "I felt nothing." I really tried. The tour was fun and beautiful since vortexes are thought to swirl in some of the most scenic spots in all of Sedona, but I did not feel the energy. I frankly got better vibes sitting on the patio at Enchantment sipping a margarita— which is one of my top recommendations for how to enjoy Sedona. In the spirit of full disclosure, I only tried the vortex tour once and have sipped many margaritas over the years at Enchantment. Maybe what I'm feeling there is the magic of Boyton Canyon. Or maybe it's the tequila.

inns, and rustic cabins. The chamber of commerce has a complete list of bed-and-breakfast establishments to please every taste. Here are just two:

Adobe Village Graham Inn. 150 Canyon Circle Dr.; (928) 284-1425 or (800) 228-1425; www.adobevillagegrahaminn.com. This elegant bed-and-breakfast is owned by Eileen and Stewart Berman. In addition to home-cooked breakfasts prepared by the hosts, guests enjoy designer touches in the individual suites and special amenities like a double Jacuzzi. This AAA Four Diamond Award–winning inn also boasts a lushly landscaped pool area. $$$.

Territorial House Bed & Breakfast. 65 Piki Dr.; (928) 204-5593 or (800) 801-2737; www .territorialhouse.com. This B&B offers a choice of 4 rooms, which include full breakfast and afternoon refreshments. The Miss Kitty room features a romantic, king-size, four-poster canopy bed; oval marble whirlpool tub with separate glass shower; and private deck. The Cisco Kid's Room features a king-size barn-wood bed and a replica of his trademark sombrero. Indian Garden is a pueblo-style room with a second-floor balcony that comes equipped with a telescope for viewing the stars. Ponderosa and Bunkhouse is a western 2-bedroom suite that is perfect for families or couples traveling together. $$.

oak creek canyon

Oak Creek Canyon is just north of Sedona on AZ 89A. Don't see one without seeing the other. Oak Creek glimmers in autumn, sparkles cool and clear in summer, and occasionally is tinged with winter snow. The drive through Oak Creek Canyon is steep enough to satisfy a roller-coaster lover, but once on the canyon floor, you may park your car and walk around the area. Plan to take this drive north to south for the most breathtaking views.

For many sightseers, the drive through Oak Creek Canyon is experience enough. More ambitious types should take a casual stroll through the wooded area along the creek. Serious hikers may prefer more rugged challenges, so if you don't mind getting wet (you'll need to wade across the creek), there are more rigorous routes described in several books on outdoor Arizona available at local bookstores.

West Fork of Oak Creek Canyon. Continue on AZ 89A about 10 miles north of Sedona between milepost 384 and 385. Watch for two large posts with a heavy chain on the west side of the road about 100 feet north of a Dos Pinos sign. The trail begins as an asphalt path. You'll pass the ruins of the old Mayhew Lodge and then emerge into a riparian wonderland of red cliffs and pungent leaves. The trail crosses Oak Creek several times, so be prepared to balance on slippery rocks or wade across. Although this is a very popular hike, the trail offers a special slice of Arizona: peaceful, green, and wet! The deeper you go into the canyon, the more verdant the scene and, during autumn, more brilliantly colored. Free.

day trip 05

north

>>> **mountains and canyons and a city that rocks:**
flagstaff

flagstaff

Often called "The City of Seven Wonders," Flagstaff is approximately 2½ hours north of Phoenix, an easy day trip by Arizona standards. The scenic highway dips through the Verde Valley, climbs over the Mogollon Rim, or "the Rim," as it's better known, and ultimately reaches this 7,000-foot-high city. This is a trip of strong natural contrast: You travel from prickly pears to pines. If you take this drive in winter, you can swim in your heated Phoenix pool in the morning, ski all afternoon in Flagstaff, and return home to Phoenix that night!

Trivia lovers may enjoy knowing that most stories concerning the origin of the name Flagstaff involved some person lopping off branches of a lone pine and running a flag up the pole. Fortunately, someone thought "Flag-staff" had a better ring to it than "Flag-pole." To celebrate the naming, a centennial flag was flown from a tall pine tree on July 4, 1876.

Today, this city is the seat of Coconino County, second-largest county in the country and home to Northern Arizona University (NAU). The northern hub of the state, Flagstaff is a bustling little city, bisected by railroad tracks, surrounded by pines, and dominated by the 12,670-foot Mount Humphreys Peak, the tallest mountain in the state. During ski season, Flagstaff's main winter attraction, the Arizona Snow Bowl, hums with the whoosh of down-hill skiers coursing down Mount Humphreys. A few years ago the downtown had a major restoration so that, today, its outdoor cafes and fun shops make this a destination. Sur-rounded by truly verdant splendor, the city of Flagstaff has gone upscale in the last number of years. New residential developments feature rustic ski-lodge themes.

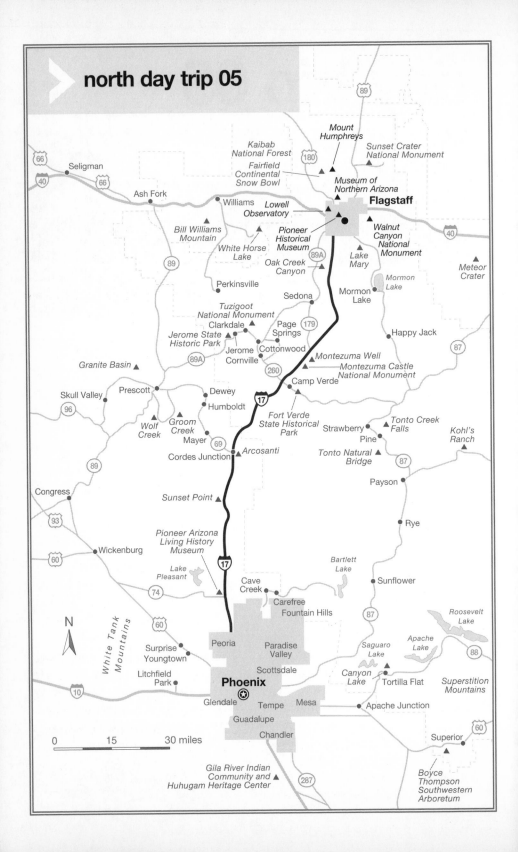

66

40 Seligman

66 Ash Fork

89

Mount Humphreys

89 180

Kaibab National Forest

Fairfield Continental Snow Bowl

Sunset Crater National Monument

Williams

Museum of Northern Arizona

Flagstaff

Lowell Observatory

Bill Williams Mountain

White Horse Lake

Pioneer Historical Museum

Walnut Canyon National Monument

89A

Oak Creek Canyon

40

Lake Mary

Meteor Crater

89

Perkinsville

Sedona

Mormon Lake

Mormon Lake

Tuzigoot National Monument

Clarkdale

Jerome State Historic Park

Jerome

Cornville

Cottonwood

Page Springs

179

260

Happy Jack

87

Granite Basin

89A

Montezuma Well

Montezuma Castle National Monument

Camp Verde

96 Skull Valley

Prescott

Dewey

Humboldt

17

Fort Verde State Historical Park

Strawberry

Pine

Tonto Creek Falls

Kohl's Ranch

Wolf Creek

Groom Creek

Mayer

69 Cordes Junction

Arcosanti

Tonto Natural Bridge

87

89

Payson

Congress

93

Sunset Point

Rye

60 Wickenburg

Pioneer Arizona Living History Museum

17

Lake Pleasant

Bartlett Lake

Sunflower

74

Cave Creek

Carefree

Fountain Hills

87

Roosevelt Lake

60

N

White Tank Mountains

Surprise

Youngtown

Litchfield Park

Peoria

Paradise Valley

Scottsdale

Saguaro Lake

Apache Lake

88

Canyon Lake

Tortilla Flat

Superstition Mountains

10

Phoenix

Glendale

Tempe

Mesa

Apache Junction

Guadalupe

Chandler

Superior

60

0   15   30 miles

Gila River Indian Community and Huhugam Heritage Center

287

Boyce Thompson Southwestern Arboretum

Because of NAU, this city is home to a hardy breed of students and outdoor types. If you love plaid flannel shirts, this may be your place. But for every visitor, Flagstaff is the ideal place to begin exploring northern Arizona. From here, a wonderland of day trips is easily accessible. (Read about these in the Flagstaff section.) Here's a sampling of the sights to see when you visit this hub of northern Arizona.

where to go

Arboretum at Flagstaff. On Woody Mountain Road off US 66, about 4 miles west of town. (928) 774-1442; www.thearb.org. The center is located in a beautiful wooded area. At an elevation of 7,150 feet, it is the highest botanic garden in the United States that does horticultural research. The display gardens offer landscaping ideas for the arid West, but even nongardeners will enjoy this quiet respite. Here are Arizona plants and flowers, many of which are rare and specially bred for this climate. Open daily Apr through Oct. Tours available. Fee; children under 3 free.

Coconino Center for the Arts. 2300 North Fort Valley Rd. (AZ 180); (928) 779-2300; www.culturalpartners.org. This regional art center offers a variety of arts programming, including exhibits, musical performances, workshops, and demonstrations, as well as a folk art program. Gallery shows of national importance are mounted. Call or visit the website for current displays and days of operation. Closed Mon. Free.

Lava River Cave. Nine miles north of Flagstaff on US 180. Turn west (left) on FR 245 and continue 3 miles to FR 171. Turn south 1 mile to where FR 171A turns left. Continue a short distance to the mile-long lava tube cave. This primitive cave was formed 700,000 years ago by molten rock that erupted from a volcanic vent in nearby Hart Prairie. If you look at the floor, you can see wavelike undulations that are the remains of frozen ripples in the last trickle of molten rock that flowed from this cave. Inside, the temperature is 42 degrees—even in summer—so dress warm. This is a rugged adventure. The entry is steep and can be slick with ice. Inside, the left route is easy; the right-hand side has very low ceilings and forces you to crawl a short distance. In winter the cave can only be accessed by skiing to it. Bring flashlights because the interior is dark, slippery, and rugged. Free. You can contact the ranger station at (928) 526-0866 or get more information at www.coconinoforest.us.

Lowell Observatory. 1400 West Mars Hill Rd.; (928) 774-3358; www.lowell.edu. Travel west on Santa Fe Avenue and follow it to the end, then climb Mars Hill. Dr. Percival Lowell built the world-famous wooden observatory in 1894. Pluto was discovered here in 1930, and today the observatory continues to be a center of important scientific work. Interesting and informative guided tours are available daily. If you visit during the summer, plan on spending Fri night here, when the observatory is open to the public. Call for hours. Fee.

The Museum of Northern Arizona. 3101 North Fort Valley Rd.; (928) 774-5213; www.musnaz.org. Three miles north of Flagstaff on US 180 at Fort Valley Road. From downtown

delightful four-season college town

When I take visitors to the Grand Canyon, our first stop is the Museum of Northern Arizona in Flagstaff. There's no better place to gain an understanding of the magnitude, geology, and history of the Colorado Plateau, the vast landmass that is drained by the Colorado River. But don't think of Flagstaff as only a stop on the way to the canyon. It's a delightful four-season college town that offers some of the best hiking in the state as well as a charming and fun downtown that's great for browsing. In recent years, the city has added some good restaurants so your choices are no longer only chain establishments or fast food.

Flagstaff, follow the signs to the Grand Canyon via US 180. A small jewel for those interested in knowing about northern Arizona—especially the Navajo and Hopi cultures—the museum offers an outstanding rug display and gift shop. This museum is a "must" for visitors who are unfamiliar with northern Arizona, as it provides a superb introduction to the Kaibab Plateau, the area that is home to the Grand Canyon. The museum has excellent interpretive exhibits for children as well as adults, and one of the best bookstores in the state. During the summer, several tribes showcase traditional arts and activities on the beautiful museum grounds. Ask to tour the Easton Collection Center, the sustainable new building that holds archival treasures for the museum. It is the second building in Flagstaff to achieve LEED Platinum Certification and is as beautiful as it is "green." Open daily. Fee; children under 6 free.

Pioneer Historical Museum. 2340 North Fort Valley Rd.; (928) 774-6276; www.arizona historicalsociety.org. From downtown Flagstaff, follow the signs to the Grand Canyon via US 180. The museum is 2 miles north of town (just a mile before you get to the Museum of Northern Arizona). Operated by the Arizona Historical Society, the facility is devoted to preserving Arizona's pioneer heritage. All kinds of artifacts depicting pioneer life are on display here to help you understand what it was like for those who settled the area. Fee; children under 12 free. Closed Sun.

Sunset Crater Volcano National Monument. (See Day Trip 01 North from Flagstaff.)

Walnut Canyon National Monument. Off I-40 east, 7½ miles east of Flagstaff at exit 204 (Walnut Canyon); (928) 526-3367; www.nps.gov/waca. A beautifully preserved Sinaguan cliff dwelling, Walnut Canyon whispers of bygone centuries. This is one of the most beautiful spots in the Flagstaff area and is a great destination for people of all ages. Almost always peaceful and sylvan, Walnut Canyon offers well-marked trails as well as more rugged adventures. Stop first at the visitor center and decide whether to travel into this time warp by strolling on Rim Walk Trail or hiking down Island Trail, a 185-foot descent. Both provide a splendid view of the 300 small cliff dwellings that are found within this 400-foot-deep canyon. If you choose the more strenuous path, prepare to take your time: It takes twice the effort to ascend as it does to descend. Open daily. Fee; children under 15 free.

Arizona Snow Bowl. (928) 779-1951; www.arizonasnowbowl.com. Take AZ 180 (Humphreys Street) north 7 miles. Turn right at Snow Bowl Road and continue climbing up that dirt road another 7 miles to the end of the path, where you'll see the lodge. Indoor types can eat at the Snow Bowl snack shop and imbibe at the bar. Weather permitting, the top of the Snow Bowl is great for a panoramic view or picnic. A ski lift runs up Mount Humphreys, Arizona's highest peak, which towers over the San Francisco Mountain range. In the summer months, the Scenic Skyride operates daily from Memorial Day through Labor Day, weather permitting. After Labor Day, the Skyride operates Friday, Saturdays, and Sundays through mid-October.

The view is dazzling. You go almost to the top of Mount Agassiz to an elevation of 11,500 feet in 30 minutes. If you do this in the summer, take a jacket, as it's cool. As you ride you can see the Grand Canyon's North Rim more than 80 miles away as well as the dormant volcano field that surrounds the city. Kendrick Peak, Wild Bill, and Wing Mountain are prominent landmarks. You'll enjoy views of Mount Humphreys, Hart Prairie, and ponderosa pines.

Once at the top, you can hike on any of a variety of interpretive trails, which have good descriptions of the vegetation and historical significance of the area.

Riordan Mansion. 409 Riordan Rd.; (928) 779-4395; http://azstateparks.com/Parks/RIMA /index.html. The mansion was built in 1904 for Timothy and Michael Riordan, who established the logging industry in Flagstaff. The interior has more than 13,000 square feet with 40 rooms, stained-glass windows, and unique window transparencies created by the renowned turn-of-the-20th-century photographer Jack Hillers. Don't miss the visitor center, which maintains an exhibit area. You can also bring a picnic and eat in the park. Open daily. Guided tours are available. As of this writing, this park is closed Tues and Wed. Many state parks are operating with additional reduced hours due to budget issues, so check the website. Fee.

Historic walking tour. From the Riordan Mansion, continue north on Milton. From the arrival of the first railroad in 1882 throughout the postwar expansion after 1945, this was the business center for most of northern Arizona. The downtown has been restored and features many shops and galleries that offer a fine array of Southwestern arts and crafts, specialty items, and clothing.

scenic drive

Around the Peaks Loop. This loop takes you all the way around Arizona's highest mountain, winding through pine forests, aspen groves, open prairies, and rustic homesteads. You can do this drive anytime when snow doesn't close the road. In spring you'll enjoy a carpet of wildflowers; in autumn the trees blaze gold. Along the way you can get out of the car and hike or camp.

To enjoy this loop, drive northeast on US 89 from Flagstaff for 14 miles. Turn west 12 miles to FR 151. Then go south 8 miles to US 180. It's 9½ miles back to Flagstaff.

The entire loop is 44 miles, and roads are suitable for cars. Plan on spending about 2 hours enjoying the magnificent scenery.

where to eat

You can't tell this from the highway, but Flagstaff is a full-service restaurant town. Everything is here from Asian to Thai, barbecue to coffee shops, natural to elegant continental dining. Macy's is a favorite for a casual morning breakfast. Ask the Flagstaff Convention and Visitor Bureau for a brochure with a complete listing of eateries. Stop in at 1 East Rte. 66 or call (928) 774-9541 or (800) 842-7293.

Beaver Street Brewery. 11 South Beaver St.; (928) 779-0079. www.beaverstreetbrewery .com. A longtime favorite for casual dining (make that beer, pizza, sandwiches, etc.), this place boasts a billiard room and an outdoor beer garden with a view of the San Francisco Peaks. Serving lunch and dinner with good food. $–$$.

Lumberyard Brewing Company Tap Room & Grille. 5 South San Francisco St.; (928) 779-2739. A sister to Beaver Street Brewery, this brewery and restaurant is located in an historic, transformed lumberyard building just south of the railroad tracks. The outdoor patio is a fun place to have a beer and a "munchies." Serving lunch and dinner. As of this writing, brewery tours are in the works.

Macy's. 14 South Beaver St. (on the south side of the Santa Fe Railroad tracks); (928) 774-2243; www.macyscoffee.net. This funky coffeehouse is a local favorite. In addition to breakfasts (they have great teas, coffees, baked goods, etc.), Macy's also serves excellent lunches and dinners. $–$$

The Museum Club. 3404 East Rte. 66; (928) 526-9434; www.museumclub.com. Built in 1931, the Museum Club is Arizona's premiere roadhouse. The floor in the historic building really does slant so when you're two-stepping, know it's not you! Known by locals as "the Zoo" for the taxidermied wildlife that dominates the walls, this club features some of the best live country-and-western music and entertainment in the area. $–$$

Tinderbox Kitchen. 34 South San Francisco St.; (928) 226-8400; www.tinderboxkitchen .com. This is the newest and hippest restaurant in Flagstaff. Chef and co-owner Scott Heinonen delivers bold flavors and beautiful, simple dishes that are wowing "foodies." A graduate of Northern Arizona University's School of Hotel and Restaurant Management, he has impressive credentials, having cooked in acclaimed kitchens throughout Oregon's Willamette Valley, California's Mendocino County, and North Lake Tahoe. In 2003 he was a private chef for Paul McCartney and ex-wife Heather during a week-long ski vacation in

Tahoe. He has partnered with his cousin, manager and co-owner Kevin Heinonen, who brings over 15 years of business experience to Tinderbox. Their Annex, next door, serves light repast and is also a great place to wait until your table is ready. $$–$$$

Satchmo's. 2320 North 4th St.; (928) 774-7292. www.satchmosaz.com. Flagstaff locals says this is barbecue to die for. It started as a tiny "hole in the wall" and then moved to these bigger digs. Inside and patio seating available. $

where to stay

All kinds of accommodations await tourists. Choose from bed-and-breakfasts and rustic cabins to modern motels and resorts. Check with the Flagstaff Convention and Visitor Bureau, 323 West Aspen Ave., Flagstaff, or call (928) 779-7611 or visit www.flagstaffarizona .org for a complete listing of hotels, motels, and other accommodations.

Kings House Hotel. 1560 East Santa Fe Ave.; (928) 774-7186 or (800) 528-1234; www .kingshousehotel.com. This very nice property features large rooms at surprisingly reasonable prices. Breakfast is included. It's won a AAA Three Diamond Award and has a heated swimming pool. Nonsmoking rooms are available, and fine dining is nearby. $$.

Hotel Monte Vista. 100 North San Francisco St.; (928-779-6971) or 800-545-3068; www .hotelmontevista.com. A historic hotel in the heart of downtown Flagstaff, the Monte Vista was built in 1926. Zane Grey donated funding to build it. This funky hotel claims to be haunted by several ghosts, and now that train whistles are silenced as trains go through Flagstaff, there is less noise level downtown so you might get to hear them. This property is not for those who like lots of amenities, but it offers a budget choice for travelers who enjoy historic places. Not every room has a private bath so ask for a room with bath if this is important to you. $$

Weatherford. 23 North Leroux St.; (928) 779-1919; www.weatherfordhotel.com. Located in the heart of downtown, this historic hotel opened in 1900 and in 1978 was listed on the National Register of Historic Places. It was a residential facility and a hostel before being reopened as a hotel. Charly's Grill is a popular, good, casual restaurant. Like the Hotel Monte Vista, the Weatherford is long on history but has some quirks. Rooms are small. $$

bed-and-breakfasts

Both of these are in beautiful old homes and are privately owned and run. Each one serves outstanding breakfasts.

Inn at 410. 410 North Leroux St.; (928) 774-0088 or (800) 774-2008; www.inn410.com. Nine suites are decorated to perfection. Some are singles; some are suites. Each has its own bathroom, and the house features fireplaces and a movie library. The breakfast is superb. $$$.

Starlight Pines Bed & Breakfast. 3380 East Lockett Rd.; (928) 527-1912 or (800) 752-1912; www.starlightpinesbb.com. This comfortable, Victorian-style home is outfitted with antiques that have been collected by the owners, who are happy to share their antiquing stories with you. All rooms are named for their grandparents. Grandma Amelia's Room boasts a claw-foot bathtub, brass-trimmed fireplace, and queen-size oak bed. Stella's Room is done in maple furnishings. Mamie's Room, on the first floor, has rich walnut furnishings, while Icie Vean's Room includes unique collectibles like a dental cabinet masquerading as an armoire and the 6-foot-long china bathtub the previous owners rescued from the Broadmoor Hotel in Denver. $$.

northeast

>>>

day trip 01

northeast

>>> **funk, glam, and outdoor fun:**
cave creek, carefree, bartlett lake

cave creek

This day trip begins at Cave Creek and offers a peek into the not-so-distant past. Along the way, you see the Phoenix urban area at its most posh. Comfortable distances and good shopping make this a relaxing, easy trip. Although the desert northeast of Phoenix is rapidly being developed, the vast Tonto National Forest is just an arrowhead's throw away. If you are concerned that this close-in desert is fast disappearing, remember that only 18 percent of Arizona is privately owned. Since most of the land belongs to the state and federal governments, it is hoped that much of it will be saved for posterity.

Cave Creek is a funky little old town that has resisted urban flash, unlike its sister city, Carefree, which was built to attract the well-heeled. A mining camp in the 1880s and a ranching community after the mines gave out, Cave Creek offers modern city dwellers an alternative to urban life. Don't miss the Town Dump, a rambling "shop" on the main road (Cave Creek Road). It's filled with curiosities and some old and new bargains.

When Tonto National Forest was established here in 1903, the first tourists started to arrive. Bartlett Dam, built in 1935, brought more people. The terrain adjacent to Tonto National Forest is dotted with lakes, punctuated by mountains, and provides an array of outdoor recreation opportunities. There is an abundance of wild game in the area, including deer, wild pig, mountain lion, duck, quail, and dove, and opportunities abound for hiking, fishing, horseback riding, and rockhounding.

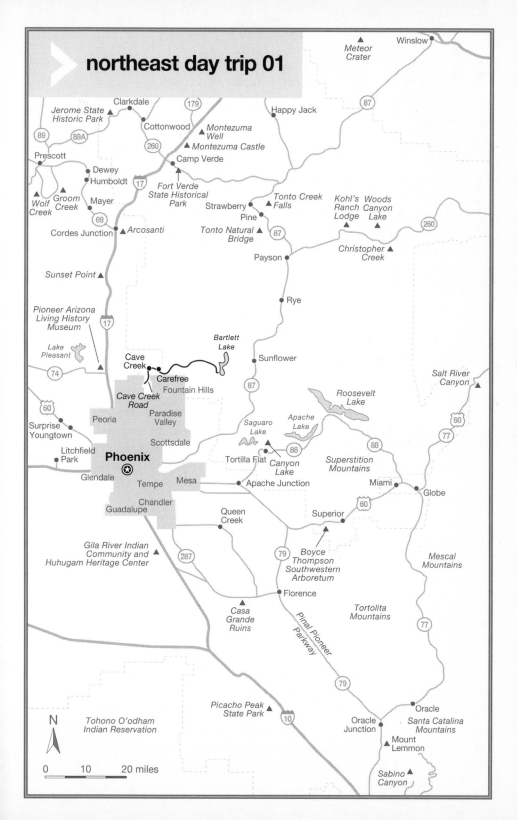

Meteor
Crater

Winslow

87

Happy Jack

Jerome State
Historic Park

Clarkdale

179

Cottonwood

Montezuma
Well

89

89A

Montezuma Castle

260

Prescott

Camp Verde

Dewey
Humboldt

Tonto Creek
Falls

Kohl's
Ranch
Lodge

Woods
Canyon
Lake

17

Fort Verde
State Historical
Park

Strawberry

Wolf
Creek

Groom
Creek

Mayer

69

Pine

Tonto Natural
Bridge

87

260

Christopher
Creek

Cordes Junction

Arcosanti

Payson

Sunset Point

Rye

Pioneer Arizona
Living History
Museum

17

Bartlett
Lake

Lake
Pleasant

74

Cave
Creek

Sunflower

Salt River
Canyon

60

Carefree

Fountain Hills

87

Cave Creek
Road

Paradise
Valley

Roosevelt
Lake

Surprise
Youngtown

Peoria

Scottsdale

Saguaro
Lake

Apache
Lake

88

60

77

Litchfield
Park

Phoenix

Tortilla Flat

Canyon
Lake

88

88

Superstition
Mountains

Miami

Glendale

Tempe

Mesa

Apache Junction

Globe

Guadalupe

Chandler

Queen
Creek

Superior

60

Gila River Indian
Community and
Huhugam Heritage Center

287

Boyce
Thompson
Southwestern
Arboretum

79

Mescal
Mountains

Florence

Tortolita
Mountains

77

Casa
Grande
Ruins

Pinal Pioneer Parkway

79

Oracle

Picacho Peak
State Park

10

Oracle
Junction

Santa Catalina
Mountains

N

Tohono O'odham
Indian Reservation

Mount
Lemmon

Sabino
Canyon

0   10   20 miles

> ## for that old west feeling

Thanks to encroaching urban development, it's getting harder and harder to experience a western horseback ride in the open desert. Happily, you can still have this kind of day in Cave Creek. At Spur Cross Ranch, cowboys and cowgirls of all ages can enjoy riding in the foothills of the vast Tonto National Forest. My family, who knows horses, reports that the steeds are as good as the scenery. Many horses were rescued from owners who could not care for them and are gentle enough for small children to ride. After a day in the saddle, head to El Encanto for Mexican food, Sonoran-style. We like to sit outside on the large patio and watch the ducks paddle on the pond. We always think, after a day like this, that Southwestern life doesn't get any better.

Keep your eye out for antiques shops. There are some intriguing places to browse. To get to Cave Creek, follow I-17 to the Carefree Highway eastbound. Turn east. It becomes Desert Foothills Drive. Individuals who cared about the desert made the 101 signs identifying the desert plants along the road. As you maneuver along the dips, take time to notice these identifying markers and learn about the unusual environment. More information is available at the Carefree/Cave Creek Chamber of Commerce, 748 Easy St.; (480) 488-3381; www.carefree-cavecreek.com.

where to go

Cave Creek Museum. 6140 Skyline Dr.; (480) 488-2764; www.cavecreekmuseum.org. The living history of the desert foothills area is presented in this small museum through displays of pioneer living, including archaeology, ranching, and mining. Open Oct to May. Closed Mon, Tues, and holidays. Fee.

Spur Cross Ranch Conservation Area. Located approximately 35 miles north of central Phoenix. www.maricopa.gov/parks/spur_cross. From the intersection of Carefree Highway and Cave Creek Road, head north on Cave Creek Road about 2½ miles to Spur Cross Road. Turn north for about 4½ miles to the public parking area. After 3 miles, the road turns to all-weather graded. Continue north on the graded road past the green house, through the tall gateposts, and on past the horse corrals to the signed public parking area on the right. This conservation area is part of the Maricopa County Park System and includes 2,154 acres of desert and the lush riparian area along Cave Creek. There are still remnants of the mining and ranching activities that occurred here and some fascinating archaeology sites. More than 7 miles of easy-to-difficult trails, ranging in length from 1.2 miles to 4.6 miles are available. All are multiuse for hiking, mountain biking, and horseback riding. This area is especially beautiful in the spring when the desert blooms with wildflowers. Open daily.

Spur Cross Stables. 44029 North Spur Cross Rd.; (480) 488-9117 or 1-800-758-9530; www.horsebackarizona.com. Located 4 miles north of the town of Cave Creek, the stables are on the edge of the Spur Cross conservation area. Custom guided-trail rides through the rolling foothills of the conservation area are available as well as special seasonal and sunset rides. During the fall and winter months, the creek flows, which adds to the beauty of the ride since flowing streams are rare in the Sonoran Desert. Minimum age for trail riding is 6 years, but the stables can accommodate younger children in their Lil' Buckaroos progam. Open daily. Call for reservations. $$.

where to eat

Binkley's. 6920 East Cave Creek Rd.; (480) 437-1072; www.binkleysrestaurant.com. It may be located in a strip mall but this tiny restaurant is a jewel. It is considered by many to be the best restaurant in the state and is another reason to come to Arizona. Owner chef Kevin Binkley earned his credentials at the French Laundry and The Inn at Little Washington and prepares casually elegant cuisine that is as inventive as it is delicious. The tasting menu is a true treat. You can choose among various entrees and courses but between courses the chef surprises you with an amazing (and seemingly endless) parade of tiny spoonfuls to tempt your palette. During the winter season, call several weeks ahead if you want to dine on Sat night. Open Tues through Sat. $$$.

El Encanto. 6248 East Cave Creek Rd.; (480) 488-1752; www.elencantorestaurant.com. Right across the street from Frontier Town, this comfortable hacienda-style restaurant satisfies that urge to binge on burritos. Request a table on the outside patio and overlook a lagoon where you can watch the ducks and sip a frosty margarita. Great respite after a busy day of sightseeing in the desert. $–$$.

The Horny Toad. 6738 East Cave Creek Rd.; (480) 488-9542. This is a gen-u-ine western joint. Fried chicken (lots of it) is a specialty, and the hamburgers are great. Lunch and dinner served daily. $$.

Harold's. 6895 East Cave Creek Rd.; (480) 488-1906; www.haroldscorral.com. Locals consider Harold's the real deal for good food, great music, and fun. It bills itself as the original Wild West saloon and restaurant and has been hosting tourists and residents for more than 70 years. The place was initially opened in 1935 to serve the workers who were building Bartlett Dam and became Harold's in 1950 when it was purchased by Harold Gavagan. Try the steaks and hamburgers or choose from the full menu. $–$$.

carefree

Another 1950s Arizona phenomenon, Carefree was a real estate developer's dream that was planned to lure those who have the means and the time to enjoy their leisure. Continue east on Cave Creek Road a mile or so, and you're there. The street names say it all—Easy Street, Nonchalant Avenue, Ho and Hum Streets, Rocking Chair Road. Carefree is an elegant little community of large homes, green golf courses, and busy boutiques set like jewels into rocky bezels.

where to go

El Pedregal. 34505 North Scottsdale Rd.; (480) 488-1072; www.elpedregal.com. Heading north on Scottsdale Road from Scottsdale, continue north toward Carefree. You'll see the bright colors of this Moroccan-inspired, fiesta-style center in the distance on the east side of the road. Park and have fun! Wander through the various boutiques and art galleries. You'll find casual dining here and, on Sun afternoons from late Sept through Nov, free concerts on center stage. Open daily.

The Sundial. Go east on Cave Creek Road to Sunshine Way and turn right. You'll see the sundial right ahead of you. This is the largest sundial in the Western Hemisphere and a Carefree landmark.

The Spanish Village. Follow Tom Darlington Drive (Scottsdale Road) south to the signs for shopping. Here you'll find narrow streets trimmed with wrought iron and lined with gift shops and restaurants.

where to stay

The Boulders Resort & Club. 34631 North Tom Darlington Dr.; (480) 488-9009 or (800) 553-1717; www.theboulders.com. Head south on Tom Darlington Drive (Scottsdale Road) and turn left just prior to the pile of boulders. Follow the signs to the Boulders Resort & Club. Breakfast, lunch, and dinner are available at the resort and club, which is one of Arizona's finest and most posh resorts. It is consistently rated as one of the best resorts in the country in terms of service, amenities, and natural beauty. The free-form architecture and desert setting are amazing and offer one of the most elegant experiences during almost any time of year. If service and superb amenities appeal to you, if you love golf and want to see the desert in its most pristine state of elegance, the Boulders is for you. Reservations are recommended at both restaurants. Also see the Golden Door Spa on property. Golf is extra. $$$.

where to eat

Cafe Bink. 36889 North Tom Darlington Dr.; (480) 488-9795; www.cafebink.com. Kevin Binkley's more casual restaurant offers a less formal menu, but the food is still outstanding. Even better, it is easier to get a table here on shorter notice. The menu changes seasonally. Open Tues through Sat, 11 a.m. to 9 p.m. $$$.

bartlett lake

To get to Bartlett Lake, continue east on Cave Creek Road about 6 miles. You'll see a fork in the road and a sign to Bartlett Dam Road. Follow the road to the right. It's unimproved, which means dirt, but if you want an adventurous drive, it's for you. The last miles are the roughest. As your teeth jounce inside your mouth, you may wonder why this section of the road isn't paved. You'll understand when you reach this relatively quiet and undisturbed body of water. Boaters and anglers love keeping Bartlett Lake somewhat inaccessible. It gives them acres of water virtually untouched. If you decide to make this trip, know at the outset that the lake is the attraction. Except for a ranger station, there are no facilities here. That's the allure—rustic beauty unmarred by concession stands.

To return to Phoenix, retrace your steps. Follow Bartlett Lake Road to Cave Creek Road and turn south on Scottsdale Road to Scottsdale. From there, it's an easy trip back to Phoenix via Lincoln Drive and Camelback, Indian School, or Thomas Roads.

day trip 02

northeast

towering pines and a great small town:
payson, tonto natural bridge,
kohl's ranch lodge
worth more time: christopher creek and
woods canyon lake

payson

Beginning with Payson, this excursion features a scenic Arizona highway, elegant in every season. You'll cross the Fort McDowell Indian Reservation, enter the Tonto National Forest, climb through the Mazatzal Mountains, and ultimately experience the carved cliffs and dramatic landscape of the Mogollon Rim country. This is an excellent summer getaway and a "must-see" in the autumn. In winter you'll see cars loaded with ski equipment as families head for the Sunrise ski area. Your main destination is Payson, considered the "Festival Capital" of Arizona. Payson can thank Zane Grey and Grizzly Adams for some of its fame, but nobody can beat Mother Nature for good press.

To reach Payson, head northeast on the Beeline Highway (AZ 87)—it's right near the border of Scottsdale and Mesa on your map. After crossing the Native American reservation, you'll enter the Tonto National Forest. The road will begin to twist and turn, and you'll pass Sunflower and Rye. Thirteen miles later, you'll reach Payson. Located in the exact center of the state in the world's largest stand of ponderosa pine, Payson sits at 5,000 feet and is a sportsman's paradise.

Founded in 1881 as a gold mining camp, Payson counts tourism as its No. 1 industry. Payson hosts myriad festivals. Stop in at the chamber of commerce (800-672-9766; www

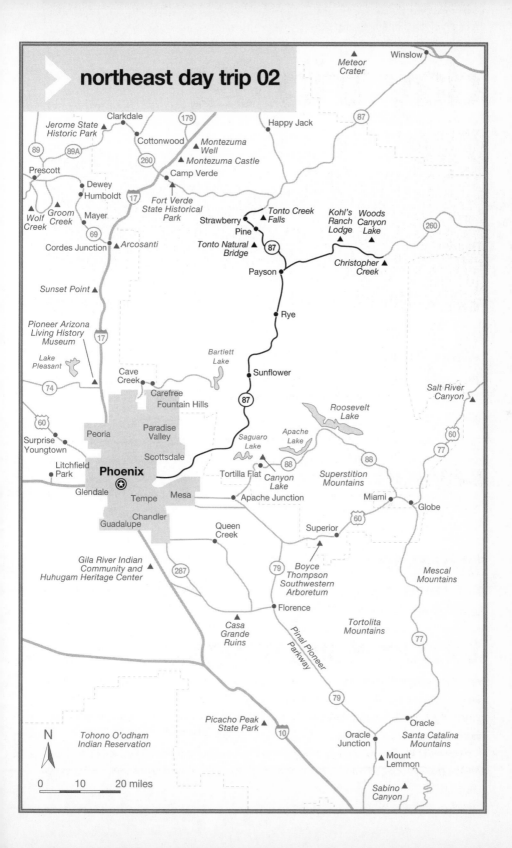

Winslow

Meteor
Crater

Clarkdale

Jerome State
Historic Park

(179)

(87)

Happy Jack

Cottonwood

Montezuma
Well

(89)

(89A)

(260)

Montezuma Castle

Prescott

Camp Verde

Dewey
Humboldt

(17)

Fort Verde
State Historical
Park

Tonto Creek
Falls

Kohl's
Ranch
Lodge

Woods
Canyon
Lake

Wolf
Creek

Groom
Creek

Mayer

Strawberry

Pine

(260)

(69)

Tonto Natural
Bridge

(87)

Cordes Junction

Arcosanti

Christopher
Creek

Payson

Sunset Point

Rye

Pioneer Arizona
Living History
Museum

(17)

Lake
Pleasant

Bartlett
Lake

Sunflower

(74)

Cave
Creek

Salt River
Canyon

Carefree
Fountain Hills

(87)

Roosevelt
Lake

(60)

(60)

Peoria

Paradise
Valley

Saguaro
Lake

Apache
Lake

(77)

Surprise
Youngtown

Scottsdale

(88)

(88)

Litchfield
Park

Phoenix

Tortilla Flat

Canyon
Lake

Superstition
Mountains

Miami

Glendale

Tempe

Mesa

Globe

Apache Junction

Guadalupe

Chandler

Queen
Creek

Superior

Mescal
Mountains

Gila River Indian
Community and
Huhugam Heritage Center

(287)

(60)

Boyce
Thompson
Southwestern
Arboretum

(79)

Florence

Tortolita
Mountains

Casa
Grande
Ruins

Pinal Pioneer
Parkway

(77)

(79)

Picacho Peak
State Park

(10)

Oracle

N

Tohono O'odham
Indian Reservation

Oracle
Junction

Santa Catalina
Mountains

Mount
Lemmon

0   10   20 miles

Sabino
Canyon

> ## full to the rim with wonders
>
> *The drive to Payson proves why Zane Grey fell in love with this special area. The town of Payson is snuggled into the heart of the dramatic Mogollon Rim, one of Arizona's most majestic landscapes. Like many of the state's small towns, the very best things to do here are done out-of-doors. Bring hiking boots or at least a pair of comfortable sneakers so you can enjoy the sights, especially Tonto Natural Bridge.*

.paysonrimcountry.com or www.rimcountrychamber.com), at Beeline Highway and Main Street, to pick up maps and information on what's doing.

where to go

The Swiss Village. AZ 87 on the north side of Payson. Friendly people, gingerbread architecture, a good doughnut shop, and lots of gift shops make this a good shopping and refreshment stop.

Rim Country Museums. 700 Green Valley Pkwy.; (928) 474-3483; www.rimcountrymuseums .com. This 3-building complex, operated by the Northern Gila County Historical Society, offers a reception area, gift shop, archaeology library, two-story exhibit building (wheelchair accessible), meeting room, and outdoor picnic area. Exhibits depict northern Gila County history, pioneer families, and archaeology. Also visit the exact replica of Zane Grey's cabin, where visitors can learn about Zane Grey and his place in history. Closed Tues. Fee.

where to eat

Pizza Factory. 238 East Hwy. 260; (928) 474-1895. Voted the best pizza in Payson for years. Family-owned by Rodney and Gail Dahlman. $$.

tonto natural bridge

About 12 miles north of Payson on AZ 87, the world's largest travertine natural bridge arches 183 feet above the streambed. Measuring 150 to 400 feet in width, it is composed of travertine, white limestone, and red coral deposits. The area is laced with ancient Native American caves. The walk down (and back up) to Tonto Natural Bridge is steep and rocky; if you aren't in good shape, you may want to reconsider. Do wear rubber-soled shoes. Be forewarned, but know that the view is well worth the trek. At the bridge, obey all signs and watch your step.

This is a small place by Arizona standards but is one that rewards the visitor with amazing views. At the bottom of this deep ravine filled with pine and sycamore trees is a cathedral-size chamber, 183 feet high, which has been carved out by a flowing creek. The natural area contains a small waterfall that cascades from the roof of the chamber and creates rainbows across the face of the rock. Natural Bridge is one of the newer of Arizona's state- and national-park standards. The 160-acre park has undergone a $5 million renovation that has paved the road, built parking lots, and renovated the lodge that was built in 1927.

The access road inclines sharply down and ends at the lodge, which is nestled in the wooded valley. To reach the trailhead, park your vehicle ($6 charge) and continue to the top of the broad bridge. From here you can look down to the deep gorge below. Turn left and navigate an incredibly steep trail with carved-in-stone steps and metal-cable railings. It is a fun but challenging trek. The Parks Department has created an alternate route down with a gentler incline and easier footing. (Pets are not allowed on trails.)

Tonto Natural Bridge was discovered by a prospector, David Gowan, who found the hidden gorge in 1877 while being chased by Apaches. He hid in one of the caves for 2 nights. Later, he convinced his nephew in Scotland to bring his family to Arizona and live on the property. The nephew, David Gowan Goodfellow, built the lodge and the bridge and opened it to tourists in 1908. The lodge houses a visitor center and a small but excellent museum filled with Gowan Goodfellow family heirlooms. It is available for rental to groups only through advance registration. As of this writing, the park is open Thurs through Mon, weather permitting. Fee; children under 6 free. (928) 476-4202; www.pr.state.az.us/parks/TONA.

where to go

Tonto Creek Falls. A half mile above the junction of Tonto and Horton Creeks, 10 miles north of Payson, is the site of this natural waterfall. The area around Payson is studded with sylvan splendor, so stop for a cool respite in a busy day of sightseeing.

kohl's ranch lodge

East Hwy. 260, Payson; (928) 478-4211 or (800) 521-3131; www.ilxresorts.com or www .diamondresortsinternational.com. Known for its rustic elegance, Kohl's Ranch is a long-time favorite with locals and visitors. Turn right onto AZ 260 at the junction of AZ 87 and AZ 260 and continue 17 miles to the ranch. Be sure to call ahead for breakfast, lunch, or dinner at this longtime Payson landmark. While you're there, enjoy Tonto Creek, which runs through the property. If you have time for a quiet retreat at this rustic lodge, burrow in for a weekend in one of the cabins that dot the property. $$.

worth more time:

christopher creek and woods canyon lake

Hikers and outdoor types will want to continue east another hour on AZ 260 to see Christopher Creek and Woods Canyon Lake. Both destinations offer excellent opportunities for camping, fishing, boating, and hiking.

Or you may prefer to head north on AZ 87 another 15 to 20 miles to see the town of Strawberry and, just 3 miles away, its neighbor, Pine. Both communities are nestled in spectacular woodsy settings and offer travelers a taste of rural, rustic Arizona at its best. Although Strawberry has the oldest standing schoolhouse in the state, most tourists come for the views rather than specific sights. If you decide to visit the area, Strawberry and Pine are geared to handle visitors.

Fossil Creek Llama Ranch. Located about 1 mile from the Fossil Creek trailhead in Strawberry, which is 15 miles northwest of Payson on AZ 87; (928) 476-5178; www .fossilcreek.com. Fossil Creek Llama Ranch offers lectures about llamas and alpacas, as well as demonstrations of cheese making and fudge making from milk produced by the herds of goats at the ranch. The ranch owners offer guided half-day and overnight hikes with llamas and have a tepee and yurt available to book for overnight stays. Open daily by appointment. Fee.

From Payson, take AZ 87 south for a direct return to Phoenix. Or branch off on AZ 188 toward Punkin Center and Roosevelt Lake and return on the Apache Trail (AZ 88), past Tortilla Flat and on into Mesa, Tempe, and Phoenix. This is a secondary road, and part of it is unpaved. The Apache Trail is renowned for its gorgeous scenery. However, if you come back this way, you're in for some steep climbing and curvy driving on a gravel road. (Refer to Day Trip 02 East from Phoenix for more information about the area.)

day trip 03

northeast

>>>

water and more water:
salt river recreation center and
saguaro lake

salt river recreation center and saguaro lake

For a real change of pace, take a short drive and a long float down the river. Drive north on AZ 87 to the Saguaro (Sa-wa-ro) Lake cutoff (Bush Highway). Follow the signs past the entrance to Saguaro Lake and the Salt River Recreation Center.

Saguaro Lake was formed by Stewart Mountain Dam and is one of the several lakes built for water reclamation purposes. You can find out all about tubing at the central office, including where to get in and out on the Salt River. Tubing is fast becoming Arizona's state sport, as a visit to the Blue Point area of the Salt River will attest on any hot day.

Follow the signs to the recreation area's parking lot. Here you'll find a place to rent inner tubes and a bus that takes you to the "put in" spot. Getting into the river involves a slippery descent. While you're tubing, pay attention to signs so you know when to get off the Salt River. At the designated spot, there will be a bus to take you back to the parking lot where you left your car. If you miss the "get off," you'll have to hike back to the bus stop.

Wear shorts or a bathing suit and tennies; pack beverages and an inner tube (or rent one there). Bring sunscreen, friends, rope, a Styrofoam cooler you can lash to an extra tube, and a hat or visor if the day is extremely warm. Be prepared for some gentle, but exciting, rapids. While the water is rarely deep, tubers can get into trouble if they don't pay attention

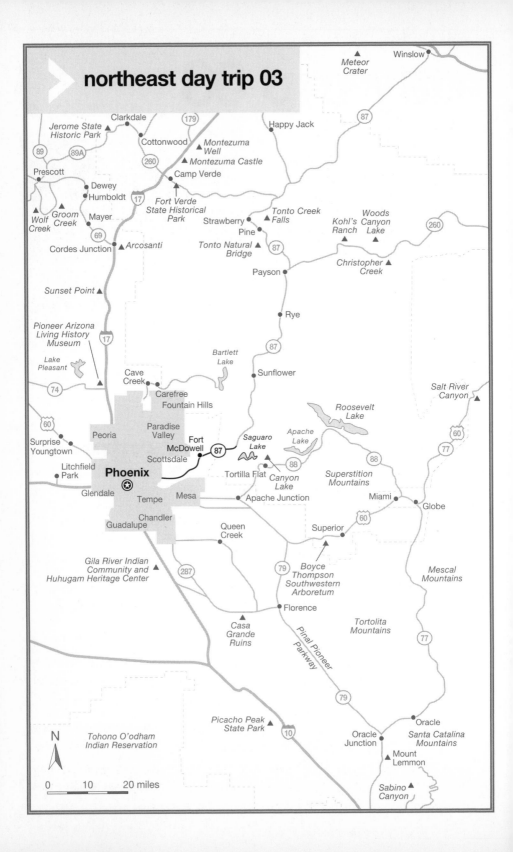

northeast day trip 03

Winslow

▲ Meteor
Crater

Jerome State ▲ Clarkdale
Historic Park
(179)   Happy Jack   (87)

Cottonwood
(89) (89A)   (260) ▲ Montezuma
Well
Prescott   ▲ Montezuma Castle
▲ Dewey   Camp Verde
Humboldt   Woods
Fort Verde   Tonto Creek   Kohl's Canyon
State Historical   ▲ Falls   Ranch Lake
Wolf ▲ Groom Mayer   Park   Strawberry   ▲   ▲
Creek Creek   Pine
(69)   ▲ Tonto Natural (87)   Christopher ▲
Cordes Junction ▲ Arcosanti   Bridge   Creek

Payson
Sunset Point ▲

Rye

Pioneer Arizona   (87)
Living History
Museum   Bartlett
Lake   Salt River
Lake   Canyon
Pleasant   Sunflower   ▲
(74)   Cave   (60)
Creek   Roosevelt
Carefree   Lake   (77)
Fountain Hills
(60)   Paradise   Apache
Surprise   Peoria Valley   Lake
Youngtown   Fort   (87) Saguaro
McDowell   Lake
Litchfield   Scottsdale   ▲   Superstition   (88)
Park   Phoenix   Tortilla Flat Canyon Mountains
⊙   Apache Lake   Miami
Glendale   Junction   (60)   Globe
Tempe Mesa
Chandler   Queen   Superior
Guadalupe   Creek   (60)
Mescal
(79) Boyce   Mountains
Gila River Indian   (287)   Thompson
Community and   ▲   Southwestern
Huhugam Heritage Center   Arboretum
Tortolita
▲ Florence   Mountains   (77)
Casa   Pinal Pioneer
Grande   Parkway
Ruins

(79)

Oracle
Picacho Peak ▲
State Park (10)   Oracle Santa Catalina
N   Tohono O'odham   Junction Mountains
Indian Reservation   ▲ Mount
Lemmon

Sabino ▲
Canyon
0   10   20 miles

tubing the salt river

Arizonans don't only like to drink a lot of water; we love to play in it whenever we can. Tubing the Salt River is an honored tradition for all ages. Wear cutoffs, old tennis shoes, and tons of sunscreen, and bring lots of water to drink. Toss in a lightweight shirt as a cover-up when the sun gets too hot. Maybe we love tubing the river so much because we live in the Sonoran Desert. Or maybe it's just because it's so much fun.

to the rocks and snags. Tubing is a great way to spend a day from May through September. Life vests are recommended for children. To check on river conditions, call (480) 984-3305 or visit www.saltrivertubing.com. Water flow and weather permitting, open Fri, Sat, and Sun from Memorial Day to Labor Day.

If getting wet and wild doesn't appeal to you, follow the signs to Saguaro Lake for a more peaceful view of water life.

where to go

Fort McDowell Casino. On the Fort McDowell Yavapai Nation, on AZ 87 (known as the Beeline Highway); (480) 837-142 or (800) THE-FORT; www.fmcasino.com. Going northeast from Fountain Hills, northeast of Scottsdale, you'll see signs announcing the casino before you approach the Saguaro Lake cutoff (Bush Highway). Like other Native American tribes, the Fort McDowell tribe has discovered a steady source of income. Games run every day and night, and the crowds pour in. Although this is no competition for Las Vegas or even Laughlin, Nevada (just across the Colorado River from Arizona), this casino is very popular.

Fort McDowell Adventures. On the Fort McDowell Yavapai Nation; (480) 816-6465; www .fortmcdowelladventures.com. Fort McDowell Adventures offers trail rides, cattle drives, hayrides, Jeep tours, overnight pack trips, desert cookouts, and trail rides. Enjoy the beauty of unspoiled open desert near the Verde River and have great outdoor fun. Open year-round.

Saguaro Lake. Eight miles north of Shea Boulevard on AZ 88 at the Saguaro Lake Marina; (480) 986-5546; www.saguarolakemarina.com. Saguaro Lake is a popular summer destination for all water sports. Open daily; closed Thanksgiving and Christmas.

Precision Boating. Call the Arizona Marine Office, (480) 986-0969 to rent a boat and fully enjoy a day on the lake. Open daily; closed Thanksgiving, Christmas, and New Year's Days.

***Desert Belle* Paddleboat.** 14011 North Bush Hwy.; for schedule information call (480) 984-2425 or visit www.desertbelle.com. Cruise the lake on an 86-foot stern-wheeler. Narrated public tours last 90 minutes. Private charters are available. Fee.

Usery Mountain Regional Park. At Bush Highway and Usery Pass Road; for useful information call (480) 984-0032 or visit www.maricopa.gov/parks/usery/. Continue on Bush Highway to Usery Pass Road. Turn left (south) onto Usery Pass Road and follow it for 2 or 3 miles to this elegant mountain park. Spend time hiking the well-marked nature trails, or riding (if you trailer in your own horses). Leashed dogs are allowed on some trails. This is one of the nicest mountain parks "out in the tules."

where to eat

Lake Shore Inn Restaurant. At the Saguaro Lake Marina. 14011 North Bush Hwy., Mesa; (480) 984-5311; www.saguarolakerestaurant.com. This full-service menu features down-home fare. Come for biscuits and gravy at breakfast, barbecued chicken and sandwiches at lunch, and steaks and seafood at dinner. Call for hours. $$.

where to stay

Radisson Fort McDowell Resort. 10438 North Fort McDowell Rd., Scottsdale/Fountain Hills; (480) 789-5300, reservations (800) 395-7046; www.radisson.com/scottsdale-ftn-hills-hotel-az-85264/azmcdowe. Located on AZ 87 (Beeline Highway), this AAA Four Diamond resort features 248 lovely guest rooms and suites. The property is owned by the Fort McDowell Yavapai Nation and includes the awarding We-Ko-Pa Golf Club. $$–$$$.

Saguaro Lake Guest Ranch. 13020 Bush Hwy., Mesa; (480) 984-2194; www.saguaro lakeranch.com. Follow Shea Boulevard to AZ 87. Continue to the Saguaro Lake turnoff and follow signs. Privately owned and operated since the 1930s, this rustic ranch is nestled beneath towering red cliffs that border the Salt River. The drive to the ranch is worth the time just for the view. This section of the Salt is scenic and serene, and wildlife abounds. Cardinals and Baltimore orioles can be seen flitting through the trees in the spring.

The 25 cabins are comfortable, clean, and air-conditioned. Many hold 4 people comfortably. The lodge includes a large room dominated by a huge river-rock fireplace, piano, and bookshelves stuffed with books. The dining room is equally spacious. There's even a small swimming pool to cool you off on a hot spring day.

Call ahead to reserve a cottage for an overnight, or make reservations for lunch or dinner as part of a day's outing.

From the ranch you can also take 2- and 3-hour trail rides that offer gorgeous views of Four Peaks, Saguaro Lake, and the desert. Kayaking and family tubing available. $$. Lodging closed from late May to Sept except for special groups.

day trip 04

northeast

a road less traveled but with lots to offer:
springerville and casa malpais pueblo,
greer, sunrise

Day Trip 04 is an "Arizona-style" trip, which means a long haul for a one-day adventure. However, if you have the stamina, it's doable. A better alternative is to plan an overnight or even a weekend, as these destinations have much to offer and include opportunities that are not found anywhere else in the state.

springerville and casa malpais pueblo

Head northeast from Phoenix on US 60, 220 miles to Springerville, home of Casa Malpais Pueblo. Springerville is a very small town set amid great beauty.

Casa Malpais. 418 East Main St.; 928-333-5375; www.springervilleaz.gov or www.wm online.com/attract/casam.htm) is located on US 60. A National Historic Landmark, this was once the site of a thriving city that was occupied for about 200 years and then mysteriously abandoned about AD 1400.

The museum opened in 1991, although the first professional anthropologist, Frank Cushing, visited the area in 1883. While the area is miles away from the Colorado or New Mexico border, the pottery found here is similar to that found in the Four Corners region.

The "House of the Badlands," or Casa Malpais, overlooks the Little Colorado River's Round Valley. There is a breathtaking view of the White Mountains, which lie to the south.

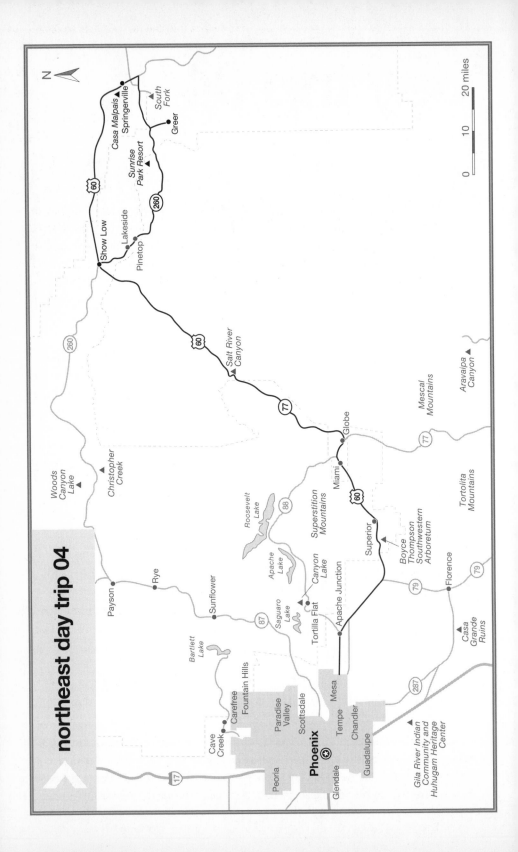

northeast day trip 04

N

0   10   20 miles

Casa Malpais ▲ Springerville
South Fork
Greer
Sunrise Park Resort ▲
60
260
Show Low
Lakeside
Pinetop
260
Salt River Canyon
60
Woods Canyon Lake ▲
Christopher Creek ▲
77
Globe
Miami
Roosevelt Lake
88
Superstition Mountains
60
Superior
Boyce Thompson Southwestern Arboretum ▲
Mescal Mountains
Aravaipa Canyon ▲
77
Tortolita Mountains
Payson
Rye
Sunflower
87
Saguaro Lake
Apache Lake
Canyon Lake
Tortilla Flat ▲
Apache Junction
79
Florence
Casa Grande Ruins ▲
79
Bartlett Lake
Cave Creek
Carefree
Fountain Hills
Peoria
Glendale
Paradise Valley
Scottsdale
Phoenix ✪
Tempe
Mesa
Chandler
Guadalupe
17
287
Gila River Indian Community and Huhugam Heritage Center ▲

What makes this archaeological site so special is that the museum and field laboratories are open to the public, Tues to Sat. Guided tours are available for a fee. Call for hours of operation. Museum entrance is free.

greer

From Springerville, head southwest for 13 miles to Greer. You'll pass by South Fork Canyon before finding this small mountain village 5 miles south of AZ 260. Greer is perched at 8,525 feet, which makes it an ideal destination year-round. The area is a sportsman's paradise that offers fishing, backpacking, ice skating, sleigh rides, and downhill and cross-country skiing. In cooperation with the USDA Forest Service, Greer has developed 35 miles of cross-country ski trails.

what to do

Butterfly Lodge Museum. Southeast corner of the intersection of AZ 373 and County Road 1126; (928) 735-7514; www.wmonline.com/butterflylodge.htm or www.springerville az.gov. Open Fri through Sun from Memorial Day through Labor Day, this historic lodge was the mountain residence and hunting lodge of author James Willard Schultz and his son, the artist Hart Merriam Schultz, known as Lone Wolf. The Butterfly Lodge Museum is listed on the National Register of Historic Places and was built in 1913–14. Schultz was an advocate for Native American rights and was influential in obtaining citizenship and voting rights for Native Americans. The authentic furnishings and artifacts illustrate the colorful careers of both father and son. Gift shop, and free children's activities at 2 p.m. on Sat. Fee; children free.

where to stay

Greer Lodge Resort. Greer. (928) 735-7216; www.greerlodgeaz.com. On AZ 260 past the turnoff to Sunrise Ski Park, turn right (south) onto AZ 373 (aka the "Greer turnoff"). Continue 5 miles on AZ 373/Main Street to the Greer Lodge Resort "check-in" facility on the right. Greer Lodge has been an Arizona tradition since the late 1940s and is family owned and operated. Originally built as a church retreat, the property includes a historic lodge and more than 50 free-standing cabins, making it a good choice for families and groups. All activities, including kayaking, stargazing, fly fishing, and mountain biking are free of charge. There's also hiking and cross-country skiing in winter. The resort's restaurant is the 373 Grill, which offers a full menu including a wine list. $$–$$$.

Hidden Meadow Ranch. P.O. Box 300, 620 County Road 1325, Greer 85927; (866) 333-4080 or (928) 333-1000; www.hiddenmeadow.com. About 10 miles north of the town of Greer, Hidden Meadow Ranch provides guests two options for driving directions, but both involve traveling a distance on a graded road. Each of the 12 luxuriously furnished log cabins

> ## ski arizona
>
> *While Payson is a popular destination, many visitors don't go beyond it. That's a shame, because northeastern Arizona has some of Arizona's most beautiful high-country scenery. During good years when we get deep snowfall, my family heads for Sunrise, the ski resort owned by the White Mountain Apache Tribe. The setting is awesome; the skiing is great for a weekend or few days of challenge. We like to stay at the tribe's hotel, which has a casino attached to it. Over the years, my husband and I took dozens of AFS exchange students to ski at Sunrise. One of our most unforgettable memories is getting a fearless Russian girl on skis for the very first time and watching her head straight down a long steep hill while we shouted, "Turn, Masha, TURN!" She never did.*

at this award-winning guest ranch is equipped with memorable amenities including a massive zinc soaking tub big enough for two. Each beautifully appointed cabin (all are nestled in the meadow) includes a main-floor master suite and second master suite in the upstairs loft area. This property has everything you could wish for, from horseback riding to fly fishing to large in-room candy jars that are filled daily. The chef is superb; the staff is friendly and unfailingly attentive, and the service overall is impeccable. With over 975 miles of trails to explore in the Apache-Sitgreaves National Forest, the ranch has been awarded best in the country by *Condé Nast Traveler* and offers four seasons of fun for children and adults. It's the West at its high-end best. $$$.

Red Setter Inn and Cottages at Greer Lodge Resort. 8 Main St., P.O. Box 244, Greer 85927; (928) 735-7216; www.greerlodgeaz.com. From Phoenix, take US 60 to Globe. Continue on US 60 to Show Low. Then take AZ 260 east to Greer Junction, AZ 373. The inn is at the end of AZ 373. This no-smoking and no-kids upscale bed-and-breakfast has 14 accommodations for anyone who enjoys seeing the great outdoors from relaxing Adirondack chairs. Now part of Greer Lodge Resort, the rate includes a full cooked breakfast and a sack picnic lunch for guests who stay 2 nights or longer. $$.

sunrise

Sunrise Park Resort. P.O. Box 117, Greer 85927; (928) 735-7669 or (800) 772-SNOW; www.sunriseskipark.com. This is a fully developed downhill ski area with a lodge, restaurant, and ski school located on the White Mountain Apache Indian Reservation. The mountains offer a variety of challenges, and the snow is often excellent. Open all year long, in the summer the area is a center for hiking and mountain biking as well as fishing and sailing on

Sunrise Lake. Horseback riding, fly-fishing school, in-line skating, archery tournaments, and volleyball are also scheduled. Also, enjoy the scenic lift ride on weekends. In the winter, call for snow conditions and reservations. *One word of warning:* The parking lot can get muddy and potholed in the winter and especially in early spring as the days warm up.

To return to Phoenix, continue west on AZ 260 to Show Low and the junction of US 60. Follow US 60 west to Phoenix.

where to stay

Hon-Dah Resort Casino. 777 Hwy. 260, Pinetop; (928) 369-0299 or (800) 929-8744; www.hon-dah.com. At the junction of AZ 260 and AZ 73, 3 miles outside of Pinetop, Hon-Dah resort is owned by the White Mountain Apache Tribe, which also owns and operates Sunrise Park. The motel-style rooms are spacious and clean, and the drive to Sunrise takes about 20 minutes in the winter, depending upon the weather. Rated by AAA as a Three Diamond property, it includes a pool and spa. Rates vary with the season. $$–$$$.

east

day trip 01

east

>>> **see (and do) it all and never leave town:**
scottsdale
worth more time: salt river pima-
maricopa indian community

scottsdale

No trip around Phoenix is complete without a day in Scottsdale, the shopping, art, and culture hub of the Valley of the Sun. It's difficult to believe that only a few decades ago Scottsdale Road was unpaved, and cowboys rode into town on Saturday night to whoop it up. Today it's a gathering spot for art aficionados, dedicated shoppers, and gourmets.

Follow Glendale Avenue east to Scottsdale. East of 16th Street, Glendale becomes Lincoln Drive. Continue east on Lincoln Drive and, as you near 24th Street and Lincoln, look to your left. There's Piestewa Peak, one of Phoenix's in-town mountain parks. Fit Phoenicians routinely climb this peak—some do it daily. If you have time and good walking shoes, turn toward the mountain at the sign to the park and explore a bit.

Continue on Lincoln Drive to Scottsdale Road. You'll pass through the town of Paradise Valley (not to be confused with the Paradise Valley area of Phoenix). This is a wealthy residential community of one-acre-plus home sites and a few well-manicured resorts. Paradise Valley is nestled between Mummy Mountain to the north and Camelback Mountain to the south.

Turn south onto Scottsdale Road and head into town for shopping and browsing. Later, you'll drive north to see other attractions. Scottsdale prides itself on its thriving downtown, outstanding art galleries, and variety of fine restaurants. During the tourist season (October through April), be prepared for traffic.

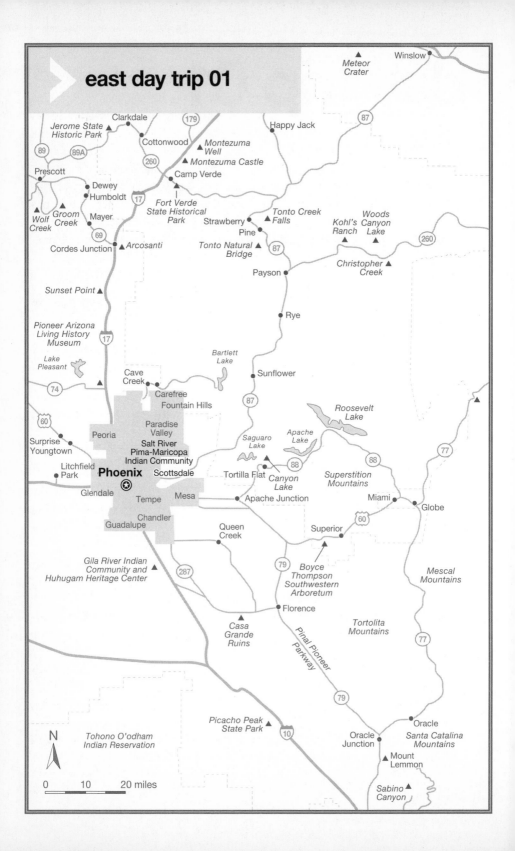

east day trip 01

Scottsdale is named for Gen. Winfield Scott and is known throughout the world as a favorite vacation spot. In the late 1800s, Scottsdale residents rented out rooms and screened sleeping porches to visitors. Today, Scottsdale is known as the city of great resorts. Its civic history is one of innovation and creativity. City fathers got on the urban redevelopment band-wagon early and turned a run-down section of downtown into a showcase for business and government. They were also instrumental in developing the flood-prone Indian Bend Wash into a series of green city parks and lakes. Today this beautiful, nationally acclaimed park runs the entire length of town along Hayden Boulevard. Every day of the year you can find activity there—from roller skating, fishing, and soccer to volleyball, baseball, and jogging.

where to go

Fifth Avenue. As you head south on Scottsdale Road, turn west onto Fifth Avenue (there's a light). There is free parking along the street. In addition, the city maintains several free park-ing lots. This shopping area has some very nice boutiques and gift shops mixed with some tacky souvenir shops. You'll also want to walk along Marshall Way, which intersects with Fifth Avenue, to see good art galleries. Ultimately Fifth Avenue connects with Indian School Road, which is one of the city's main east–west thoroughfares.

Local Talent.7050 East Fifth Ave.; (480) 874-1000; www.localtalentaz.com. See the work of talented Arizona designers and artisans: fashion for men, women, and children, and art pieces for the home. The 3,000-square-foot shop is a first for the state, which has many fashion designers but has not had a retail store dedicated to their art. Owner Shannon McRae has collected more than a dozen fine Arizona designers to showcase. Open daily.

Marshall Way. Intersects with Fifth Avenue, 1 block west of Craftsman's Court. Marshall Way is an art street with some of the city's best contemporary galleries. Some don't-miss places to visit include:

Art One. 4120 North Marshall Way; (480) 946-5076; www.artonegalleryinc.com. Emerging artists are featured in 2 galleries that always are fun to explore. Some featured artists are students at Arizona State University. Open daily; call for times.

Bentley Gallery. 4161 North Marshall Way; (480) 946-6060. Bentley carries pro-vocative, fine contemporary art and sculpture in an elegant gallery setting. A "must" for contemporary-art lovers. Closed Mon.

Calvin Charles Gallery. 4201 North Marshall Way; (480) 421-1818; www.calvincharles .com. International contemporary art is shown in an amazing art space.

Lisa Sette Gallery. 4142 North Marshall Way; (480) 990-7342; www.lisasettegallery .com. The most "New York" space in Scottsdale, this outstanding gallery features very fine and very contemporary art and photographs. Museum-quality shows are mounted. Owner Lisa Sette is knowledgeable and approachable. Closed Sun and Mon.

SouthBridge. www.southbridgescottsdale.com. An architecturally unique pedestrian bridge designed by Paolo Soleri connects the Waterfront retail area with SouthBridge. This new development features high-end boutiques and hip restaurants. Parking is available on the street and in an underground parking structure that is accessed from Stetson Avenue.

The Waterfront. 7135 East Camelback Rd.; http://scottsdalewaterfrontshopping.com. Located at Camelback Road between Marshall Way and Scottsdale Road, this is another of the city's new retail centers, also with a variety of fine shops and trendy restaurants. Underground parking is free and plentiful.

main street

During your stroll through the Fifth Avenue area, be sure to wander along Stetson Drive, Goldwater Boulevard, and 6th Avenue. Then you can move on to Main Street, which is lined with more art—western to contemporary. Scottsdale boasts, more than 125 galleries, museums, and festivals, enough to please even the most dedicated art enthusiast.

Pay attention to the sidewalk and you'll see the Art Walk "line". These sidewalk markers point the way to a self-guided tour of the Scottsdale Arts District. There are 21 stops that include art galleries and wearable art. You can download a map for this walk by visiting www.scottsdalecvb.com/arts-and-culture/art-walk. During the season (fall through spring), enjoy the Thursday night Art Walk, when the galleries along Main Street and the Marshall Way area stay open and stage special exhibitions. You can meet artists, mingle with art lovers, and enjoy refreshments and live music.

To reach Main Street, drive east on Fifth Avenue to Scottsdale Road. Turn south on Scottsdale Road and turn west at Main Street. Later you'll turn east to visit Old Town Scottsdale and its shops.

East of Scottsdale Road, Scottsdale's Old Town area projects an "Old West" image, recalling Scottsdale's history. The pedestrian crossing areas are set off in simulated brick, and the sidewalks along Main Street are shaded by wooden-shingled porticos extending from the buildings. These serve a practical as well as an aesthetic purpose. During the hot summer months, when temperatures climb upward to 110 degrees, the roofs afford essential shade. West of Scottsdale Road, it's all about art.

where to go

Main Street west of Scottsdale Road. Like Marshall Way, Main Street is lined with art galleries. Styles range from western American realism to contemporary, with everything in between. Here are a few favorites:

Faust Gallery. 7100 East Main St.; (480) 200-4290; www.faustgallery.com. The owner is the nephew of the legendary Lovena Ohl, and he continues her tradition of showcasing the finest contemporary Native American artists. Among the "name" artists who show here are Larry Golsh and the late Harvey Begay, both acclaimed as masters of contemporary

Native American jewelry. Faust Gallery includes a superb collection of collector Native American textiles, intriguing sculpture and sculptural furniture, paintings, kachina dolls, and an outstanding collection of historic art. Extraordinarily knowledgeable, owner Bill Faust is a gentle man who knows his art and his artists and displays only the highest quality work. Even collectors not interested in Native American art should make this shop a "must" on any Scottsdale tour. Open daily during the season (fall through spring). During the summer, the gallery is open Tues through Sat.

Gebert Contemporary Gallery/Chiaroscuro; 7160 Main St.; (480) 429-0711; www .gebertartaz.com. Founded in Santa Fe, New Mexico, as Chiaroscuro by the Gerbert family, this gallery has several locations. Gerbert/Chiaroscuro carries internationally known contemporary artists and a few emerging artists in this beautiful and spacious gallery.

Joan Cawley Gallery. 7135 East Main St.; (480) 947-3548; www.jcgltd.com. Showcases American contemporary and Southwest imagery. A longtime favorite. Closed Sun.

Overland Gallery. 7155 Main St.; (480) 947-1934 or (800) 920-0220; www.overland gallery.com. Overland Gallery carries well-known western and representational artists including Gary Ernest Smith, Ed Mell, and Martin Grelle. In 1991 the gallery introduced Russian impressionist paintings by master artists from the 1930s to the 1980s. Closed Sun.

Main Street east of Scottsdale Road. Park on Main Street east of Scottsdale Road, walk east to Brown Street, and then turn north. This area is a treasure trove of stuff for tourists to explore. Shops range from junk to funk—with some fine jewelry and clothing shops that feature western wear tossed in for good measure.

Stroll north on Brown Street toward Indian School Road for more browsing at **Pima Plaza**. Located on 1st Avenue between Scottsdale Road and Brown, Pima Plaza has restaurants, art galleries, and unusual shops, including one devoted to music boxes.

civic center mall

The Civic Center Mall area backs up to Old Town. An impressive government complex includes the Scottsdale City Hall, City Court, Library, and Center for the Arts, all designed by local architect Bennie Gonzales. The rolling lawns of the mall also act as an outdoor art museum for an impressive collection of contemporary sculpture.

Heading east on 2nd Street brings you to **Los Olivos** restaurant, established by the Corral family more than 50 years ago. It was named for the olive trees that lined the street, which were planted in 1895 by Gen. Winfield Scott, the town's founder. From here the tour continues to the Scottsdale Center for the Arts, Scottsdale Library, and Scottsdale Historical Museum.

Scottsdale Historical Museum. 7333 Scottsdale Mall; (480) 945-4499; www.scottsdale museum.com. In the area of Brown and Main Streets, this museum includes photographs, furniture, and other items that depict Scottsdale's early days. Free.

The Scottsdale Library. 3839 Civic Center Plaza. Stop in to enjoy the architecture and ambience. Visit the Arizona room as well. Here you'll see displays featuring items from Arizona history—from rare books to silver saddles.

This is worth a trip just to enjoy the architecture. Note the dove of peace that "floats" high above the entrance; the image is naturally projected by sunlight. Also marvel at the magnificent quill pen that hovers above the inkwell. The children's section is fun and offers enticing places to get turned on to books and reading.

The Scottsdale Center for the Performing Arts. 7380 East 2nd St.; (480) 994-ARTS; www.scottsdalearts.org. This facility boasts 2 theaters and a visual arts gallery. Both theaters and the gallery feature outstanding, nationally known artists. In addition, special events are sponsored during the year, including an outdoor crafts show. There's also a unique gallery shop for browsing. Admission to the center is free, but performances have fees; exhibits are often free. The gift shop is one of the best secrets of the city. Shop for unusual objets d'art, jewelry, books, and other unique items—all very well priced. Check with the box office for schedules.

Scottsdale Museum of Contemporary Art. 7374 East 2nd St.; (480) 994-2787; www .smoca.org. Located next to the Scottsdale Center for the Performing Arts, the museum building is the work of well-known Phoenix architect Will Bruder and is worth a visit just to see Bruder's vision. Inside is a sometimes controversial but always interesting collection of fine contemporary art, architecture, and design. The museum is billed as a "laboratory" for exploration and inquiry. Closed Mon. Fee.

Trailside Galleries. 7330 Scottsdale Mall; (480) 945-7751; www.trailsidegalleries.com. Western-art lovers will find much to enjoy at this gallery, where a variety of works by important artists is featured.

where to go

Historic Old Town Walking Tour. At the Little Red Schoolhouse on Civic Center Mall, pick up a self-guided walking tour guide to 14 destinations, including the Center for the Arts and the Scottsdale Library. The Little Red Schoolhouse is almost in the center of the original Scottsdale town site. It was built in 1909 at a cost of $4,500 and had 2 classrooms for grades 1 through 8.

From the 1920s until the 1960s, the area around the schoolhouse contained a barrio, or neighborhood, that began when Mexican laborers and their families arrived to work in the cotton fields that surrounded Scottsdale.

Walking west to Brown Street, you can see the next points of interest at the corner of Brown and Main Streets. **Bischoff's Shades of the West** is a western collectibles store today, but in 1897 it was the site of the first general store. By the 1940s it was an arts and crafts center called Arizona Craftsmen. **Affordable Elegance/Cactus Cones** still has a portion of the original adobe wall visible. Walking south on Brown Avenue, you see **Our Lady of Perpetual Help Catholic Church**, which today is the home of the Scottsdale Symphony. Built in 1933 by volunteer labor and donated materials, it consists of 14,000 adobe blocks, each weighing 50 pounds.

Continuing south on Brown to **Cavalliere's Blacksmith Shop** brings you to what was the edge of town. The original building was tin. The Cavallieres still own and operate it and, along with conventional smithing, produce ornamental wrought-iron items.

fashion square area

For more shop-'til-you-drop, head for Fashion Square at Scottsdale Road and Camelback. What used to be 2 malls is now a megamall that ranks as the largest in the valley. Wander through several department stores and browse through row upon row of boutiques. Dine at fine and casual restaurants.

This mall stretches across Camelback Road with a "bridge" of new shops that connects Nordstrom to the main mall. Parking is ample and available near all the fine anchor department stores that include Nordstrom, Neiman Marcus, Barney's, and Macy's. The mall looks massive, and it is. Inside are all the best nationally known stores, from Tiffany to the newest concept store for Banana Republic along with some one-of-a-kind Arizona-only shops. If you need help navigating the miles of retail shopping, the concierge desk is always available to you.

the borgata

North on Scottsdale Road to one traffic light north of McDonald Drive is an Italian village on the left. This is the Borgata. Why Italy in the midst of Arizona? Who knows? As you stroll through the interior brick courtyard, you'll find a clutch of chic shops and restaurants. On Friday afternoons starting in October and continuing through May, there's a fun farmers' market with live music.

McCormick-Stillman Railroad Park. 7301 East Indian Bend Rd.; www.therailroad park.com. Located at the southeast corner of Indian Bend and Scottsdale Roads. In 1967, Anne and Fowler McCormick donated 100 acres of McCormick Ranch to Scottsdale stipulating that it be used as a park. Almost a decade later, the 30-acre park opened in 1975. This is a great destination for families with young children. Everyone can climb aboard the train that travels around the perimeter of the park. There's also a carousel, and model-railroad clubs exhibit here. Of course there's a fun playground. Guy Stillman, son of the McCormicks, offered his 5/12-scale Paradise and Pacific Railroad to the city as the centerpiece for the park, which Walt Disney had tried to purchase for a theme park he was developing. In addition to model railroads, several full-size train cars are on exhibit. Free, but fee for the train and carousel.

north scottsdale

North Scottsdale offers a wealth of experiences including architectural tours at the Cosanti Foundation and Taliesin West and some of the region's best hiking. With the exception of the Cosanti Foundation, most of these destinations are located north of Shea Boulevard and east of Scottsdale Road. Shoppers will want to stop at Scottsdale Road and Doubletree Ranch Road, which is about a ½ mile south of Shea, to visit the SHOPS Gainey Village. Plan to browse the upscale boutique and enjoy a casual meal.

what to do

The Cosanti Foundation. 6433 Doubletree Ranch Rd.; (480) 948-6145; www.cosanti .com. As you leave the Borgata, go north on Scottsdale Road to Doubletree Ranch Road at the 4th stoplight. Turn west and watch for the sign to the Cosanti Foundation on the south side of the street. Wander through Paolo Soleri's enchanted studio. You'll be fascinated by the Soleri wind bells; made and sold on the premises, they make wonderful Arizona keepsakes. You can see the scale model for Arcosanti, the prototype community that Soleri is building in the desert north of Phoenix. Open daily. Enjoy a self-guided tour or call ahead to arrange group tours. View the hot bronze pour between 10 a.m. and noon, Mon through Fri.

Taliesin West. 12621 North Frank Lloyd Wright Blvd.; (480) 860-2700, ext. 494; www .franklloydwright.org. Follow Scottsdale Road to Shea Boulevard. Turn east on Shea for about 4/10 mile and make a left at Via Linda. Go approximately 4/10 mile and turn left at North 108th Street. Follow that to Taliesin West.

Taliesin West is the headquarters for Taliesin Associated Architects and an architectural school that teaches the design principles and philosophy of Frank Lloyd Wright, one of America's most respected architects. Wright died in 1959, but his belief that environment and structure should blend in total harmony continues to influence architects throughout the world. Call for information on night nature-walk tours.

"Under construction" since the 1930s, Taliesin West has been built and maintained by professionals and students who live and work there. (The original Taliesin was built in Wisconsin in the early 1900s.) The structures serve as a living testimony to Wright's enduring genius.

The compound is constructed of native Arizona materials, and the main building is positioned and designed to take full advantage of the warm winter sun. Hour-long tours given by Taliesin staff and students are available daily. These talks are exceptionally informative. Ask about the other tours that are available, such as tours of apprentice homes and studios. Be sure to save plenty of time to browse through the bookstore—it is a treasure trove of memorabilia about Mr. Wright as well as a great resource center for architecture. Open year-round. Call for information. Fee.

Arizona Cowboy College. 30208 North 152nd St.; (480) 471-3151; www.cowboycollege .com. If the cowboy life entices, Arizona Cowboy College offers the real thing in workshops that run as one-week camps. It operates on a ranch in North Scottsdale and a working cattle ranch in northern Arizona. Classes often are scheduled to coincide with fall and spring roundups. Fee.

McDowell Sonoran Preserve and Gateway Trailhead. 18333 North Thompson Peak Pkwy.; www.scottsdaleaz.gov/preserve. Strollers as well as serious hikers should plan to visit Gateway Trailhead at McDowell Sonoran Preserve to experience the full beauty of our desert. The preserve is a long-time dream of one woman, Carla (she uses this as her legal name), who convinced the city to invest and create this spectacular preserve. While there are other access points into the preserve, this trailhead is the largest and showcases hiking Scottsdale style. You'll find lots of parking, informative signage, and even chic (believe it!) bathrooms—all this and a great variety of trails. When completed, the McDowell Sonoran Preserve is expected to make up about one-third of Scottsdale's land base, maintaining scenic views and protecting this desert resource for future generations. Eventually a Desert Discovery Center will be built here. What is especially great is that this trailhead includes an easy and well-signed nature-trail loop that is ideal for children as well as adults, along with access to some of the best hiking trails in the state. There are also some areas for sitting and admiring the dramatic views. The website has detailed maps, but trails are well marked and accommodate all levels of hiking. Open daily. Free.

where to eat

Scottsdale boasts the most vibrant restaurant scene in the entire valley. Depending upon your taste you can enjoy sophisticated urban cuisine to cowboy grub and never leave town. Of course, there's also great Mexican food. Here are a few special places, many located near the heart of Old Scottsdale.

Arcadia Farms. 7025 1st Ave.; (480) 947-2596; www.arcadiafarmscafe.com. Tucked away near the heart of Old Scottsdale, Arcadia Farms is a good choice for lunch with its cottage and patio setting. The restaurant uses local organically grown, pesticide-free, hormone-free, and trans-fat-free ingredients in all recipes. As a member of Chefs' Collaborative, Arcadia Farms promotes sustainable cuisine by supporting local farmers and inspiring the public to make healthy food choices. It serves delicious breakfast and great lunches. Open daily. $$.

Cowboy Ciao. 7133 East Stetson Dr.; (480)946-3111; www.cowboyciao.com. The menu is modern American with Southwestern and global influences, which makes for quirky and delicious combinations. The setting is upscale western urban chic—Roy Rogers meets Donna Karan—yet it is always comfy. Save room for desserts that are designed to "satisfy your inner child." Check out the wine list to satisfy your "inner adult." Serving lunch, dinner, and Sun brunch. Open daily. $$–$$$.

Eddie's House. 7042 East Indian School Rd; (480) 946-1622; www.eddiematneys.com. Eddie is one of Arizona's best and most beloved chefs. His food is inventive and often hearty with a strong flavor of the eclectic Southwest. $$–$$$.

El Chorro Lodge. 5500 East Lincoln Dr., Paradise Valley; (480) 948-5170; www.elchorro lodge.com. Originally a school for girls and later a small guest ranch, El Chorro is a longtime landmark restaurant best known for serving great sticky buns. A local philanthropist and new owner gave it a much-needed renovation and enhanced its charm. The original buildings have been restored, and outdoor patios expanded. A new indoor-outdoor bar is a fun focal point. The "new" El Chorro personifies Southwestern elegance and serves continental cuisine with Southwestern accents. Serving lunch, dinner, and Sun brunch. Live music Thurs through Sat nights. Open daily. $$–$$$.

elements. 5700 East McDonald Dr.; (480) 948-2100; www.sanctuaryoncamelback.com. Located in one of Scottsdale's most hip resorts (Sanctuary Camelback Mountain), elements is clearly one of the valley's finest restaurants thanks to the talents of its chef, Beau MacMillen. Foodies will recognize his name as he is an Iron Chef winner and frequent TV celebrity. Complementing Beau's inventive and superbly prepared cuisine are the sweeping views of Paradise Valley. The restaurant, nestled high on Camelback Mountain, has the best setting in town. Don't miss the Jade Bar. Open daily. $$–$$$.

Frank & Lupe's. 4121 North Marshall Way; (480) 990-9844; www.frankandlupes.com. Great for casual New Mexican–style cuisine food that not super spicy. All recipes are from Frank and Lupe's families. The patio is a great place for dining. It's misted, making it comfortable almost all year around, and the funky setting feels like Old Mexico. Serving lunch and dinner. Open daily. $–$$.

Greasewood Flat. 27375 North Alma School Pkwy.; (480) 585-9430; www.greasewood flat.net. The ultimate Arizona casual bar and steak house, everyone eats outside on picnic tables. The place is historic; the hamburgers are good, and on cool evenings the campfire is roaring. Live music. Open daily for lunch and dinner; Sun lunch is always a scene. $–$$.

Los Sombreros Cafe & Cantina. 2534 North Scottsdale Rd.; (480) 994-1799; www.los sombreros.com. Located at Virginia and Scottsdale Road in South Scottsdale, Los Sombreros recreates regional Mexican cuisine from San Miguel, Mexico, the owner's home town. It's a neighborhood cafe located in a restored 1920s-era farmhouse. You can eat inside or have a margarita and dinner on the intimate patio. Serving lunch and dinner. Open daily. $$.

Pinnacle Peak Patio Steakhouse & Microbrewery. 10426 East Jomax Rd.; (480) 585-1599; www.pppatio.com. This huge rambling complex is famous for mesquite-broiled steaks as well as for cutting off the neckties of unsuspecting "dudes" who come into a cowboy place too dressed up. Open daily. $$.

where to stay

Scottsdale is a mecca for luxury resorts.

Camelback Inn, a JW Marriott Resort and Spa. 5402 East Lincoln Dr.; (480) 948-1700 or (800) 24-CAMEL; www.camelbackinn.com. This resort has maintained its four-star, five-diamond rating since the award was introduced. It features spacious grounds, elegant pools, and one of the most complete and beautiful spas in the valley. Despite all the renovations, the essential beauty remains. Casitas are tucked away under the shadow of Mummy Mountain. $$$.

Fairmont Scottsdale. 7575 East Princess Dr.; (480) 585-4848; www.fairmont.com. Grand and impressive, this ultralarge, Moorish-style resort features world-class golf and tennis, patios that go on forever, and sumptuous dining. $$$.

Four Seasons Resort at Troon North. 10600 East Crescent Moon Dr.; (480) 515-5700 or (800) 819-5053; www.fourseasons.com/scottsdale. Set on 40 acres of vibrant desert blooms, the five-diamond Four Seasons appears like a contemporary pueblo village terraced against the mountainscape of North Scottsdale. With priority golf privileges at nearby Troon North golf course, this ultraposh but super-comfortable resort features an intimate and award-winning contemporary steak house, a full-service and elegant spa, 4 tennis courts, and a lagoon-style swimming pool. A special feature is the children's pool, where pint-size teak lounge chairs are positioned next to Mom's and Dad's. $$$.

Hotel Valley Ho. 6850 East Main St.; (480) 248-2000; www.hotelvalleyho.com. Hotel Valley Ho was cool when it opened in 1956, and the reimagined midcentury-modern version of the Valley Ho is just as hip today. Choose from stylish rooms and suites; indulge at Café ZuZu and Trader Vic's. Or stay in the new tower (it was in the original plans but was never built) that is a hotel within a hotel. The round swimming pool and full-service spa add to the glam. $$$.

Hyatt Regency Scottsdale at Gainey Ranch. 7500 East Double Tree Ranch Rd.; (480) 444-1234; www.scottsdale.hyatt.com. Contemporary architecture, great golf, tennis, and a pool featuring a sand beach are part of the charm here. There is also a fine-dining restaurant.

Another reason to stay at this hotel is the Native American and Environmental Learning Center. The hotel has made a strong commitment to Native Americans. A small exhibition is run by Hopi "hosts" who share some of their culture with hotel guests. A visit to the learning center is the next best thing to a trip to the Hopi or Navajo reservations. $$$.

The Phoenician. 6000 East Camelback Rd.; (480) 941-8200; www.thephoenician.com. It features rolling golf courses, 9 swimming pools, and a nature trail with more than 300 kinds of cactus along the way. The Centre for Well-Being Spa is excellent. Rooms are oversize; suites are vast. Sun brunch is the best in the valley. $$$.

Sanctuary Camelback Mountain. 5700 East MacDonald; (480) 948-2100; www.sanctuary az.com. This renovated, upscale boutique resort is a luxurious hideaway high on the north face of Camelback Mountain. Hillside casitas are part of the compound, along with an intimate spa, pool, and fine-dining restaurant (elements). $$$.

worth more time:

salt river pima-maricopa indian community

The Salt River Pima-Maricopa Indian Community is surrounded by Scottsdale, Tempe, Mesa, and Fountain Hills. Established in 1879, it is home to 2 tribes, the Pima and the Maricopa. About 6,000 people live within the community, which covers a little more than 52,000 acres.

To learn about the heritage and culture of these 2 tribes, visitors can tour the small Huhugam Ki Museum (10005 East Osborn Rd.; 480-362-6320; www.srpmic-nsn.gov). The words *Huhugam Ki* mean "house of those who have gone" and refer to the Pimas' ancestors, the Hohokam Indians, who were the original residents of the Salt River Valley.

The small museum is constructed of adobe and desert plants and contains interpretive exhibits that describe these tribes' heritage. Baskets, pottery, photographs, and other historic articles are on display, and community members are often at the museum demonstrating their skills as potters and basket weavers. Open Mon to Fri. Free.

This tribe owns several business enterprises, including Casino Arizona (with 2 locations, one at Loop 101 and McKellips and the other at Loop 101 and Indian Bend Road), Talking Stick Resort, and Pavilions at Talking Stick shopping center at Indian Bend and Pima Roads, as well as Salt River Fields at Talking Stick.

Both locations of Casino Arizona are open 24 hours a day and feature dining rooms, gift shops, and other amenities. In addition to slot machines, poker, and other games of chance, these facilities include fine-dining rooms and theaters that showcase outstanding performers. Both facilities are open to the public with or without a visit to the gaming rooms. Tribal officials point out that revenues generated from both casinos fund government, social, health, and educational services for the tribe. For information on Casino Arizona, call (480) 850-7777 or visit www.casinoaz.com.

Visitors are always welcome at powwows, which are held in April and Nov. For information call the Huhugam Ki Museum at (480) 362-6320. For general information about the community, contact Tribal Administration at (480) 362-7400 or www.srpmic-nsn.gov.

what to do

Pavilions at Talking Stick. Loop 101 and Indian Bend Rd.; www.scottsdalepavilions.com. This open air shopping mall was one of the first major retail malls developed by a Native

American tribe. Currently you'll find big-box stores like Target and small one-of-a-kind boutiques as well as several restaurants. As of this writing, the Pavilions is under redevelopment
and new stores will be added soon.

Salt River Fields at Talking Stick. 7555 North Pima Rd.; (480) 270-5000; www.saltriver
fields.com. Located at Loop 101 and Indian Bend, next to the Pavilions at Talking Stick
shopping center, Salt River Fields at Talking Stick is the first major league baseball spring-
training facility built on tribal land. The complex is home to the Arizona Diamondbacks and
Colorado Rockies teams. Both teams practice here during the year and play Cactus League
ball games in the huge shaded stadium. The park's design puts visitors up close to their
favorite players so you can watch batting practice or practice games. Interpretative signage
makes this 140-acre site double as an outdoor museum, introducing visitors to the cultures
of the O'odham (Pima) and Piipaash (Maricopa).

Talking Stick Golf Club. 9998 East Indian Bend Rd.; (480) 860-2221; www.talkingstick
golfclub.com. Designed by Bill Coore and Ben Crenshaw, this 36-hole golf club consistently
ranks as one of the best in the state. The course is owned by the Salt River Pima-Maricopa
Indian Community and operated by Troon. Wildhorse Grille is open to the public and serves
excellent food. Open daily. $–$$.

Talking Stick Resort. 9800 East Indian Bend Rd.; (866) 877-9897. This resort and casino
includes a 15-story tower that is topped by the Orange Sky restaurant, a memorable fine-
dining experience with 360-degree views of the valley. Be there at sunset for the full effect.
The resort-spa-casino complex includes a floor full of gaming, a big state-of-the-art show-
room with live concerts and performances, multiple lounges, spa, and a full range of dining
options. Open daily. $$–$$$.

day trip 02

east

>>>
the east valley swings and twists and turns:
tempe, mesa, queen creek, apache junction, tortilla flat, the lakes

tempe

Years ago, most of eastern metropolitan Phoenix was open space. Snowbirds, or winter visitors, as they are more politely called, flocked to the East Valley. Cotton was king, but much of that is history now. Today as you drive east toward Tortilla Flat, you'll see many new residential developments. But gradually, as you leave the urban area behind and continue along the famous Apache Trail, you'll find yourself in open country where you can marvel at the wild natural beauty that is still here, so close to the city. When your day is done, you'll even know the answer to those ubiquitous bumper stickers that ask: where the hell is Tortilla Flat?

Tempe, along with Mesa, is one of the major cities in the East Valley. The city is home to one of the nation's largest universities—Arizona State University (ASU). Originally called "Hayden's Ferry," the city's history owes its past, present, and future to Judge Trumbell Hayden, a miller, educator, and all-around promoter who established a ferry across the Salt River in 1872. By 1877, the community that quickly followed was known as Tempe. Almost immediately, Judge Hayden began lobbying the territorial government to establish a teacher's college in Tempe. That tiny college grew up to be ASU.

Today Tempe continues to be a pioneering sort of place. Most notably, the city constructed the Tempe Town Lake, a large recreational lake in the once-dry Salt River bed. Lined by adjacent parks and new urban development, it is the first successful demonstration

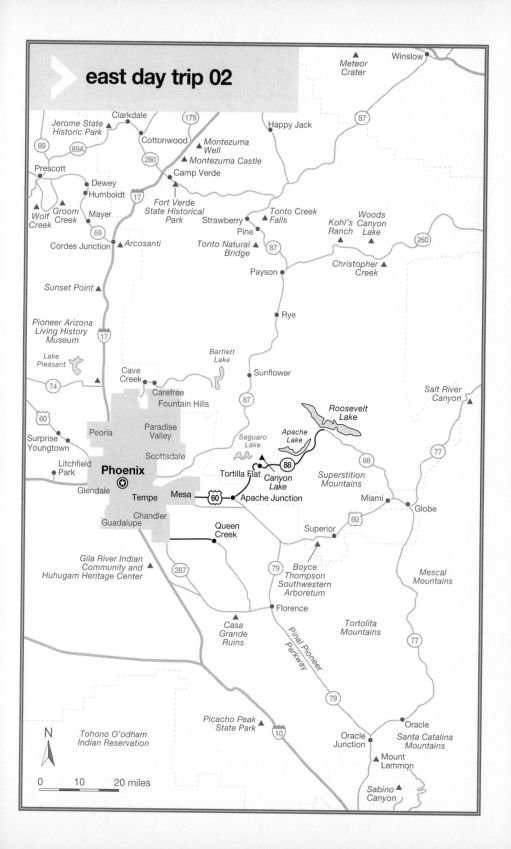

of the Rio Salado project and created an entire new center for town as offices and recreation uses lined the river banks. In 2010, the rubber dam that created the lake ruptured, temporarily disrupting the lake experience. But the city quickly began to repair the dam and bring back the Town Lake. In addition to the Town Lake, Tempe is a center for festivals. Twice a year the town hosts a huge art and craft festival along Mill Avenue.

Tempe's biggest claim to fame is ASU. To see the campus, park in one of the visitor lots and walk the palm-lined malls. See the library, which is built mostly underground, and the school of architecture with its exterior red shade grid. The most famous building is the Grady Gammage Memorial Auditorium, designed by Frank Lloyd Wright.

To get a sense of Tempe's past and future, drive through the downtown. Follow Mill Avenue south past ASU Gammage. You may wish to make a quick jog east to see Tempe City Hall at 31 East 5th St. Turn east off Mill Avenue onto East 5th for a short half block to get a glimpse of this unusual contemporary structure. Designed in the shape of an inverted pyramid, the glass-and-steel building shades itself from the glaring Arizona sun.

where to go

Arizona State University Grady Gammage Memorial Auditorium. On the corner of Mill Avenue and Apache Boulevard; (480) 965-5062; www.asugammage.com. This was the last public building Frank Lloyd Wright designed. Although he did not live to see it completed, it's

switching gears: hip and happening to rugged beauty

One word of warning: During the fall, when there's a home football game, don't even try to visit downtown Tempe. ASU is a football school and traffic gets re-routed to accommodate fans who show up hours early to tailgate in the parking lot of Sun Devil Stadium. Tailgating is an elaborate ritual here, complete with bar-becue grills and gourmet feasts.

If you want to get the full flavor of ASU, stroll along Mill Avenue on a weekend night when the students are out in force. You'll love it or hate it, but you won't forget it.

A completely different experience awaits you on the Apache Trail. This is an amazing ribbon of road that twists and turns through some of the desert's most breathtaking landscape. It was a marvel of engineering in its day and still is impressive. Whenever I drive it, I remind myself that this area has been a tourist destination since automobiles arrived in Arizona and were able to climb the steep hills. I can never think too long about what that must have been like because there's always another sharp curve to navigate.

a hallmark of Wright's vision. Follow Scottsdale Road south into Tempe, where it becomes Rural Road. Turn west onto University Drive and south on Mill. You'll see the center's distinctive pink color and scalloped roofline just beyond the curve on Mill between University and Apache. The public may purchase tickets to events at Gammage—there's a full season of music, dance, theater, and lectures. Half-hour tours of the building are available on a limited basis. Call for information. Free.

If you want to spend more time on campus, pick up a map from an attendant at any of the visitor parking lots. The map will direct you to other points of interest, such as:

The J. Russell Nelson and Bonita Nelson Fine Arts Center. At 10th Street and Mill Avenue on campus. ASU boasts a magnificent visual-and-performing-arts complex by noted architect Antoine Predock. This Egyptian-inspired group of buildings is definitely worth a visit. Within the complex you'll find the University Art Museum, which has one of the finest American ceramics collections in the country. The various traveling shows as well as the permanent collection are all outstanding. The complex also includes the Paul V. Galvin Playhouse, the University Dance Laboratory, and other interior and exterior exhibition and performing space.

Sea Life Aquarium. Arizona Mills, 5000 Arizona Mills Circle; (480) 478-7600; www.sealife us.com/phoenix/phoenix-home. From I-10, exit Baseline Road East; from US 60, exit Priest Drive South to Arizona Mills. This is one of some 30 aquariums developed in 11 countries by an international aquarium company, and it is the first Sea Life Aquarium in the United States. The exhibit, which is part of Arizona Mills outlet center, includes 26,000 square feet of display tanks and habitats that showcase more than 5,000 creatures in 200,000 gallons of water. Even better, Sea Life actively promotes conservation. Open daily. Fee.

Tempe Center for the Arts. 700 West Rio Salado Pkwy.; (480) 350-2822; www.tempe .gov/tca. Strikingly beautiful, this center was designed by Tempe-based Architekton and award-winning Barton Myers Associates of Los Angeles. Facing Tempe Town Lake, the building houses a state-of-the-art, 600-seat proscenium theater, a 200-seat studio theater, and a 3,500-square-foot gallery. Internationally known Childsplay performs here along with the Tempe Symphony Orchestra and chorus and dance ensembles.

mesa

To get to Mesa from Tempe, follow Apache Boulevard east. As it enters Mesa, Apache becomes Main Street. Once known primarily for its wide streets—wide enough for an ox team to turn around—Mesa is a fast-growing big city that is proud of its excellent schools, churches, and heritage. The Chamber of Commerce and Mesa Convention and Visitors Bureau is located at 120 North Center. You can find information on the community center, the historical and archaeological museum, little theaters, and the youth museum. (480) 827-4700; www.visitmesa.com.

where to go

The Arizona Museum for Youth. 35 North Robson St.; (480) 644-2468; www.arizona museumforyouth.com. One of only two children's museums in the country that focuses on the fine arts, this is a special family place. The museum is owned by the city of Mesa and the Arizona Museum for Youth Friends Inc. It opened in 1981 in a temporary facility, moved to its permanent facility in 1986, and has been nationally honored in a *USA Today Weekend* magazine article as the "Most Outrageously Artful" children's museum in America.

The exterior of the brick building gives no hint of the exciting interior environment designed to titillate the imagination, stimulate the mind, and captivate the eye. Three exhibits are mounted annually, one for each of the fall, spring, and summer school semesters. Artwork is installed at a child's eye level, and traditional museum displays are interspersed with participatory activities to enhance and reinforce the visual experience.

Closed Mon. The museum is also closed for 2 weeks every spring, summer, and fall. Fee.

Arizona Museum of Natural History. 53 North MacDonald St.; (480) 644-2230; www .azmnh.org. Arizona's premier natural history museum, the Arizona Museum of Natural History, formerly the Mesa Southwest Museum, explores the Southwest's history from the time before the dinosaurs to the present day. See the largest collection of dinosaur fossils in the state, visit a Spanish mission, look for the lost Dutchman's treasure, pan for gold in the History Courtyard, experience the diversity of Arizona's earliest inhabitants, see beautiful examples of Native American pottery, "star" in a made-in-Arizona movie, and much more. Closed Mon and holidays. Call for hours. Fee.

Mesa Arts Center. 1 East Main St.; box office: (480) 644-6500; administration: (480) 644-6501; www.mesaartscenter.com. This is the largest arts complex in the state and an architectural treat that shouldn't be missed. Drop-in tours of the campus are held at noon on Mon and 5 p.m. on Thurs. The center features performing and visual arts. Open daily.

The Mesa Temple Visitors Center. 525 East Main St.; (480) 964-7164; www.mesa templevc.weebly.com or www.lds.org and select "Places to Visit." This imposing structure serves as Arizona headquarters for the Church of Jesus Christ of Latter-Day Saints. Although the sanctuary is open only to Mormons, the visitor center welcomes guests. You may learn something about the Mormon faith and hear about the Mormon men and women who came west to establish homes, farms, and communities. Tours of the temple's visitor center are available anytime. Call for more information.

Usery Mountain Recreation Area. Follow Usery Pass Road 12 miles northeast of Mesa to the main entrance; (480) 984-0032; www.maricopa.gov/parks/usery. This 3,324-acre recreation area provides trails for hiking and horseback riding, camping and picnic areas, and an archery range. Eleven hiking trails are lush with desert vegetation and are of varied difficulty. The most popular are Wind Cave Trail and Pass Mountain Trail. Open daily. Fee.

where to eat

Rockin' R Ranch. 6136 East Baseline Rd.; (480) 832-6793; www.rockinr.net. Mosey on over to Arizona's Wild West town. The specialty is chuck-wagon suppers, and the restaurant serves huge steaks as well as fish, ribs, and chicken. Enjoy horse-drawn wagon rides, pan for gold, watch staged gunfights, and take in some entertainment by the Rockin' R Wranglers. Good family entertainment. Reservations are requested. Dinner theater available. Open Sat only in the summer. Call for information and reservations. $$–$$$.

queen creek

There are 2 good reasons to visit Queen Creek: the Queen Creek Olive Mill and Schnepf Farms. Fortunately both are very near each other, so you can cover Queen Creek in an easy day.

Queen Creek Olive Mill. 25062 South Meridian Rd.; (480) 888-9290; www.queencreek olivemill.com. From Mesa/Tempe take AZ 101 south to US 60 and transition onto eastbound US 60. Take US 60 approximately 18 miles to Ironwood Road, exit 195, and turn south. Travel approximately 11 miles to Combs Road and turn right (west). Travel 1 mile and turn right (north) on Meridian Road. The Mill entrance is on your left.

Arizona's only working olive farm and mill produces wonderfully flavored olive oils for sale in the large store. Visitors can tour the mill and sample artisan olive oils and other delicious products. Order lunch and enjoy al fresco dining on the grounds. Open daily.

Schnepf Farms. 24810 South Rittenhouse Rd. (480) 987-3100; www.schepffarms.com. From Mesa, take US 60 east to the Ellsworth Road exit. Turn right on Ellsworth and drive south to Rittenhouse Road. Turn left on Rittenhouse and follow it about 3 miles to the farm's entrance on right. Mark and Carrie Schnepf and their 4 children are the sole operators of Schnepf Farms, and they produce a full calendar of festivals along with offering tours and gourmet dinners. Visit the website or call for hours and events.

apache junction

Continue east on US 60 to Apache Junction, which calls itself "The Gateway to the Super-stition Mountains." This range has fascinated people for more than a century, ever since German immigrant Jacob Waltz arrived in Arizona in 1863 to prospect for gold. According to legend, Waltz found, or possibly stole, one of the very rich Peralta gold mines deep in the Superstition Mountains. Try as he did, however, he never again was able to find the mine and prove his claim.

Because people mistakenly thought that the immigrant was from Holland, as Waltz continued his search, the story grew about the "Dutchman's Lost Mine." In time, the unproven claim became known as "The Lost Dutchman's Lost Mine," a misstatement that no one has bothered to correct.

Apache Junction itself is a sprawling conglomeration of commercial property and mobile homes set against the spectacular Superstition range. Drive through it and continue on AZ 88 to begin the Apache Trail, a section of Arizona that even impressed President Theodore Roosevelt. Observing that it combined the grandeur of the Alps, the glory of the Rockies, and the magnificence of the Grand Canyon, he called it "the most awe-inspiring and most sublimely beautiful panorama Nature has ever created." Clearly others agreed. Teddy Roosevelt predicted in 1911 that the Salt River Valley would boom and attract people from throughout the country, and he was right.

where to eat

The Mining Camp Restaurant and Trading Post. 6100 East Mining Camp Rd.; (480) 982-3181; www.miningcamprestaurant.com. Turn left onto AZ 88 at Apache Junction and continue north for 4 miles.

This landmark restaurant is built of rough-sawn ponderosa pine that was hauled from Payson. A replica of the old mining camp cook's shanty sits at the base of the Superstition Mountains.

The interior has also been copied with amazing authenticity. A trading post sells authentic Native American relics, legendary maps, and photos of early mining days. All-you-can-eat food is served family-style. If you like never-ending amounts of hearty western food amid a rustic gold-mining atmosphere, this place is for you. Open Nov 1 through May 31. Call for reservations. $$.

tortilla flat

Travel 18 miles northeast on AZ 88 to reach Tortilla Flat, one of the last true outposts of the West. Here visitors will find a rustic dining room that features hamburgers and chili, a weatherbeaten-looking small hotel, and a public restroom. This is a fun place to stop.

Although tiny by anyone's standards, Tortilla Flat is the last town between Apache Junction and Roosevelt Dam. A few miles east of Tortilla Flat, the Apache Trail turns into a rough gravel road. If you decide to continue east to Roosevelt Lake, prepare yourself for a rugged and even hair-raising trip.

AZ 88, also known as the Apache Trail, is one of the most crooked roads in the nation. It was named for the Apache Indians who helped build the very scenic, winding road that ends at Roosevelt Lake. It was constructed to haul materials for Theodore Roosevelt Dam. The route snakes through some of the prettiest mountains and desert in the Phoenix area. Along the way is Tortilla Flat, the only surviving stagecoach stop on the route. The buildings were destroyed by fire some years ago but have since been rebuilt. Today you can stop at the general store, cafe, and post office. The prickly pear cactus ice cream and the chili are specialties.

where to go

Goldfield Ghost Town. 4650 North Mammoth Mine Rd.; (480) 983-0333; www.goldfield ghosttown.com. Four miles northeast of Apache Junction on AZ 88, just past mile marker 200. Go on a mine tour, pan for gold, and explore specialty shops. The town sells antiques, has a museum, and sports a steak house with spectacular views of the Superstition Mountains. You can also take a 20-minute ride on the state's only narrow-gauge railroad.

the lakes

If you're ready for more scenery, follow the Apache Trail on AZ 88 east 28 miles through the chain of man-made lakes on the Salt River that includes Canyon Lake, Apache Lake, and Roosevelt Lake, which is much larger than the other two. Roosevelt Lake is located on the gravel road after the pavement ends. The unpaved stretch is notable not only for its rough surface but also for its steep descent into Fish Creek Canyon. Adventurous tourists are advised to make this trip by traveling east, not west, in order to easily see approaching automobiles.

The Apache Trail is a trip of unforgettable beauty in all seasons. The trip winds through scenic desert mountain vistas, climbs in hairpin turns, and finally plunges into Fish Creek Canyon. Because of the condition of the road, it is slow going in places. But that only gives travelers more time to enjoy the breathtaking views of desert lakes, saguaros, and mountain landscapes.

Fish, water-ski, relax, swim, or just enjoy the desert lake views. Each lake offers services for travelers.

where to go

Canyon Lake. Follow AZ 88 for 16 miles north of Apache Junction to the Canyon Lake Marina; (480) 827-9144; www.dollysteamboat.com. Like all Arizona lakes, Canyon Lake is a hotbed of summertime activity, from power boating to waterskiing to Jet Skiing. Those who prefer to have a less strenuous experience will enjoy *The Dolly,* a 103-foot stern-wheeler. The day cruise takes 1½ hours and is narrated. Lunch is available, and box lunches may also be purchased. Romantics may prefer the dinner cruises, which are priced according to the changing menu. Call ahead for reservations and menu information. Canyon Lake also caters to visitors with the Lakeside Restaurant and Cantina, a family restaurant at 9593 East Anasazi Place (480-288-8290; www.canyonlakerestaurant.com). $$; fee for the cruises. Call for reservations.

Apache Lake. (928) 467-2511; www.apachelake.com. You'll find a full-service resort and marina with boats for fishing and tackle. Check with the Apache Lake Resort for more information.

Roosevelt Lake. (928) 467-2245; www.nps.gov/tont/culture/roosevelt.htm or www.rlmaz .com. Roosevelt Lake is your ultimate destination and is well worth the trip, which traverses paved and unpaved roads that snake through some of the best desert scenery in central Arizona. Although the road through Fish Canyon is not paved, it is graded. The Apache Trail is a magnificent drive at all times of the year but especially beautiful in the spring and fall. A year-round haven for unwinding, Roosevelt Lake is popular among skiers, bass anglers, and campers. There's a full-service marina. The visitor center is definitely worth a visit as it tells the story of how Roosevelt Dam was constructed through models, exhibits, and outstanding photographs. It also affords a magnificent view of the panorama of Roosevelt Dam, one of the major masonry dams in the world.

Roosevelt Dam. Roosevelt Dam remains one of the most important reclamation projects in the United States. Without the dam's ability to stop flooding and provide a well-managed source of water, the Phoenix metropolitan area would not have developed as it has. The dam is also a sight of amazing beauty.

Tonto Basin Ranger Station and Visitor Center. (928) 467-3200; www.fs.fed.us/r3/tonto. Located at Roosevelt Lake, this visitor center tells the story of Roosevelt Dam through models and exhibits. A good bookstore provides you with additional information about the dam and this riparian area. If you are interested in camping, the center has current information on Roosevelt Lake's modern campgrounds. Some even have solar-heated showers. Open daily. Fee.

day trip 03

east

take a shine to copper country:
superior, miami-globe
worth more time: salt river canyon
and show low

superior

Pick up this trip in Apache Junction and travel southeast on US 60 toward Superior. The approximately 50-mile drive from Mesa to Superior takes you deep into copper-mining country. Arizona owes its history to the mines and the railroads, for the presence of precious minerals—gold, silver, and copper—lured people west. The railroads opened the land so that men could carry those treasures out and, in the process, made the territory accessible to settlers.

The main street of this small town follows Queen Creek, which is nestled among the copper-stained mountains. In 1875 this was a bustling silver- and gold-mining center. Today its future hangs on a precarious copper thread.

where to go

Boyce Thompson Southwestern Arboretum. US 60, just a few miles west of Superior; (520) 689-2723 or (520) 689-2811; http://ag.arizona.edu. As you drive toward Superior on US 60, turn right at the sign and follow the driveway into the arboretum. This vast (1,076-acre) living museum was the dream of William Boyce Thompson, a mining magnate and philanthropist. He endowed not only this site but also a sister institution, the Boyce Thompson Institute for Plant Research. The Arizona arboretum is all the more intriguing because of its Sonoran Desert location.

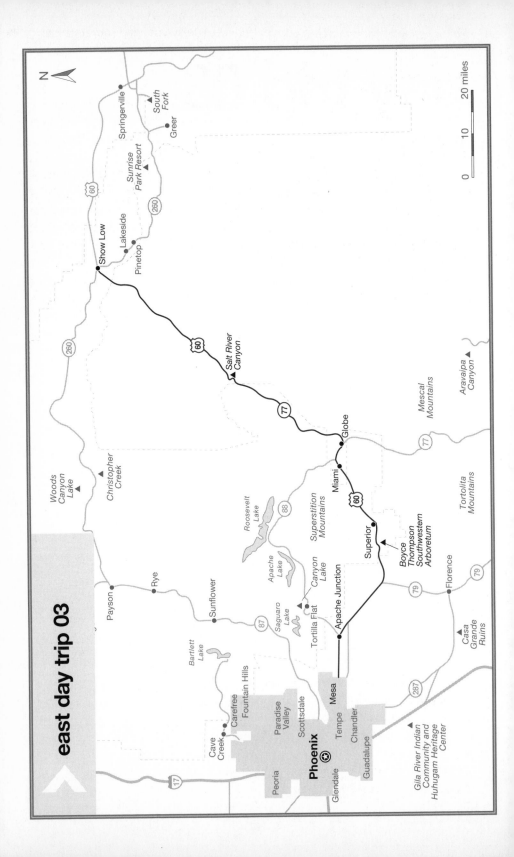

east day trip 03

N

20 miles
0   10

Springerville

South
Fork

Greer

Sunrise
Park Resort

Lakeside

Pinetop

Show Low

260

60

260

Woods
Canyon
Lake

Christopher
Creek

Salt River
Canyon

60

77

Globe

Mescal
Mountains

77

Aravaipa
Canyon

Payson

Rye

Sunflower

Roosevelt
Lake

88

Apache
Lake

Superstition
Mountains

Canyon
Lake

Miami

Superior

Boyce
Thompson
Southwestern
Arboretum

Tortolita
Mountains

Bartlett
Lake

Saguaro
Lake

Tortilla Flat

Apache Junction

60

79

Florence

79

Cave
Creek

Carefree

Fountain Hills

Paradise
Valley

Scottsdale

Mesa

Tempe

Chandler

Guadalupe

287

Casa
Grande
Ruins

17

Peoria

Glendale

Phoenix

Gila River Indian
Community and
Huhugam Heritage
Center

This is one of the most special spots in Arizona. The grounds are well marked and, in most places, wheelchair accessible. The long loop trail will take you an hour to 2 hours depending upon how long you stay at each designated stop along the way. There are a myriad of side loops to follow depending upon your interest and the season.

If you have never meandered through a shady and fragrant eucalyptus grove, stared at the numerous twisted arms of a 200-year-old giant saguaro cactus, or tried to figure out how the bizarre boojum tree grows, you've missed some of the desert's best pleasures. Begin your tour at the visitor center and get acquainted with this living garden before heading out on the well-marked trails. They begin with some "easy-does-it" walks and graduate to more challenging terrain.

One fascinating section is devoted to old-world trees, including the pomegranate, Chinese pistachio, and olive, that are of major economic importance in various parts of the world. You will be amazed to learn how many different trees can grow in the Arizona desert. Also available are display greenhouses, herb gardens, and a demonstration garden. Open daily except Christmas. Picnic grounds with grills. Fee.

rolling desert and small mining towns

This area is called the Tonto Basin since it is surrounded by the 3 million–acre Tonto National Forest. It is the ancestral territory of the Yavapai Apache people, but it is also copper country, as you'll see when you discover the small mining towns. This is also the land of the vast San Carlos Reservation and Fort Apache Reservation, which are home to the San Carlos Tribe and the White Mountain Apache tribe. If you make this day trip, include a stop at one of my favorite Indian ruins, Besh-Ba-Gowah Archaeological Park. It has been so carefully reconstructed you can feel the presence of the people who once lived in this pueblo. I also highly recommend that you drive the steep and narrow Salt River Canyon. Be prepared for spectacular mountain and canyon views. We have done this many times, but my favorite memory of the Salt River Canyon is driving this high desert highway alone after a big winter snowstorm and seeing the prickly pear cactus and agaves that grow along the road thick with snow. If I wasn't driving our extended-cab diesel pickup, I would have pulled over and taken pictures. On the return trip that day, I was more comfortable handling the truck, but the snow had already melted.

miami-globe

Continue on US 60 east to Miami and Globe. As you enter Miami, look for the sign noting the site of the Bloody Tanks Massacre of Apaches. Proceed east to Globe, the seat of Gila County and a center for cattle and mining. Globe began as a mining town in 1886, but now it is the trading center for the San Carlos Apache Indian Reservation and a favorite headquarters for wild pig (javelina) hunting. Apart from the natural setting, the main attraction here is mining, although in recent years the town has become a focus for historical renovation. A historical home tour is held each February, and the whole town participates. Pick up a self-guided walking and driving tour map at the chamber of commerce. Visit the Globe-Miami Chamber of Commerce, 1360 North Broad St., US 60, Globe; call (928) 425-4495 or (800) 804-5623 for information; or visit www.globemiamichamber.com.

Be sure to include the **Gila County Historical Museum** (1330 North Broad St.; 928-425-7385; www.arizonahistoricalsociety.org or www.globeaz.gov) in your tour. This small museum holds a treasure trove of pioneer and mining artifacts collected throughout the region. Closed Sun. Call for hours. Free.

where to go

Besh-Ba-Gowah Archaeological Park and Botanical Gardens. 1324 South Jess Hayes Rd.; (928) 425-0320; www.globeaz.gov. Take Broad Street through historic downtown Globe for approximately 1½ miles. You'll see the turnoff for the park. Besh-Ba-Gowah is the remains of a prehistoric village that overlooks Pinal Creek in the shadow of the Pinal Mountains. The walls and structure are made of rounded river cobble and mud, and the careful reconstruction lets you experience the plazas and living quarters as they must have been centuries ago. Artifacts, including a weaving loom, grinding stones, and even a large squash, are carefully positioned in some of the reconstructed rooms.

Besh-Ba-Gowah means "a place of metal" or "metal camp." This pueblo consists of more than 300 rooms and once housed 400 people. It was built and occupied from about AD 1225 to AD 1400 by the Salado Indians. These people were accomplished farmers and grew crops including corn, beans, and squash along the banks of Pinal Creek.

The community also functioned as a trading center. The Salado made pottery and traded widely. They also wove baskets of sotol and yucca fibers as well as fine cotton cloth, and they adorned themselves with bracelets and necklaces made of shells they acquired by trading their pottery and baskets.

As with many pueblos, it is suspected that drought drove the people out. Besh-Ba-Gowah lay abandoned for years but underwent excavation and stabilization in the 1980s. The park opened in 1988. There is an excellent small museum on the grounds that displays artifacts relating to this site. Group tours by arrangement. Open daily. Fee.

where to shop

Antiques and collectibles. In recent years, the Globe-Miami area has attracted many antique shops. Sullivan Street in Globe is known as antique alley, and the town of Globe touts its "antique trail." Local favorites include the Hill Street Mall at 383 South Hill St., the Pickle Barrel Trading Post at 404 South Broad St., and Pretty Patty Lou's at 551 South Broad St. Quilters delight in visiting Johnny's Country Corner, 383 South Hill, with its outstanding array of quilts and quilting supplies. Pick up a brochure from the chamber of commerce for more information.

The Cobre Valley Center for the Arts. 101 North Broad St., Globe; (928) 425-0884. This cooperative is housed in the historic Gila County Courthouse, which has been renovated to its original splendor. The arts and crafts exhibited are by local artists. Free.

where to stay

Noftsger Hill Inn. 425 North St.; (928) 425-2260 or (877) 780-2479; www.noftsgerhillinn .com. Call for directions. This is a bed-and-breakfast housed in an old elementary school that sits on a hilltop overlooking Globe. $$; no credit cards accepted.

worth more time:

salt river canyon and show low

From the Miami-Globe area, continue northeast on AZ 77/US 60 another 87 miles for a magnificent plunge through the wild beauty of the Salt River Canyon and a visit to the community of Show Low. Plan to spend the night in Show Low or head southeast for approximately 5 miles on AZ 160 to Lakeside or Pinetop and stay there.

The Salt River Canyon begins about 30 miles northeast of Globe on AZ 77/US 60 and is often called "The Mini Grand Canyon." Take this drive during the daytime so you can appreciate the spectacular sights. The highway twists and turns for 5 miles from the top of the canyon to its floor.

This is one of the most scenic stretches in all of Arizona. Along the way, you can pull off at several lookout points to admire the artistry wrought by millions of years of erosion. If you have packed a light lunch, picnic at one of the several shady spots provided at the bottom of the canyon. This area is well marked. Pull off, park, and walk down a flight of steps to the riverbank. Adventurous adults and children will want to explore the river, swim, or fish. If you travel 7 miles downstream on a dirt road, you'll see the amazing **Salt Banks.** The formations tower 1,000 feet above the river, looking like giant ocean waves frozen in time and about to crest.

When you're ready for the long climb out of the canyon, continue approximately 60 miles northeast on AZ 77/US 60 to Show Low. This small community is a hub of activity with the 4 million acres of the White Mountain Recreation Area, which include 500 miles of trout streams and 50 lakes. It is also home to **Sunrise Park,** the state's most complete ski center and resort.

Show Low enjoys a high, cool climate and a backdrop of exceptional forest land. Its name reputedly came from an incident involving C. E. Cooley, who had been a government scout with Gen. George Crook. Cooley married the daughter of Chief Pedro of the White Mountain Apaches and, in 1875, established a home on what is now called Show Low Creek. His place became a favorite spot for travelers. Marion Clark was Cooley's partner, but at some point in the relationship, Clark decided to end their hotel venture. To settle on who should stay and who should leave, the two agreed to play a card game of Seven-Up. When the hand was dealt, Cooley lacked a single point to win. As they prepared to draw cards, Clark is reputed to have said, "If you can show low, you can win." Cooley tossed his hand down and said, "Show low it is." Clark moved up the creek to what is now Pinetop, and thanks to the deuce of clubs, Cooley stayed. More important, the name stuck.

Today Show Low is the trade and service center for southern Navajo County and portions of southern Apache County. Tourists use it as a jumping-off point for recreation in the White Mountains. You'll find modest facilities here, including motels, cabins, and campgrounds. For more information write the Show Low Chamber of Commerce, 951 West Deuce of Clubs, Show Low 85901; call (928) 537-2326 or (888) SHOWLOW; or visit www .showlowchamberofcommerce.com.

southeast

day trip 01

southeast

>>> **experience cowboys, indian-style:**
gila river indian community,
casa grande, florence

gila river indian community

Follow I-10 east to exit 162, Wild Horse Pass Boulevard. The Gila River Indian Community tribal land lies south of metropolitan Phoenix and borders the cities of Phoenix, Mesa, Gilbert, Coolidge, Casa Grande, Avondale, and others. It covers nearly 400,000 acres. In addition to farming, the tribe operates casinos, owns a Native American–inspired resort, has built a 36-hole golf course, and operates a heritage center.

what to see

Rawhide at Wild Horse Pass. 5700 North Loop Rd., Chandler; (480) 502-5600; www .rawhide.com. From I-10 south, exit at 162, Wild Horse Pass Boulevard, to 48th Street. Turn south on 48th Street. Head west on North Loop Road. This authentic 1880s town is a great stop for families. It has shops, a museum, rides, and attractions including a rock climb, stagecoach ride, mechanical bull, and desert train ride. The Six Gun Theater presents a rough and tough stunt show, and the Spirit of the West Theater showcases western acts. For many years this attraction was located in Scottsdale, but in 2005 it moved to the Gila River Indian Community. The Rawhide Steakhouse features good western fare like ribs and steaks. Open daily. Call for hours. Free admission. Fee for some attractions.

Sheraton Wild Horse Pass Resort and Spa. 5594 West Wild Horse Pass Blvd., Chandler; (602) 225-0100; www.wildhorsepassresort.com. This resort has received raves for its

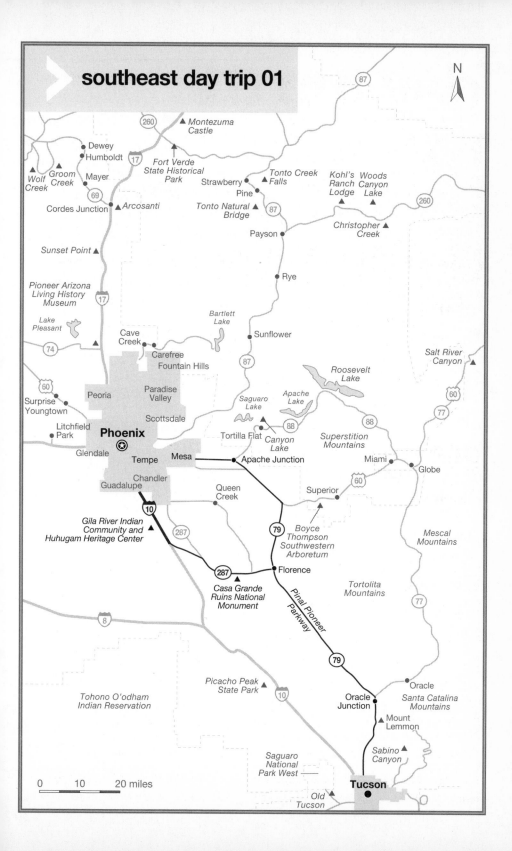

southeast day trip 01

N

Montezuma Castle ▲

260

Dewey
Humboldt

17

Fort Verde
State Historical
Park

Strawberry

Tonto Creek Falls ▲

Kohl's
Ranch
Lodge ▲

Woods
Canyon
Lake ▲

Wolf
Creek ▲

Groom
Creek ▲

Mayer

69

Pine

87

260

Cordes Junction

Arcosanti ▲

Tonto Natural
Bridge ▲

Payson

Christopher ▲
Creek

Sunset Point ▲

Rye

Pioneer Arizona
Living History
Museum

17

Bartlett
Lake

Sunflower

Roosevelt
Lake

Salt River
Canyon ▲

Lake
Pleasant

74

Cave
Creek ▲

87

60

Carefree
Fountain Hills

Saguaro
Lake

Apache
Lake

77

Surprise
Youngtown

60

Peoria

Paradise
Valley

Tortilla Flat

Canyon
Lake ▲

88

Superstition
Mountains

88

Litchfield
Park

Scottsdale

Phoenix ⊙

Glendale

Tempe

Mesa

Apache Junction

Miami

Globe

Guadalupe

Chandler

Queen
Creek

Superior

60

Mescal
Mountains

10

Gila River Indian
Community and
Huhugam Heritage Center ▲

287

79

Boyce
Thompson
Southwestern
Arboretum

287

Florence

Tortolita
Mountains

77

Casa Grande
Ruins National
Monument ▲

Pinal Pioneer Parkway

8

Picacho Peak
State Park ▲

10

79

Oracle

Oracle
Junction

Santa Catalina
Mountains

Tohono O'odham
Indian Reservation

Mount
Lemmon ▲

Saguaro
National
Park West

Sabino ▲
Canyon

0   10   20 miles

Tucson ●

Old
Tucson

native american culture

Since gaming facilities opened on tribal land, Indian tribes in the metropolitan areas have become significant "players" in economic development, especially tourism. This day trip takes you to the Gila River Indian Community reservation. Once considered remote, today the reservation seems amazingly close to the East Valley as the valley has grown east. Well served by I-10, it's just 15 minutes from Phoenix Sky Harbor International Airport. Although this community continues to develop new hotels and other venues, it is also committed to preserving its past. To learn about its history, visit the beautiful Huhugam Museum. For cowboy culture, stop at Rawhide, a favorite Old West tourist attraction that is now located on this reservation. I suspect this one of the few places in the United States where you can see cowboys presented Indian-style.

sensitive interpretation of Native American life. Canals bordered with native grasses wind throughout the property. Guests can ride in boats to participate in resort activities. The fine-dining restaurant, which features Native American–inspired cuisine, is superb. A stable on the property offers riding and western events. $$–$$$.

Huhugam Heritage Center. 4759 North Maricopa Rd. (within the Gila River Indian Community); (520) 796-3500; www.huhugam.com. Located near the hotel and the casino, the heritage center is an interpretation of "The Big House" at Casa Grande and combines a research institution with a museum. In addition to exhibits, an outdoor area, modeled after ancient Indian ball courts, is used for outdoor festivals and performances. Open Wed through Fri. Fee.

where to eat

Kai at Sheraton Wild Horse Pass Resort and Spa. 5594 West Wild Horse Pass Blvd., Chandler; (602) 225-0100; www.wildhorsepassresort.com. Kai has garnered nearly every prestigious award—including the AAA Five Diamond Award and Forbes Five-Star Award—and, along with Binkleys, is considered to be one of the finest restaurants in the state. The inventive menu incorporates the essence of the Pima and Maricopa tribes and uses locally farmed ingredients from the Gila River Indian Community. The cuisine, service, and ambience make this an exceptional Arizona dining experience. Ko'Sin, the more casual restaurant, is also excellent and incorporates Native American traditional foods. Open Tues to Sat. $$$.

where to stay

Sheraton Wild Horse Pass Resort and Spa. 5594 West Wild Horse Pass Blvd., Chandler; (602) 225-0100; www.wildhorsepassresort.com. This was the first property that the Community built. The 500-room luxury property was designed to reflect the heritage and culture of both the Pima and Maricopa people. The Aji Spa is first rate. $$–$$$.

Wildhorse Pass Hotel & Casino. 5040 Wild Horse Pass Blvd., Chandler; (800) 946-4452; www.wildhorsepass.com. The 242-room property is located in a ten-story tower and is part of the Gila River Indian Community's Wild Horse Pass casino complex. It offers visitors a luxurious urban experience. $$–$$$

casa grande

Casa Grande was traditionally an agricultural and manufacturing town that has now expanded into the retail industry with 2 major shopping outlet centers located conveniently along I-10. The community is located midway between Phoenix and Tucson and was founded in 1879. This is the largest community in Pinal County.

where to go

Casa Grande Valley Historical Society. 110 West Florence Blvd.; (520) 836-2223; www .cgvhs.org. Located in downtown Casa Grande, this museum presents many historical facts about the area. Exhibits focus on the history of the region from the arrival of the railroad in 1879 to the present. Fee. Call for hours.

florence

Continue east on AZ 287 to Florence, approximately 9 miles from Coolidge. Florence has two main claims to fame: its courthouse and the prison. The fifth-oldest city in the state, it was established in 1866 by a local Native American agent, Levi Ruggles. The community grew rapidly and became the county seat when Pinal County was chartered in 1875. In spite of its desert setting, Florence is an agricultural community. Local crops include cotton, cattle, sugar beets, grain, and grapes. Poston Butte, named for Charles Poston, the "Father of Arizona," is a nearby landmark.

If you want to continue to Tucson (see Day Trip 03 Southeast from Phoenix), you may take US 79 south (Pinal Pioneer Parkway) for a 42-mile scenic stretch between Florence and Oracle Junction and then continue south to Tucson. This drive takes you through a unique natural garden where virtually every type of Arizona desert flora is displayed. Depending upon your time and botanical interest, you can explore easily accessible side roads along the way.

To return to Phoenix from Florence, take US 79 north for 16 miles to its junction with US 60. Turn west and follow US 60/US 89, 47 miles to Phoenix through Apache Junction, Mesa, and Tempe (Day Trip 02 East from Phoenix).

where to go

Pinal County Visitor Center. 330 East Butte, P.O. Box 967, Florence 85232-0967; (520) 509-3555 or (888) 431-1311; www.pinalcountyaz.gov/visitors. Located in the heart of the historic district, the visitor center has an official guest book that visitors are asked to sign. This is the place to get maps and brochures about special events that take place during the year as well as inquire about the local businesses and restaurants. Open weekdays 8 a.m. to 4 p.m.

day trip 02

southeast

>>> **back to the future:**
casa grande ruins national
monument, biosphere 2

casa grande ruins national monument

Get ready to go "back to the future" with a full day touring an ancient Native American ruin and then jetting into a space-age environment. From Phoenix take I-10 east to exit 175 through Sacaton. From Sacaton take AZ 287 southwest for approximately 14 miles to Coolidge. As you approach Coolidge, you will come to the Casa Grande Ruins National Monument, an 11-room, 11-family, 600-apartment building built by the ancient Hohokam and Pueblo Indian farmers. This structure was constructed of hardened mud blocks that are 5 feet long, 2 feet high, and 4 feet thick. Today it is protected by a giant steel "umbrella." While its original use is still debated, this is the only four-story Native American ruin structure found in the United States, and the only example in Arizona of a structure from the Classic Period (AD 1300–AD 1400).

Discovered in 1694 by Father Kino, the structure had already been burned when he came upon it. The Pima Indians had a custom of burning the inside of their buildings when they abandoned them. The ruins were explored in 1882 by Dr. J. Walter Fewks of the Smithsonian Institution. Dr. Fewks returned to do more exploration in 1906 and 1908.

As you wander through these imposing ruins, pay special attention to the calendar holes. Two small openings in the east and center rooms are placed so the sun's rays come

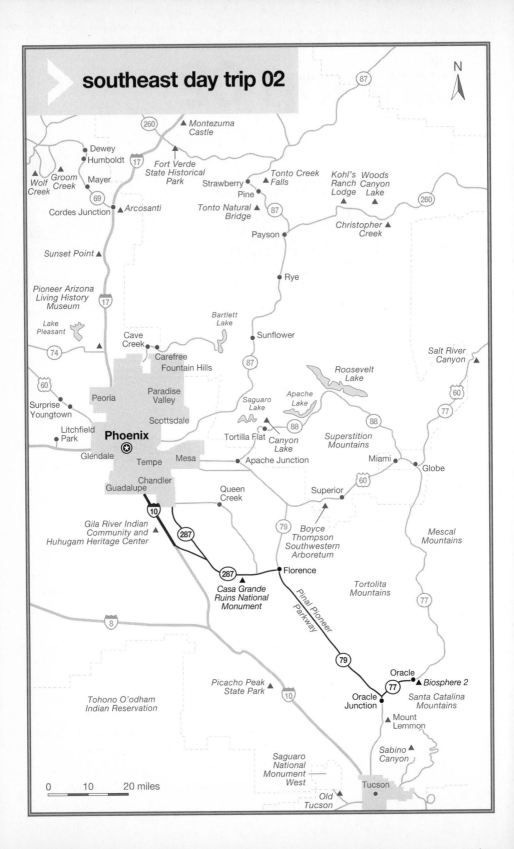

> ## miniworlds
>
> *This trip is short on scenery, but once you arrive at Casa Grande Ruins, you'll forget the miles of flat, scrubby desert and housing developments. In this pre-Columbian world, you are transported into the society of the Huhugam (Hohokam). I think it's fun to pair this with a tour of Biosphere 2, the only glass-enclosed, human-size eco-system world in the country. The project was built with high hopes as an experiment (with the goal of being a prototype for long distance space travel) to understand how to live in a contained environment. I was fortunate to follow it closely, from pre-groundbreaking to closure, covering it for magazines including* Life *and* Metropolitan Home. *The night before Biosphere 2 was officially sealed for the first attempt to sustain life within a closed-loop environment, I was among invited guests who toured the enclosure from tropical mountaintop to savanna, farm fields to "ocean"—all the while marveling at the miniworlds within its glass-enclosed walls.*

through. The streak of light passing through both holes and lining up on a target occurs near the spring and fall equinoxes.

If you visit with smaller children, ask for the special trail guides that are available for youngsters. The guides are free, but a donation is always appreciated. Open year-round, except Christmas. Fee. (520) 723-3172; www.nps.gov/cagr.

biosphere 2

From Casa Grande Ruins National Monument, continue on AZ 287 west to Florence. Then travel south on US 79 to Oracle Junction and join AZ 77. Follow AZ 77 to mile marker 96.5 at Oracle and follow the signs to Biosphere 2 and SunSpace Ranch. (520) 838-6200; www.b2science.org.

This 3½-acre enclosure is a microcosm of Earth. The project has been under way since 1984. It was built as a human experiment in which 4 men and 4 women lived inside in a sealed and re-created "earth environment" for 2 years. Stocked with nearly 4,000 species of plants and animals, the project replicates 7 life zones, or biomes, including a tropical rain forest, marshland, desert, savanna, mountains, and ocean. Next to the dramatic structure are several domelike buildings that act as the "lungs" for the project.

A walking tour takes visitors around the site and inside the "miniworld." The tour begins in the theater, where visitors learn about the philosophy that guided this experiment. Inside, virtually everything is recyclable and nothing is disposable. The tour continues around the grounds of the project to give visitors a sense of its magnitude. Open daily for tours except Thanksgiving and Christmas. Fee.

day trip 03

southeast

drive down and up to the old pueblo:
picacho peak

picacho peak

The best reason to take a day trip to Picacho Peak State Park is to plan a leisurely hike around the area—especially in the spring when the wildflowers are in bloom. Happily, there are several trail options that accommodate serious hikers and casual walkers alike. If you are not a hiker, you can still admire this landmark, craggy formation from the vantage point of your car as you speed by on the interstate. But enjoying it requires taking the time to drive into the park, get out of the car, and walk or hike the trails.

Picacho Peak State Park. (520) 466–3183; www.azstateparks.com. Picacho Peak State Park is located 60 miles southeast of Phoenix, just off I-10. From the ranger station, follow the Barrett Loop to the trailhead of Hunter Trail.

Located halfway between Tucson and Phoenix, this landmark soars to 3,400 feet. Calloway Trail (⁷⁄₁₀ mile) and a short nature loop (½ mile) offer pleasant excursions, but hotshot hikers should head for Hunter Trail and a steep 2¹⁄₁₀-mile trek to the summit.

The ascent begins immediately on a clearly marked, difficult path. In 45 minutes, even the semifit can reach the saddle, where a panoramic view of the Sonoran Desert extends beyond the Picacho Mountains to the Catalinas near Tucson. In spring the desert floor may be carpeted with bright orange Mexican poppies, adding vibrant color to the stands of sun-bleached ocotillo and saguaro.

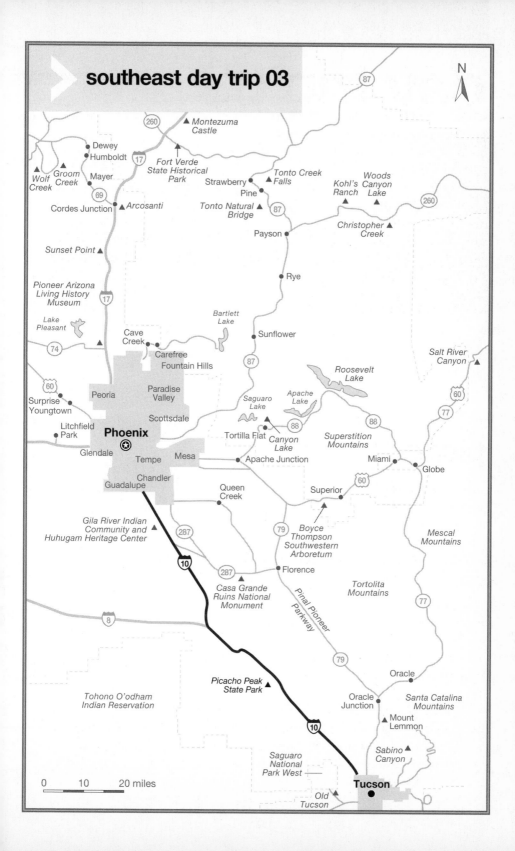

southeast day trip 03

From the saddle the trail gets rough, plunging down 300 feet before climbing to the summit. Twelve sets of cable, anchored into bare rock, provide handholds. Hardy hikers will discover that the view from the top is glorious. Carry water, wear boots and gloves, and expect a rugged, 3- to 5-hour round-trip. Hikers should avoid the summit trail during June, July, and August.

Long a beacon for wayfarers, Picacho Peak was known to prehistoric Hohokam Indians who traveled here on trade routes. Later Pima or Papago Indians and Spanish missionaries camped on this site. On April 15, 1862, two advance Union and Confederate units clashed near Picacho in the westernmost battle of the Civil War. Reports of casualties vary, but it's known that three Union soldiers were killed. A monument commemorates the skirmish, and the battle is reenacted every March.

A second memorial within the park honors the Mormon Battalion, which built the first wagon road across the Southwest in 1846. Fee.

day trip 01

southwest

>>>

arizona's historic river city:
yuma

yuma

Follow I-10 southeast out of Phoenix to the junction of I-8. Continue west on I-8 to Yuma (about a 4-hour drive). Situated in the southwestern corner of the state, Yuma has an interesting heritage. History confirms that the area was visited as early as 1540 by the Spaniards. By the 1870s this community was the key southwestern city in the territory. First called Colorado City (for the river), then Arizona City (for the territory), and eventually Yuma City, the name finally was shortened to Yuma.

Yuma won a permanent place in Arizona Territory by 1870. Today the residents of this city rely on the same river waters to support agriculture, commerce, recreation, and the military. Located close to San Diego and Mexico, this small city attracts thousands of winter visitors to its sunny environs.

Today some historic buildings commemorate what was once the busy Yuma Crossing. The Colorado and Gila Rivers converged here before the Gila changed its course. Eighty years before the Pilgrims landed, beginning in 1540, Spanish explorers rode through this land in search of the Seven Cities of Gold.

As time passed, countless trails met at this junction. Kit Carson guided American troops. The Mormon Battalion trudged through, carving the first road from Santa Fe to San Diego, and during the gold rush days, more than 30,000 people seeking their fortunes trekked across the river here on their way to California.

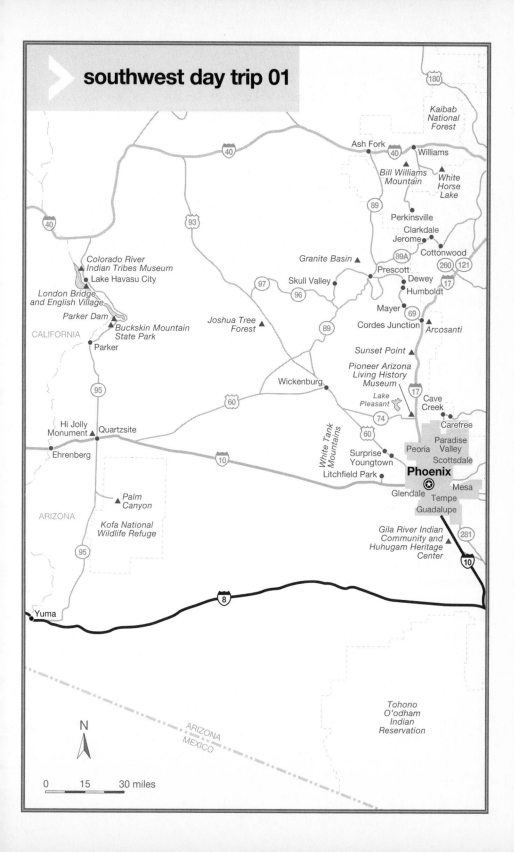

southwest day trip 01

> ## recommended overnight excursion
>
> *A disclaimer is in order before you read further. This isn't a day trip by most standards, but in Arizona, we are used to longer distances. The drive to Yuma is about 3½ hours one way, so I recommend you plan this as an overnight excursion. But because so much history happened here, Yuma is definitely on my recommended visit list. The westernmost city in Arizona, Yuma used to sit quietly on the banks of the Colorado River, except during the winter months, when the population boomed with winter visitors who came for the sunshine and easy lifestyle.*

In the 1850s the shallow draft steamboat opened the Colorado River to shipping, and Yuma became a major port of entry for Arizona. The Fort Yuma Quartermaster Depot swarmed with the bustle of a military supply hub. During the 1860s, 1870s, and 1880s, during the height of the Apache Wars, the Yuma Quartermaster Depot supplied military posts throughout the region. Then the train arrived in 1877, and the depot was abandoned in 1883.

For more information call the Yuma Convention and Visitor Bureau at (928) 783-0071 or (800) 293-0071, or visit www.visityuma.com.

where to go

Peanut Patch. 4322 East County 13th St.; (928) 726-6292 or (800) USA-PNUT; www.the peanutpatch.com. This store was opened in 1977 on the Didier family farm and sells some of the finest peanut products in the West. Tours of the plant are available. Open Oct through May. Closed Sun. Free.

Sanguinetti House Museum. 240 South Madison Ave.; (928) 782-1841; www.arizona historicalsociety.com. One of Yuma's most historic buildings, this was the home of pioneer merchant E. F. Sanguinetti. A regional museum of the Arizona Historical Society, it holds historical documents, photographs, and artifacts. Walk through the gardens and aviaries on the grounds. Open daily except closed all federal holidays. Fee.

U.S. Army Quartermasters Depot/Arizona State Park. On 2nd Avenue behind City Hall. The depot was established in 1864 and served the entire Southwest as a matériel transfer and distribution point for troops stationed at the military outposts throughout the Arizona Territory. The depot saw much activity during the 1870s and 1880s at the height of the Apache Wars, but it was abandoned in 1883 after trains arrived here in 1877. Both the quartermaster's office and the stone water reservoir have been restored to their original condition. This state park is open as of this writing.

Yuma Art Center. 254 South Main St.; (928) 373-5202; www.ci.yuma.az.us/parksandrec/artcenter.htm. Located in a restored Southern Pacific Railroad depot, the center presents exhibitions of contemporary Arizona and Native American artists. Closed Sun and Mon. Donation suggested.

Yuma River Tours. 1920 Arizona Ave.; (928) 783-4400; www.yumarivertours.com. One of the best ways to enjoy Yuma is by jet boat river tour. The boats travel past ruins and petroglyphs, ferry crossings, and homesteads. You'll see steamboat landings and mining camps and visit a wildlife refuge, one of the few untouched refuges in the entire country. Also offered are beautiful lunch and dinner cruises aboard a stern-wheeler. This is a special experience that shouldn't be missed. Reservations required. Fee.

Yuma Territorial Prison State Historic Park. Giss Parkway and Prison Hill Road, off I-8 near the Colorado River; (928) 783-4771; www.historicyumaprison.com or www.azstateparks.com. Now a state park, the prison operated from 1876 to 1909 and had a miserable reputation. Western bad men (and women) used it as their address—folks such as Buckskin Frank Leslie and "Heartless" Pearl Hart. Museum exhibits document the story of the prison cells, which are authentically furnished and add a hands-on sense of reality. You can also take a ranger-guided tour of the facility. Open daily except Christmas. Fee; children 6 and younger free.

Pick up a self-guided tour pamphlet from the Yuma County Chamber of Commerce, 180 West 1st St. in the old city hall building (928-782-2567; www.yumachamber.org), for more to see in Yuma.

where to eat

Chretins. 505 East 16th St. (928) 782-1291; www.chretins.com. This family-owned Mexican restaurant is huge, old, and funky. Expect to wait if you arrive on a weekend during the winter, but the Mexican menu is homemade and worth it. The atmosphere is old Yuma with a touch of Mexico. Open daily. $$.

La Fonda Tortilla Factory. 1095 South 3rd Ave.; (928) 783-6902; www.lafondarestaurantandtortillafactory.com. This place serves excellent Mexican food. The service is slow, but the tortillas are delicious. $$.

Mi Rancho. 188 South 4th Ave.; (928) 783-2116. Authentic Mexican food is served here. Posole and soft tacos are highly recommended. $–$$.

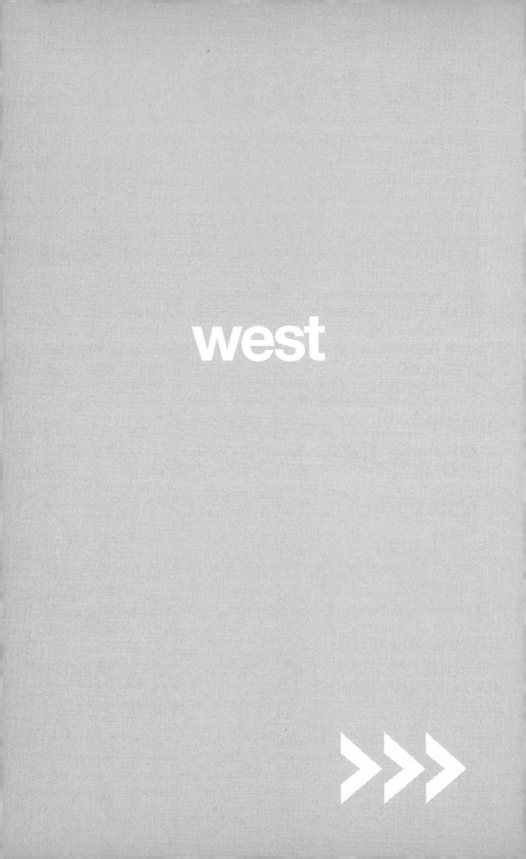

west

>>>

day trip 01

west

>>> **collector rocks to a rockin' river:**
quartzsite, palm canyon, parker,
lake havasu city

quartzsite

The main event of this day trip, Lake Havasu City, is a 4½- to 5-hour drive—one way. Obviously this trip is best done as an overnight. Head west out of Phoenix on I-10 past Litchfield Park. Eventually, after 112 miles, I-10 intersects with AZ 95 to Quartzsite, your first stop.

Situated in the Mohave Desert, Quartzsite is best known for its great numbers of "snowbirds" (as winter visitors are called), who flock to this community each year in vast numbers, pulling mobile homes with them. Visitors appreciate the sunshine and inexpensive, quiet living Quartzsite affords. The town hosts an annual rock-and-mineral show in February that attracts more than 850,000 people.

where to go

Hi Jolly Monument. Quartzsite, in the Quartzsite City Cemetery. Go west on West Main Street from the center of town about ¼ mile and follow the signs to the road leading to the city cemetery. Here you will see an unusual reminder of a pioneer experiment.

In the 1850s the U.S. War Department decided to introduce camels into the desert. The Hi Jolly Monument honors Hadji Ali, one of the Arab camel drivers who was brought here to drive the beasts. The experiment was successful, but the cavalry members disliked riding the disagreeable, smelly animals and wanted to disband the camel corps. The official

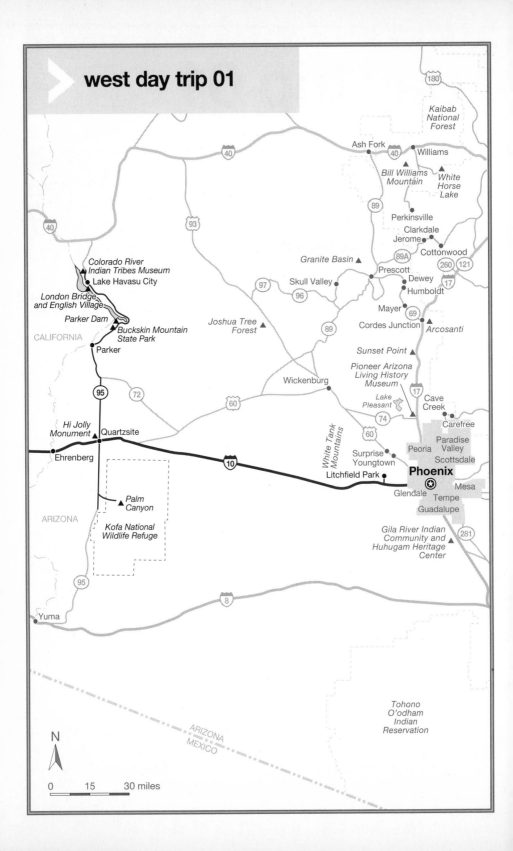

report stated that the beasts got sore feet from walking over the desert, when in actuality the cavalry got sore from riding the camels!

When the camel experiment ended, most of the other drivers went home, but Hadji Ali, or Hi Jolly, as he was called, stayed to become a prospector. He is buried in the city cemetery.

Nineteen miles west of Quartzsite is Ehrenberg, a haven for rock hunters looking for agates, limonite cubes, and quartz—all abundant in the area.

palm canyon

Hikers will want to detour south for about 20 miles on AZ 95 to the Kofa National Wildlife Refuge. Watch for the sign 18⁷⁄₁₀ miles south of Quartzsite that reads PALM CANYON and KOFA GAME RANGE. (It's an old sign; it should say PALM CANYON and KOFA NATIONAL WILDLIFE REFUGE.) Turn east and follow the gravel road leading to the canyon. You must drive slowly for about 9 miles. There's a parking area at the end of this road. You can hike ¼ mile through the towering narrow canyon on a trail to Palm Canyon. Nestled in the Kofa Mountains is Arizona's only native stand of palm trees. The Kofa National Wildlife Refuge is home to 800 to 1,000 bighorn sheep and many species of birds. The refuge includes more than 660,000 acres.

During the hot summer months, temperatures soar, and you'll sizzle. Hiking is best during the spring and autumn. Free. (928) 783-7861.

parker

Retrace your route by driving north on AZ 95 to its intersection with AZ 72. Follow AZ 72 northwest to Parker, which is 35 miles north of Quartzsite. If you have time to explore, stop at the Parker Chamber of Commerce, 1217 California Ave. (928-669-2174; www.parker areachamberofcommerce.com), to pick up information. There are a variety of events held during the year, including several boat races, so check to see what's going on.

Parker is a river town—part California beach, part Arizona river rat—and exists for power and water sports. Late summer can be brutal. August temperatures climb to 120 degrees. Each year the community hosts an international inner tube race in mid-June. It attracts hundreds of dedicated tubers, who travel along the 7 miles in a variety of outlandish outfits. Check www.coloradoriverinfo.com/parker for details.

where to go

Buckskin Mountain State Park. Twenty miles north of Parker on AZ 95; (928) 667-3231; http://azstateparks.com/Parks/BUMO/index.html. This park is open as of this writing, but call or check the website before visiting. Situated along a grassy, shady section of the riverbank, this park offers a quiet respite in often-raucous Parker. Enjoy the many campsites

off the beaten path

By day tripping standards, this is way off the beaten path. But it's a shame to miss the London Bridge. Like the trip to Yuma, this involves a long drive and is best done as an overnight. I admit that, when I first heard about the London Bridge, the thought of this antique English bridge arching over the Colorado River in the Arizona desert seemed like a stretch. But the old bridge is beautiful and the town, with its beach and river, is fun to visit.

and hiking trails. There is a concession operation, but you might prefer to bring a picnic lunch. Fee.

Colorado River Indian Tribes Museum. 1007 Arizona Ave.; (928) 208-4211. This museum displays the world's largest collection of Chemehuevi Indian basketry. In addition, visitors will see Mohave pottery and exhibits that interpret the four tribes in the area: Mohave, Chemehuevi, Hopi, and Navajo. It is the only museum in La Paz County. Inquire about how to see the Blythe Intaglios, ancient Mohave figures that are etched in the nearby desert. A donation is suggested.

Parker Dam. On AZ 95 in Parker Dam, California, 17 miles north of Parker, Arizona. Continue on AZ 95 through Parker and turn right at Agency Road. There's a stoplight. Continue on that road to the dam. As you cross the river onto the dam, you'll enter California; the Colorado River is the state boundary.

Parker Dam was built on the Colorado in 1934 and is one of the deepest dams in the world. You'll see only about one-third of the structure; the rest is under the water's surface. With a height of 320 feet and base thickness of 100 feet, it's an imposing edifice. Behind it is Lake Havasu, which contains 648,000 acre-feet of water. (An acre-foot is the amount of water it takes to cover 1 acre at a depth of 1 foot.)

You can take a self-guided tour of the dam, which includes stops from the top of the dam to the generating station below the water. Taped speeches describe what you're seeing. If you've never visited a desert dam and you have a spare half hour, treat yourself to the experience and marvel at the technology. Free. For more information call the Parker Chamber of Commerce in Arizona at (928) 669-2174 or visit www.parkerareachamber ofcommerce.com.

lake havasu city

From the dam, drive north for an hour on AZ 95, which winds along the riverbank to Lake Havasu City. This area, like neighboring Parker, is best known for water-based recreation.

You can make the Phoenix–Lake Havasu City trip in a day, but then it's more of a marathon than a day trip. It is better to plan this trip as an overnight, or even 2 overnights, so you have time to enjoy the area.

Lake Havasu City, established in 1963, was designed as a self-sufficient, planned community for several thousand residents. Although somewhat isolated from the rest of the state, it continues to attract newcomers and is growing into an attractive community for people who love a quiet, water-recreation lifestyle. Don't expect to see any "big city" stuff here. Come to relax, not for fine dining. Lake Havasu City is strictly small town.

Geologically, the area around Lake Havasu and Lake Havasu City is a gold mine. Within a 10-mile radius there are specimens of volcanic rock, geodes, jasper, obsidian, turquoise, and agate. Native American relics and abandoned mines also make this trip worthwhile for adventurous backpackers. If colored chips interest you more than pretty rocks, you're just 150 miles from Las Vegas and less than an hour from Laughlin, Nevada, across the Colorado River.

Make the Lake Havasu Convention and Visitors Bureau your first stop in town. As you enter Lake Havasu City, you'll come to a stoplight. Head away from the lake and drive to the top of the hill. Turn left, and then take the first immediate left into the parking lot. The visitors bureau is located at 314 London Bridge Rd. Call (928) 453-3444 or (800) 2-HAVASU, or visit www.golakehavasu.com.

where to go

The *Dixie Bell*. (928) 453-6776 or (928) 855-0888; www.londonbridgeresort.com. Anchored at the dock near London Bridge. Lake Havasu is a dream for fans of water sports. Nearly every form of boating is available, from canoeing and waterskiing to Jet Skiing to paddle wheelers. The *Dixie Bell* is a replica of an Old South stern-wheeler. It's the largest boat of its kind on the Colorado River and maintains a regular cruise schedule. Fee. Operates daily; reservations are highly recommended.

Lake Havasu and Lake Havasu State Park. (928) 855-2784; www.azstateparks.com This lake, which was formed when Parker Dam was built on the Colorado River, is 45 miles long and attracts anglers, boaters, water-skiers, Jet Skiers, and nature lovers. From town, follow Lincoln Bridge Road, which sweeps along the western boundary of Lake Havasu City. As you drive, you'll see signs for many public beaches that are owned and operated by the state. All types of facilities are offered—from camping to resort living.

You can rent a houseboat, Jet Skis, or a speedboat and cruise the blue lake expanse, or you can just drive to a beach, roll up your pant legs, and wade around to your heart's content. The beachfront is rocky, so those with tender toes should take tennis shoes.

The 13,000-acre park, which was developed along the 23 miles of shoreline surrounding Lake Havasu, contains beaches and campgrounds. Three beaches are especially popular. **Pittsburg Point,** at Lake Havasu City, is across from the London Bridge and has a variety of concession facilities. Follow McCulloch Boulevard across the bridge and continue on McCulloch as it loops around and becomes Beachcomber Boulevard. **Windsor Beach,** north of the London Bridge on the mainland, is a good day facility and has boat-launching ramps. From McCulloch Boulevard, turn north onto London Bridge Road and go north to Windsor Beach. **Cattail Cove State Park,** 15 miles south of Lake Havasu City on AZ 95, has boat and trailer rentals nearby and is easily accessible to the lake. Fee. For more information call Lake Havasu State Park.

London Bridge. At McCulloch Boulevard and AZ 95, spanning Thompson Bay. Gimmicky? Of course. But there is a thrill to walking, bicycling, or driving over the London Bridge, as incongruous as it seems suspended over the Colorado River in Arizona.

How did it get there? In 1967 the city of London decided that the London Bridge was too small for the current volume of traffic, so after 136 years of use, the bridge was offered for sale. Robert P. McCulloch Sr., the founder of Lake Havasu City, purchased it, had it dismantled in England with every block numbered, and shipped it to the United States. Three years later, the reconstruction was finished at a total cost of $7.5 million. It was a publicity stunt of grand proportions that instantly put Lake Havasu City on the map. The London Bridge formally opened in Arizona in October 1971 to the delight of everyone who sees it.

The English Village. This is the area around the bridge that sports a full-size village featuring gift shops and restaurants. Somehow, under the shadow of the London Bridge, it doesn't seem incongruous in its Arizona desert setting. Wander around or stop to eat at one of the restaurants or cafes.

northwest

>>>

day trip 01

northwest

>>>

antiques, the old west, and water sports:
glendale, peoria, wickenburg,
joshua forest parkway, lake pleasant

glendale

Unlike most Arizona drives, this excursion is not scenic at first. But take heart—the gorgeous desert foothills await. Along the way you'll pass through urban Phoenix and get a taste of the Old West. Be prepared for city driving and long, open stretches. You'll cross the Agua Fria River (which may or may not have water in it depending upon the season) and view the White Tank Mountains in the distance.

Drive northwest on Grand Avenue (US 60) from Phoenix through Glendale, once called "The City of Perpetual Harvest." Established in 1885 as a church community, Glendale soon became a farming town. Today it is one of the largest shipping points for fresh garden vegetables in the country.

In recent years Glendale has found its niche as a center for antiques and quaint shops. It purposefully looks back to the days when life was simpler and people were friendlier. Tourists are discovering Glendale's historic downtown, which looks like a turn-of-the-20th-century village. Antiques buffs appreciate finding a concentration of antiques shops as well as assortment of craft galleries, restaurants, and tearooms. Of special interest is the candy factory, which is open to tours.

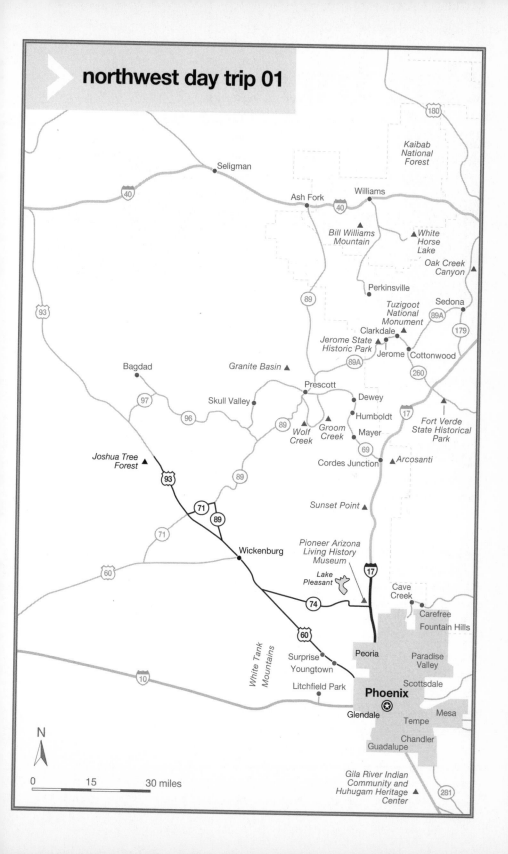

Kaibab
National
Forest

180

Seligman

40

Ash Fork

40

Williams

Bill Williams
Mountain

▲ White
Horse
Lake

Oak Creek
Canyon ▲

Perkinsville

89

Tuzigoot
National
Monument

Sedona

89A

Clarkdale ▲

179

Jerome State ▲
Historic Park

Jerome

Cottonwood

93

89A

260

Bagdad

Granite Basin ▲

Prescott

Dewey

17

Skull Valley

97

96

89

Wolf
Creek

Groom
Creek

Humboldt

Mayer

Fort Verde
State Historical
Park ▲

Joshua Tree
Forest ▲

93

71

89

89

Cordes Junction

69

▲ Arcosanti

71

Sunset Point ▲

60

Wickenburg

Pioneer Arizona
Living History
Museum

Lake
Pleasant

17

74

Cave
Creek

Carefree

Peoria

Fountain Hills

60

White Tank Mountains

Surprise

Paradise
Valley

10

Youngtown

Scottsdale

Litchfield Park

Phoenix ⊛

Mesa

Glendale

Tempe

Chandler

Guadalupe

Gila River Indian
Community and
Huhugam Heritage ▲
Center

281

N

0   15   30 miles

> ## antiques, football, and the old west

If you enjoy browsing through antiques shops, Glendale is a "must" destination. Considered a suburb of Phoenix, Glendale is also the home of the Coyotes arena (our hockey team) and the University of Phoenix stadium where the Arizona Cardinals play. The stadium is an architectural and engineering feat and has created a national "buzz" for its innovative design. There are scheduled public and private tours. Continuing farther northwest, I'm partial to Wickenburg, with its charming small museum, Desert Caballeros Western Museum. Each time I visit I find new things to enjoy here. The museum has an excellent permanent collection, and the staff mounts outstanding shows. Less well known than some of the larger museums, this is one of my recommended "treasures" to family and friends.

where to go

Catlin Court Historical District. Located near the heart of Glendale, Catlin Court is bordered by white picket fences and brick-trimmed sidewalks. There are gazebos and gaslights and gardens as well as historic craftsman bungalows, which have been beautifully restored. Catlin Court contains tearooms, where visitors can turn back the clock to more gracious times, and rows of antiques shops and craft boutiques. For information call or visit the Glendale Visitor Center at 5800 West Glenn Dr., Suite 140, Glendale; (877) 800-2601or (623) 930-4500; www.visitglendale.com.

Cerreta Candy Company. 5345 West Glendale Ave.; for tours call (623) 930-1000; www.cerreta.com. This family-owned business makes candy for Disneyland, Magic Mountain, and Knott's Berry Farm, among others. Candymaking and free tours of the factory are offered. The wrapped candies are terrific. Free.

Sahuaro Ranch Park. Located on 59th Avenue north of Olive. Sahuaro Ranch includes a 16-acre park and preserves one of the Phoenix area's finest and oldest homesteads. The ranch has 7 original buildings, a lavish rose garden, and a flock of peacocks that roam the grounds. It is listed on the National Register of Historic Places. Tours of the guest house are available through the Glendale Historical Society at (623) 435-0072.

The Bead Museum. 5754 West Glenn Dr.; (623) 931-2737; www.thebeadmuseum.org. The museum is easily accessible from I-17 by exiting west on Glendale Avenue and traveling a few miles to 58th Avenue. Turn north (right) on 58th and travel 1 block, and the museum will be clearly visible on the northeast corner of Glenn Drive and 58th Avenue. Beads from all over the world are on display, proof of the ingenuity and imagination that have gone into human adornment throughout history. Special exhibitions are mounted, and there is even a reference library. The Bead Museum Store sells a full range of beads, beading supplies, and books. Open Tues to Sat; extended hours on Thurs. Fee.

peoria

Peoria was founded in 1885 by four farming families who came from the Midwest and named the town for their hometown in Illinois. According to the city's history, these early settlers either built adobe homes or used large tents. Half the tent contained a floor and served as the living quarters while the other half housed grain, hay, spare furniture, and tools. Rattlesnakes, scorpions, and desert rats often sought refuge from the hot desert sun under the floor. Life became more difficult when floods washed out the canal diversion dam, forcing a 6-mile trek to the Grand Canal for water that they hauled in barrels back to town.

As production at the Vulture Mine in Wickenburg increased, traffic got busier along the route leading to the Grand Canal. In 1887 the road was named Grand Avenue. By 1888 Peoria had a post office and a population of 27. By 1970 Peoria sported only 2,500 people, but in the following decade growth soared. Today, Peoria is a fast-growing city of more than 100,000 people, more in spring, when the Peoria Sports Complex hosts spring training for the Seattle Mariners and San Diego Padres.

where to go

Challenger Space Center. 21170 North 83rd Ave.; (623) 322-2001; www.azchallenger .org. One of more than 40 learning centers in the United States, Canada, and Great Britain, the Challenger Space Center of Arizona offers kids and grown-ups the thrill of space travel without ever leaving Earth. The center is located within a striking architectural building that blends with the Sonoran Desert. Inside, adults and children experience special flight simulations, viewings, and multimedia presentations. If you've never visited one of these centers, you are in for a treat. Tucson is also home to a Challenger Space Center if you're touring that part of the state. Call ahead for information on special opportunities and camps. Fee. Open Mon through Sat.

The Wildlife World Zoo & Aquarium. Three miles west of Litchfield Road on Northern Avenue; (623) 935-WILD; www.wildlifeworld.com. Follow Grand Avenue (US 60) and turn right on Litchfield Road. At Northern Avenue, turn right again. The zoo is 4 miles west on Northern. Walk through an aviary with more than 30 species of tropical birds and see the largest collection of marsupials (kangaroos and wallabies) in the country, all five types of the world's ostriches, and America's most complete pheasant display. The park also offers a safari train ride through exhibits, a giraffe feeding station, Arizona's first white tiger, a skyride, and a carousel. The aquarium campus opened in 2008 and exhibits nearly 150 aquatic species from South American leaf turtles to warm-weather penguins and sharks. There's also a 40-foot-high log flume ride for those who want still more water. Open daily. Fee.

wickenburg

Follow US 60 north to Wickenburg for a taste of the old and new West. As you proceed, you'll enter rolling foothills dotted with saguaros, ocotillos, and mesquite.

Wickenburg is located approximately 54 miles northwest of Phoenix and sits at the foot of the Bradshaw Mountains on the banks of the Hassayampa (Hah-sa-yampa) River. Legend has it that anyone who drinks from the Hassayampa never tells the truth again. As you approach the Hassayampa, you may wonder how anyone ever drinks out of the river anyway, since usually it is a wide, dry, sandy riverbed. But look again. The green, lush area around it demonstrates the power of a desert river. Even a sporadic flow of water creates fertile soil out of dusty ground, and a stretch of the river flows underground.

Wickenburg was established by Henry Wickenburg, who searched for an elusive vein of gold for 10 years. There are numerous stories about how he finally found that treasure. Some may be more truthful, but this legend is the best: When the failed prospector landed in what is now called Wickenburg, he was discouraged and alone. His partner had no faith in him, and to make matters worse, Wickenburg's balky burro refused to move. Looking up, the prospector saw a vulture circle, land, and eye the stubborn beast. In utter disgust, Wickenburg picked up a rock to throw at the bird. When the rock dropped, it split in half and revealed gold.

Regardless of the veracity of that tale, Wickenburg did stumble over the richest gold lode in Arizona and named it the Vulture Mine. Although his claim has long been exhausted and is no longer open, the town of Wickenburg retains its rustic gold rush image. Visit Wickenburg's official website at www.outwickenburgway.com.

where to go

Frontier Street. This area is preserved as it was in the 1800s, with a fine railway station, a former hotel, and other buildings. Follow US 60 west as it crosses the Hassayampa River. Frontier intersects with US 60. Wander at will.

Desert Caballeros Western Museum. 21 North Frontier St.; (928) 684-2272; www.western museum.org. Turn left onto Frontier from US 60. Parking is next to the railroad tracks. Staffed and built by dedicated volunteers, this museum contains works by well-known western artists, including Frederic Remington and George Phippen. In addition to the art gallery, visit the Hall of History, period rooms, mineral room, and Mexican room. This museum is one of the state's lesser known gems, and the collection and the facility are both outstanding. The museum can be toured in an hour and is very much worth the trip. Fee.

Old 761. At Apache and Tegner Streets behind the Town Hall. From the museum, follow Frontier Street northwest to Apache Street. Turn right on Apache to just north of Tegner Street. Here you will see the original steam engine and tender that chugged along the tracks from Chicago to the West.

Jail Tree. Tegner and Center Streets. From Old 761, follow Apache Street south. Turn left onto Tegner Street. You'll come upon a large, 200-year-old mesquite tree. Since Wickenburg didn't have a jail, the law used this tree to tether rowdies who caused trouble. You can see the leg irons, still attached to the tree, which accomplished the task. Law-abiding citizens can stop, clamp on the irons, and have their pictures taken.

Hassayampa River Preserve. On US 60, 3 miles southeast of Wickenburg; (928) 684-2772. The preserve entrance is on the west side of the highway near mile marker 114. Although the Hassayampa River flows underground for most of its length, it comes to the surface near Wickenburg. Owned by the Nature Conservancy, the area has been restored to its natural state as a shady, life-filled riparian area. Today the Hassayampa Preserve consists of 4 miles of one of Arizona's last and finest Sonoran Desert streamside habitats. It supports 230 species of birds.

When the Nature Conservancy purchased the property in December 1986, much of the land had been overgrazed and returned to desert. With care, it has become an invaluable biologic riparian resource.

A 1-mile nature trail leads through the leafy, gladed area next to the river. There's a less scenic but shorter loop trail around Palm Lake. In addition to the self-guided walks, naturalists lead hikes on a seasonal schedule. These tours last about 1½ hours and are quite informative.

The Hassayampa Bookstore is located in a lovely adobe structure and has books and guides on plants and animals of the Southwest, including history, travel guides, and gift items. There's also a reference library the public can use.

There's no picnicking, and pets must be left at home. However, this peaceful, serene setting is comfortable even on a warm spring day. Open Wed to Sun. Closed major holidays. Fee; children under 13 free.

Vulture Mine. Located on Vulture Mine Road; (602) 859-2743. Follow US 60 west 2½ miles out of Wickenburg to the Vulture Mine Road. Turn south. Proceed 12 miles to the mine. The self-guided tour of this ghost town, once known as Vulture City, begins at the Vulture's Roost, a wood-framed building that holds a collection of mining memorabilia and ore samples from the mine and surrounding area. Visitors follow a "treasure map" of the town to explore it, stopping at the assay office and manager's headquarters, where you see the walls, which were built from low-grade ore. They contain an estimated $600,000 in gold and silver. The tour includes living quarters and the stamp mill and eventually leads to the Glory Hole. Although Henry Wickenburg held the original claim to the rich mine, he ended up with only pennies in his pocket and a bullet in his head on the bank of the Hassayampa River. Nearby, the Glory Hole is the main shaft of the mine. Two hundred million dollars in gold was removed from this mine. The wooden headframe still rises over the entrance to the main shaft, but the opening is partially boarded up to protect visitors. Still, you can peer into the tunnel and imagine what it was like for miners who worked inside its depths. The trail continues past the blacksmith shop and other sites. Open Thurs through Sun, fall and winter; Fri through Sun, spring and summer. Fee.

where to eat and stay

Chaparral Ice Cream & Bakery. 45 North Tegner; (928) 684-3252; www.chaparral-ice cream.com. This ice cream parlor features homemade ice cream. The best flavor is Hassayampa Mud. You can have lunch or an early dinner here of soup, sandwiches, and pastries. The atmosphere is authentic 1950s with red-and-white checked tablecloths, roomy wooden booths, and a friendly staff. Open daily with weekend entertainment. $–$$; no credit cards accepted.

Kay El Bar Guest Ranch. Box 2480, Wickenburg 85358; (800) 684-7593; www.kayelbar .com. This is a charming historic guest ranch that is listed on the National Register of Historic Places. Beautifully maintained, it offers visitors an authentic western experience from trail riding to family-style dining. The setting is uniquely territorial-style Arizona. A 2-night minimum stay is required, however, to get the full flavor of this special getaway guest ranch, visitors will want to spend a week. Children must be 7 years old to participate in the riding program. The Kay El Bar is open from Oct 12 to May 1. $$$.

Rancho de los Caballeros. 1551 South Vulture Mine Rd. (928) 684-5484 or (800) 684-5030; www.sunc.com. Five miles west of Wickenburg and 2 miles south of US 60 on Vulture Mine Road. Located in an especially scenic high desert setting, this "Ranch of the Gentlemen on Horseback" combines a luxurious resort setting with the relaxing ambience that is the hallmark of Southwestern hospitality. A unique combination of golf and riding allows guests to ride through miles of magnificent desert trails and tee off on rolling, challenging fairways in the same day without leaving the grounds. An elegant resort, Rancho de los Caballeros boasts a superb golf shop on its premises. Fine dining is available, along with hearty western favorites. Open mid-Oct through mid-May. Reservations required. $$$.

joshua forest parkway

Northwest on US 93, 20 miles beyond Wickenburg, you'll be greeted by one of nature's more unusual welcoming committees: a strange, dense forest of Joshua trees. Located on both sides of the highway, hordes of thick-trunked cacti crowd the landscape and mesmerize passing tourists.

Joshua trees, which are actually tall, bristly yucca plants, were named by Mormon pioneers who thought the upright branches pointed toward the promised land. These slow-growing trees provide homes for 25 species of birds. In addition, pack rats gnaw off spiny leaf blades, and night lizards find that the rotted-out bark of wind-toppled Joshua trees provides their entire world. Usually found in the Mohave Desert, Joshua trees are rarely found in the Sonoran Desert, which makes this dense stand all the more exciting.

lake pleasant

To complete your day, what better excursion than to head for Lake Pleasant? To reach this recreation site, go southeast on AZ 89 and backtrack for about 11 miles. At the junction of AZ 89 and AZ 74, follow AZ 74 east to Lake Pleasant, one of the many manufactured lakes dotting the Arizona desert. Arizonans take water seriously and dam rivers for flood control, surface water, and recreation. You may be surprised to know that Arizona has one of the highest boats-per-capita ratios in the country.

Lake Pleasant was formed when the Waddell Dam was constructed on the Agua Fria River. Today 24,000 acres of lake await, featuring every outdoor and water sport from camping and fishing to scuba diving, parasailing, and ultralight gliding. Watercraft can be rented at the marina. Picnic, rent Jet Skis, or just enjoy the rocky landscape and cool views before returning to Phoenix. When you're ready to end your day, travel east on AZ 74 to I-17. Follow I-17 south to Phoenix. Or backtrack west on AZ 74 and pick up US 60 southeast to Phoenix. www.maricopa.gov/parks.

where to go

Lake Pleasant Regional Park. 41835 North Castle Hot Springs Rd., Morristown; (928) 501-1710; www.maricopa.gov/parks. Nineteen miles northwest of Peoria on AZ 74 off Castle Hot Springs Road. Hiking, boat rentals and 140 campgrounds make this an ideal nature getaway. There's a visitor center and plenty of boat ramps available. Open 24 hours. Dillon's restaurant has great barbecue and traditional fare and is open daily for lunch and dinner.

>> part ii: tucson

Tucson is the second-largest city in Arizona, after the state capital Phoenix, and is also the Pima County seat. Yet it continues to wear its Hispanic heritage like an elegant mantilla. With Mexico just 60 miles to the south, the Mexican influence is strong and can be seen in the architecture and tasted in the food. Actually, 4 cultures are clearly felt in Tucson: Spanish, Mexican, Native American, and, of course, contemporary American.

The city is surrounded by five mountain ranges: the Santa Catalinas rise to the north, the Rincons to the east, the Santa Rita Mountains to the south, the Tucson Mountains to the west, and the Tortolita Mountains to the northwest. With an elevation of 2,410 feet above sea level (about 1,000 feet higher than Phoenix), the "Old Pueblo," as Tucson is called, has a drier and slightly cooler climate than its big sister, Phoenix.

One of Tucson's claims to fame is that it is the oldest inhabited city in the country. Spanish missionaries and soldiers arrived in the area in the late 1600s. The Presidio San Agustín del Tucson was established in 1775. "The Old Pueblo," as the adobe-walled Tucson Presidio became known, gave Tucson its nickname. Originally a Mexican city, Tucson became part of the United States in 1854.

Although both Phoenix and Tucson are casual southwestern cities, they are quite different. Phoenix shines with glass and chrome while Tucson glows with pink adobe and wrought iron. Where Phoenix can be wide-open western, Tucson can slip back in time and roll its *r*'s. Whether you stroll through the Barrio, the old, mostly Mexican-American neighborhood, or walk along the "movie-set" campus of the University of Arizona (U of A), you'll be acutely aware of how this half-old, half-new city pursues its blended destiny.

where to go

Metropolitan Tucson Convention and Visitors Bureau. 100 South Church; (800) 638-8350; www.visittucson.org. Pick up additional information about the Old Pueblo to learn how the original walled Presidio of San Agustín del Tucson was built by the Spaniards in 1776. You can see a piece of that wall preserved under glass on the second floor of the old Pima County Courthouse at the corner of Washington Street and Main Avenue. You'll also learn about the 4 flags that have flown over Tucson. In 1776 the Spanish claimed it. Later, it belonged to Mexico. In 1853 Arizona was included in the Gadsden Purchase, and

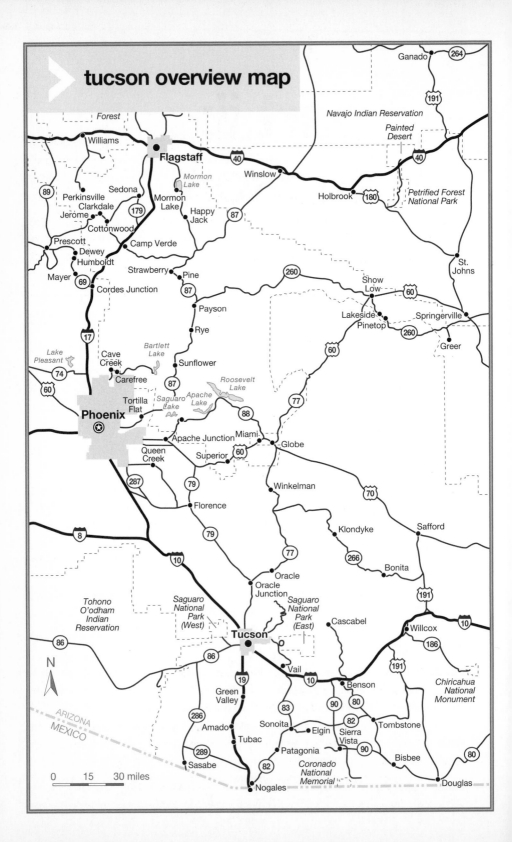

tucson overview map

Tucson became part of the United States. Then, during the Civil War, the city became part of the Confederate territory.

Arizona Historical Society/Tucson. 949 East 2nd St.; (520) 628-5774; www.arizonahistoricalsociety.org. This museum features changing and permanent exhibits that tell Arizona's history from Spanish Colonial times through the territorial years. There's also a research library and gift shop, and docent-led tours are available by reservation. Closed Sun. Fee.

Center for Creative Photography. On the University of Arizona campus; (520) 621-7968; www.creativephotography.org. During the week, park in the garage at Speedway and Park on the northeast corner and walk across the street to the center. A collection of more than 80,000 photographs are housed in this striking, contemporary building. The archives of Ansel Adams are catalogued and displayed here. A research library is open to the public. Open daily. Free.

DeGrazia Gallery in the Sun. 6300 North Swan; (520) 299-1381; www.degrazia.org. Ted DeGrazia was a legendary Tucson artist, character, and a master at marketing his art. Reproductions of his Mexican children were ubiquitous during the height of his popularity in the 1970s and 1980s. Most people never get to see his original works of art which are powerful, moving, and, yes, charming. Six collections are housed in this very special gallery that was hand built by DeGrazia. I consider its architecture one of his best works of art. Of course there's a gift shop so you can take home DeGrazia art. Open daily. Free.

Fourth Avenue. Unique shops and some great restaurants await your pleasure in this district. Here are some of the more unusual ones.

Arroyo Design. 224 North 4th Ave.; (520) 884-1012; www.arroyo-design.com. The husband-and-wife team that owns this wonderful furniture-design store creates the handmade furniture using native hardwoods like mesquite and ironwood. The pieces are works of art and highly collectible.

Handcrafted Tile Inc. 347 North 4th Ave.; (520) 624-0506. Beautiful handcrafted tile, for big and small jobs, are exhibited and sold here.

Native Seeds/Search. 526 North 4th Ave.; (520) 622-5561; www.nativeseeds.org. Native Seeds/Search is dedicated to preserving heirloom seeds and has gained international fame for its work. You can buy seeds here along with natural goods, books, and posters.

International Wildlife Museum. 4800 West Gates Pass Rd.; (520) 617-1439; www.thewildlifemuseum.org. Nearly 300 mammals and birds from 6 continents are realistically displayed in natural habitats with many excellent interactive exhibits that provide additional information. While the building looks like a misplaced castle-fortress in the desert, the collection is complete and well displayed. There are guided tours, wildlife films, videos, and restaurants. Open daily. Fee.

Tohono Chul Park. 7366 Paseo del Norte; (520) 742-6455; www.tohonochulpark.org. This park is beautifully landscaped with natural vegetation and gardens that feature nature

tucson, a lush desert

If you spend any time in Arizona, you'll quickly see that Tucsconians consider themselves fortunate not to live in Phoenix. The same is not true for us Phoenicians. We actually like Tucson. Tucson folks, for instance, insist that, since the elevation of their city is about 1,200 feet higher than Phoenix, they enjoy a cool climate while we sizzle in the summer. They will say in all honesty, "So you came to Tucson to cool off?" when the temperature difference is maybe 5 degrees. They also consider that the U of A is the real university in the state and that their basketball team and football team are far superior to ASU's. All of these are highly arguable points. But what they don't boast about enough is the beauty of their desert. Tucson is completely surrounded by magnificent mountain ranges, and the higher elevation does make their desert more lush.

In the interest of full disclosure, when we first moved to Arizona we lived in Tucson while my husband was stationed at Davis-Monthan Air Force Base. I love the small town feeling of the city and even its lack of freeways, which mean that you almost are always driving on city streets. Traffic can be slow and heavy. Still, despite years of living in Phoenix, part my heart beats in rhythm with the Old Pueblo.

trails, demonstrations, and ethnobotanical gardens. There's also a geological re-creation of the nearby Catalina Mountains, a recirculating stream, ramadas, an art gallery with good quality arts and crafts displayed, and an exhibit hall. The gift shop is worth browsing through, and a tearoom is available for refreshments. This is a great destination for a breakfast or lunch respite. Open daily. Fee.

Tucson Botanical Gardens. 2150 North Alvernon Way; (520) 326-9686; www.tucson botanical.org. Enjoy a collection of gardens that includes a historical Tucson area, arid landscaping, herbs, irises, tropical greenhouses, wildflowers, Native American crops, and vegetables. Fee.

University of Arizona Museum of Art. On the campus of the U of A; (520) 621-7567; www.artmuseum.arizona.edu. A permanent collection of art spans the Middle Ages through the 20th century. There are changing exhibitions that feature student, faculty, and guest artists. Closed Mon. Fee; ages 18 and younger free.

where to eat

Tucson has wonderful restaurants that serve all varieties of ethnic food. Mexican food is served Sonoran-style and is slightly spicier than the Phoenix version. Continental cuisine is as elegant as that found in any city three times its size. Here are a few favorites, each with special historic or cultural significance:

Arizona Inn. 2200 East Elm St.; (520) 325-1541 or (800) 933-1093; www.arizonainn.com. Continental fare is graciously served at this landmark hotel. Located in the central city, the dining room is quiet and relaxing. Furnishings are all original and were made by the return- ing veterans of World War I. You can eat indoors or outdoors, where you face the lovely gardens. The food is as terrific as the setting. $$–$$$.

Cafe Poca Cosa. 110 East Pennington St.; (520) 622-6400; www.cafepocacosatucson.com. A local favorite, chef Suzana Davila's cooking has garnered raves from *Gourmet* magazine, the *New York Times,* and others. She's a native of Guaymas, Sonora, and her cuisine and hip restaurant take Mexican food to another level. Serving lunch and dinner. Closed Mon. $$.

El Charro Cafe. 311 North Court Ave.; (520) 622-1922; www.elcharrocafe.com. Estab- lished in 1922, this restaurant is still owned and operated by the same family that opened it, which makes it the oldest family-owned Mexican restaurant in the United States. There are several locations, but the original is the most charming with its collection of rooms and patios. Plentiful plates of Sonoran-style Mexican cuisine is served here. Serving lunch and dinner. Open daily. $–$$.

Janos. 3770 East Sunrise Dr.; (520) 615-6100; www.janos.com. Located in a freestanding building on the grounds of the Westin La Paloma Resort & Spa, Janos is considered one of the city's best restaurants. Its owner, Janos, is considered one of the city's best chefs. His cuisine is inventive Southwest with French techniques. Open for dinner; closed Sun. year- round and Mon from May through Sept. $$$.

where to stay

Like Phoenix, Tucson is famous for its resorts. If you have a "hankerin'" for a dude ranch, Tucson is bursting with them. There are more guest and dude ranches in southern Arizona than anywhere else in the country. If you prefer a quick overnight in a basic motel, you can find that, too. But if you want to stay in an out-of-the-ordinary accommodation, read on. For a more complete list of accommodations, write the Arizona Hotel & Lodging Association, 1240 East Missouri Ave., Phoenix 85014-2912; call (602) 604-0729; or visit www.azhla.com.

Arizona Inn. 2200 East Elm St.; (520) 325-1541 or (800) 933-1093; www.arizonainn.com. If you like historical Tucson at its most serene, you'll enjoy this world-famous hotel. There is no flash or glitz here, just unhurried, unchanged hospitality served up at its best. In the heart of town, the Arizona Inn has served an illustrious clientele over the years. Ask the staff about the celebrity guests who like the paneled, hacienda mood of this homey inn.

The inn has 80 rooms, all individually decorated, and many have private patios. The atmosphere is 1930s with modern amenities. The library in the main sitting room is filled with books, the living room is stately but inviting, and the 60-foot heated pool is sheltered on all sides. The restaurant is one of the city's best and features continental cuisine. But while the main dining rooms are lovely, plan to have breakfast on the patio. Then be sure to stroll around the grounds to enjoy the gardens of this gracious hotel.

The history of the Arizona Inn is fascinating. Take time to read the small book placed in each room that tells its story. This is one of the best places to stay in the city if you enjoy a very civilized approach to vacationing. Even one evening here can do a lot to unwind a harried guest. Prices are reasonable in the winter and a downright bargain in the summer. $$–$$$.

The Ritz-Carlton, Dove Mountain. 15000 North Secret Springs Dr., Marana; (520) 572-3001; www.ritzcarlton.com. The newest luxury property in southern Arizona, the Ritz Carlton Dove Mountain is located northwest of the city, less than 20 minutes from downtown Tucson. Guests enjoy a glorious setting plus a Jack Nicklaus Signature golf experience, spa, and every upscale amenity including 3 swimming pools, hiking and stargazing. The property includes 209 guest rooms and 44 casita suites. $$$.

guest ranches

The Tucson area has a number of excellent guest ranches within an hour or two of the city. For a complete listing call the Metropolitan Tucson Convention and Visitor Bureau at (520) 624-1817 or visit www.visittucson.org. Most guest ranches are small and accommodate no more than 60 guests. Some offer opportunities for "dudes"; others are for more rugged riders. Names to know include the Lazy K Bar Guest Ranch, 16 miles northwest of Tucson, and White Stallion Ranch, 17 miles northwest of Tucson. Both are close to the city.

Tanque Verde Guest Ranch. 14301 East Speedway; (520) 296-6275 or (800) 234-3833; www.tanqueverderanch.com. This year-round ranch, a Tucson landmark, features comfortable, western accommodations; 150 horses; tennis courts; an indoor health spa; and gourmet dining. You'll need to stay longer than overnight to get a flavor of all that this ranch has to offer. The ranch backs up to a national forest filled with saguaros. Riding trails wind through unspoiled desert. Lessons are included with the rides, and all levels of riders can be accommodated. The breakfast trail ride is a special treat. Mountain biking, hiking, fishing, exercise rooms, spa, and pool are available. Don't be surprised to hear many languages being spoken here, as this is a favorite with international guests.

The atmosphere is western casual. The patios and dining areas are spacious. It's great in the winter, spring, and fall. The ranch has 74 rooms. Summer packages make this an affordable destination for families and international guests. Fully supervised children's programs are offered for those ages 4 to 12. $$$.

bed-and-breakfast

El Presidio Inn. 297 North Main Ave.; (520) 623-6151. This is an award-winning luxury B&B in a historic Victorian adobe mansion built in 1880. The garden is romantic and lush, and the appointments are superb. Located within walking distance of Tucson's historic downtown, El Presidio's guests enjoy a complete breakfast, evening treats, and elegant surroundings. Four suites with private baths are available. $$–$$$; no credit cards accepted.

northeast

>>>

day trip 01

northeast

>>> **the peak of perfection for outdoors enthusiasts:**
sabino canyon, mount lemmon

sabino canyon

Begin your drive in Tucson, surrounded by the urban scene. But as you head out toward the Santa Catalina Mountains, you'll leave the city behind. One of the beauties of this day trip is that you can enjoy some of the area's most magnificent wilderness so close to a major city. To do Sabino Canyon and Mount Lemmon justice in a single day, you'll need to leave early and not linger long at either place. Frankly, this is a problem because both areas have endless trails to hike and acres of serenity to enjoy. So think about doing each of these separately.

Although this day trip stars Mother Nature at her finest, she is fickle. Take a wrap along. Depending upon the season, carry a windbreaker, heavy sweater, or even a ski jacket. As you climb to the summit of Mount Lemmon, you'll experience a major change in climate. You also need comfortable walking shoes so you can get out and walk around once you've arrived. If you plan to drive to the top of Mount Lemmon during the winter months, call ahead to check on the weather. If it's cloudy or rainy in Tucson, it could be snowing at the summit. Although the road to Mount Lemmon is paved, snow can make it impassable. Even the most adventurous types wouldn't get caught without chains or a four-wheel-drive vehicle.

New York City has Central Park, but Tucson has Sabino Canyon, a woodsy respite close to town. Nestled in the foothills of the Santa Catalina Mountains, Sabino Canyon is a hiker's, picnicker's, and outdoors lover's dream. With its streams and waterfalls, hiking and

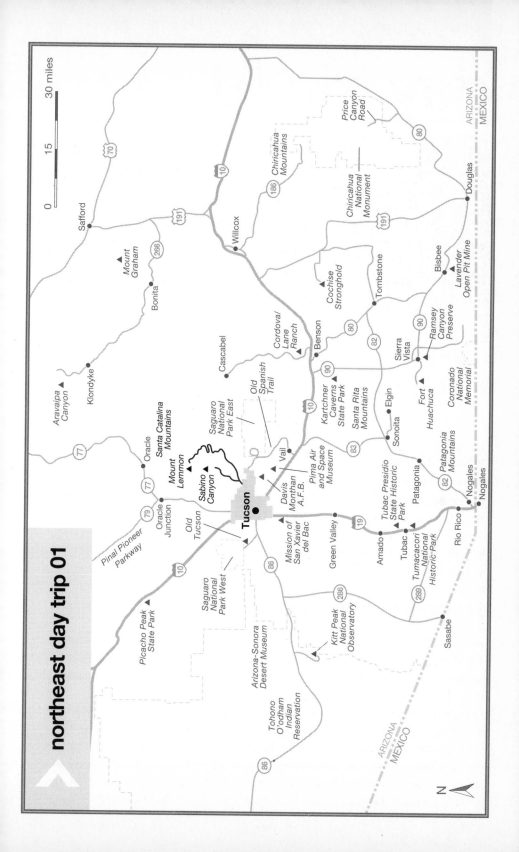

northeast day trip 01

30 miles

ARIZONA
MEXICO

Price Canyon Road

Chiricahua Mountains

Chiricahua National Monument

Douglas

Lavender Open Pit Mine

Bisbee

Ramsey Canyon Preserve

Coronado National Memorial

Fort Huachuca

Sierra Vista

Tombstone

Cochise Stronghold

Benson

Kartchner Caverns State Park

Santa Rita Mountains

Elgin

Sonoita

Patagonia

Patagonia Mountains

Nogales

Nogales

Rio Rico

Tumacacori National Historic Park

Tubac

Tubac Presidio State Historic Park

Amado

Green Valley

Mission of San Xavier del Bac

Sasabe

Kitt Peak National Observatory

Arizona-Sonora Desert Museum

Tohono O'odham Indian Reservation

ARIZONA
MEXICO

N

Safford

Mount Graham

Bonita

Aravaipa Canyon

Klondyke

Santa Catalina Mountains

Oracle

Mount Lemmon

Sabino Canyon

Saguaro National Park East

Willcox

Cascabel

Old Spanish Trail

Cordova Lane Ranch

Vail

Pima Air and Space Museum

Davis Monthan A.F.B.

Tucson

Old Tucson

Oracle Junction

Pinal Pioneer Parkway

Saguaro National Park West

Picacho Peak State Park

biking trails, this natural area manages to absorb the hordes of visitors who turn to it every day for a needed dose of calm and quiet.

To get there, follow Wilmot Road north to where it joins with Tanque Verde Road. Head northeast on Tanque Verde and across the Pantano Wash to its intersection with Sabino Canyon Road, which takes you to the visitor center. You must park your car here and proceed either on foot or by tram for the 4-mile trip to the first of several recreation areas. The tram runs frequently, and there are regular moonlight rides offered from April through December. Fee. No credit cards or personal checks. (520) 749-2861 or (520) 749-2327; www.sabinocanyontours.com.

where to go

Pick up a trail map at the visitor center. As you walk along, you'll see many different trees growing. Pine and fir forest the slopes above the streambed. Deep within the canyon, you'll find willow, box elder, and alder. In the lower elevations Sabino Canyon is host to cactus, paloverde, and even saguaros, while along the streambed you'll find shady sycamore, cottonwood, ash, and walnut trees.

Why the name Sabino? No one is exactly sure. One school of thought insists that the name comes from a plant called sabino or savino. The more accepted story is that it was named for a Mexican rancher who lived in the area in the 1870s.

Formed about 200 million years ago, the canyon has established itself as an ideal getaway no matter what season. The tram was installed to help preserve the air quality and environment. Along the way it stops at designated observation sites, and during the summer months, moonlight excursions offer a totally different experience. If you've never taken a guided tour in a national park at night or seen a wild area after sunset, you should do this. Tickets are available next to the visitor center parking area. For more information write Sabino Canyon Shuttle, 5900 North Sabino Canyon Rd., Tucson 85750; call (520) 749-2861; or visit www.sabinocanyon.com.

mount lemmon

To get to Mount Lemmon from Sabino Canyon, follow Sabino Canyon Road south to Tanque Verde Road. Turn east on Tanque Verde to Catalina Highway. Follow Catalina Highway northeast to Mount Lemmon. This is an extremely popular area and is well marked. Watch for signs to Mount Lemmon.

As you drive along Tanque Verde toward Catalina Highway, you will see some elegant residential areas. Tucson is famous for its low-slung, hacienda-style homes and bright blue pools hidden among the saguaros and ocotillos.

Catalina Highway, also called the road to Mount Lemmon, climbs the mountain's southern slope. From this point, the 30-mile drive will take about an hour up the 9,157-foot mountain. Although the road is perfectly safe for automobile traffic, those who can't look down from a tall building may not enjoy this experience. Queasy passengers who still want a view should just look up.

As you head up this beautiful mountain road, you'll pass scenic viewpoints and areas marked for camping and picnicking. You can even stop and fish; signs will lead you to a lake stocked with trout. Along the way you'll get a real-life lesson in physical geography since this drive takes you through five distinct life zones—areas that support specific types of vegetation. You'll begin in the Sonoran Desert and climb through piñon and juniper. Soon you'll be into elevations that support fir trees and, eventually, aspen trees. This is the same vegetation change you would observe were you to drive from Arizona to the Canadian border. Not surprisingly, the drive is especially gorgeous in autumn and spring.

You will have to pay a $5 toll for the privilege of driving this road. While few people enjoy handing over $5, the money goes to support the state's park system. At Summerhaven you will pass some commercial development—bars and restaurants. This area can be crowded during weekends and holidays.

Construction of this road began in 1933 and was not completed until 1950. Much of the road clings to a narrow ledge or skirts high ridges. During years when southern Arizona gets hit by storms, the road can get washed out in places, but it is quickly repaired. Three miles from the tollbooth is the overlook for Seven Cataracts, which, when it's running, is a cascading stream. One other word of warning: The temperature at the top is usually about 20 degrees cooler than the bottom of Mount Lemmon, so it's a good idea to bring sweaters or jackets if you plan to hike around.

Once at the top, enjoy the view and do walk around. If you've packed a picnic lunch, spread it out and relax. Enjoy the crisp, cool air and the views that stretch forever.

back road, rough road

I will never forget my first drive up Mount Lemmon. We had just moved to Tucson and were anxious to explore it all. With our golden retriever in the back of our convertible, we headed for a day of adventure. The higher we drove, the rougher the road became. Along the way, we saw a sign that said not recommended for sedan travel, but we figured that it didn't mean us since we were driving with the top down. By the time we arrived at the top of the mountain, about an hour later, our dog had turned green. We found a tiny gas station and, as we filled up the car, talked with the attendant (pre-pump-your-own-gas days), who wondered how we got up there. We gestured to the road behind us. He was flabbergasted and said that we'd traveled the back road to Mount Lemmon, which was only designed for four-wheel drive. We figured that we were still okay since our car had four wheels. But the next time we took the preferred road and were amazed at how much easier it was.

Remember, while perched in this northern clime, that you are just 1 hour—and some 7,000 feet—away from the desert floor.

To return to Tucson, retrace your steps down the mountain and follow Tanque Verde Road back into town.

where to go

Mount Lemmon Ski Lift. 10300 Ski Run Rd.; (520) 576-1321; www.skithelemmon.com. In the winter, if the snow is right, Mount Lemmon becomes the southernmost ski area in the United States. In the summer, ride the lift for the breathtaking view. The 30-minute round-trip covers approximately 1 mile. You'll depart near the base area and enjoy a scenic view of San Pedro Valley, the Reef of Rocks, and the towns of Oracle and Mammoth. Closed Tues and Wed. Fee.

where to eat

Iron Door Restaurant. 10300 Ski Run Rd.; (520) 576-1321. In Ski Valley, at the base of the Mount Lemmon ski area. Come for salads, sandwiches, homemade soups, chili, and corn bread. The restaurant is named for a lost mine with an iron door that, legend has it, was operated by Jesuit padres in the Catalinas during the 1700s. According to the story, Apache raiders killed the Native American mine workers and the Jesuits. Lunch only. Closed Tues and Wed. $$.

east >>>

day trip 01

east

>>>

flight, space, and saguaros:
davis-monthan air force base and
pima air and space museum,
saguaro national park (east)

davis-monthan air force base and pima air and space museum

It's difficult to imagine that this immense base started as a municipal airport established by civic-minded citizens in 1919. Located on Craycroft Road at Golf Links Road in Tucson, Davis-Monthan is named for Lts. Samuel H. Davis and Oscar Monthan, two early Air Corps officers from Tucson.

The Army Air Corps made its first investment in D-M in 1931, and modern paved roads and runways followed in the mid-1930s. Shortly before Pearl Harbor, $3 million was earmarked for expansion, and D-M soon became one of the best heavy-bombardment training stations in the nation.

After World War II, the base was nearly deserted until it was designated an Air Technical Service Command storage area. Because of the arid climate, hundreds of aircraft are stored here now.

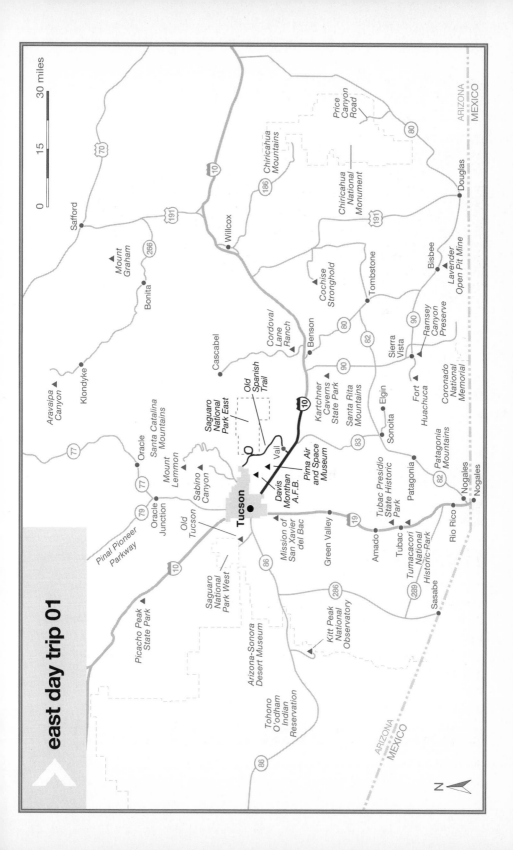

east day trip 01

30 miles

N

ARIZONA
MEXICO

ARIZONA
MEXICO

Safford

Mount Graham

Bonita

Klondyke

Aravaipa Canyon

Oracle

Santa Catalina Mountains

Mount Lemmon

Sabino Canyon

Oracle Junction

Old Tucson

Tucson

Pinal Pioneer Parkway

Picacho Peak State Park

Saguaro National Park West

Arizona-Sonora Desert Museum

Tohono O'odham Indian Reservation

Kitt Peak National Observatory

Mission of San Xavier del Bac

Green Valley

Amado

Tubac

Tumacacori National Historic Park

Sasabe

Rio Rico

Nogales
Nogales

Patagonia

Patagonia Mountains

Tubac Presidio State Historic Park

Sonoita

Elgin

Fort Huachuca

Coronado National Memorial

Sierra Vista

Ramsey Canyon Preserve

Bisbee

Lavender Open Pit Mine

Douglas

Santa Rita Mountains

Kartchner Caverns State Park

Davis Monthan A.F.B.

Pima Air and Space Museum

Vail

Old Spanish Trail

Saguaro National Park East

Cordoval Lane Ranch

Cascabel

Benson

Tombstone

Cochise Stronghold

Chiricahua National Monument

Chiricahua Mountains

Price Canyon Road

Willcox

Safford

the "bone yard"

Aviation buffs wax rhapsodic when you take them to the "bone yard," an expanse of open desert that serves as a massive parking lot for mothballed airplanes. Now part of the Pima Air and Space Museum, this is still one of my favorite destinations. Like our desert signature plant, the saguaro, this amazing collection of planes is one of Arizona's most unique icons. What's fun about this day trip is that within an easy drive, you celebrate the history of flight and the heritage of saguaro forests, two specialties of southern Arizona.

Currently D-M is a diversified military installation. It is home to the largest outdoor aircraft storage facility in the world, and A-10 combat crew training and OA-37 Forward Air Control operations also are conducted.

where to go

Pima Air and Space Museum. 6000 East Valencia Rd., just east of I-10, 1 mile from the interstate; (520) 574-0462; www.pimaair.org. It houses more than 5,000 military planes, ranging from bombers to drone fighters, on 2,600 acres. More than 70 different aircraft types may be seen.

Although not technically part of Davis-Monthan, the facility works closely with the base. The third-largest air museum in the country, it is exceeded in size only by the Smithsonian Institution's National Air and Space Museum in Washington, D.C., and the Wright-Patterson Air Museum in Dayton, Ohio. Ask if a special volunteer is available to take you through the presidential aircraft located on the grounds. Base tours are provided by the museum Mon through Fri, excluding Christmas and Thanksgiving. Fee.

Challenger Learning Center of the Southwest. (520) 618-4823; www.challenger.org. On the campus of the Pima Air and Space Museum, this center provides children and adults with invaluable experience in the fields of math, science, and technology by providing simulated space missions that kids "fly." The program is part of an international effort to bring the wonders of space within the reach of youngsters. Open daily. Call for operations of "mini missions." Fee.

saguaro national park (east)

As you look at your map of this area, note that the Saguaro National Park is actually two parks. The larger one, the Rincon Mountain Section unit, is located due east of Tucson, while the smaller park, the Tucson Mountain District unit, lies to the west. Both parks were established March 1, 1933, for the protection of a remarkable stand of saguaro (pronounced sa-wa-ro) cactus found here. Be apprised that there are no accommodations available other than picnic tables at either of these facilities.

Return to I-10 when you leave the Pima Air and Space Museum. Go east on I-10 to exit 275 and continue north on this road to Old Spanish Trail. Turn east on Old Spanish Trail for 2 miles to the entrance and visitor center of Saguaro National Park East or Rincon Mountain Section unit. The park is open from 7 a.m. to sunset. The visitor center is open from 8 a.m. to 5 p.m. daily.

Driving through a stand of saguaros is unlike driving through any other kind of forest. The profusion of angles will constantly delight you. Some saguaros signal with their arms in crazy directions; others stand almost perfectly symmetrical with arms reaching up in supplication. Although a stately plant, saguaros nevertheless strike some humorous poses.

As you walk or drive through the 62,499 acres of this section of Saguaro National Park, you'll be amazed at the endless variety and sheer numbers of the plants. The visitor center has information on the native vegetation and nature trails, and you'll get an overview of the biology and geology found in this area of the state. Hopefully you'll come away with a better understanding of how plants and animals adapt to an arid existence. Above all, you'll gain a new appreciation for a wondrous plant, the saguaro.

The saguaro cactus is remarkable. A natural desert condominium, it provides homes for a variety of creatures. Several species of birds eat its seeds, live in its walls, and build nests in its arms. By the time a saguaro grows to 20 feet and has its first branch, the plant has lived through 75 years of strenuous desert sun, wind, and rain. With a root structure stretching for miles just barely beneath the surface, the plant is an unparalleled natural balancing act. Superbly adapted to make the most of an unpredictable desert water supply, the plant's accordion-style pleats allow it to shrink during droughts and plump up after rains. This queen of the desert can grow to 50 feet and live to age 200.

Birders will have a field day at Saguaro National Park. More than 50 species of reptiles also roam around the park. If you've thought of the desert as an empty place, think again. As you wander through this rolling, saguaro-studded landscape with its endless shades of sun-bleached green, look for desert tortoises, gophers, coach-whip snakes, ground squirrels, peccaries, coyotes, and mule deer. Listen, too, for the whistle of the curve-bill thrasher, the churring of the cactus wren, and a yipping coyote chorus.

If you visit between February and May, you may be fortunate enough to witness an outstanding wildflower display. These fragile blooms are dependent upon winter rain, so a superb show is not guaranteed each year. If you're there when these blossoms peak, you're in for a special desert experience.

Outdoor types may prefer hiking in the forest of the Rincon Mountains. A backpacking permit is required in the backcountry. Fee. (520) 733-5153; www.nps.gov/sagu.

day trip 02

east

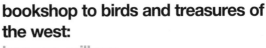

bookshop to birds and treasures of the west:
benson, willcox

benson

Follow I-10 east to Benson, about 45 miles from Tucson. This small community, like its neighbor Willcox, was founded along the main line of the Southern Pacific Railroad. During the late 1800s it served as a shipping point for the livestock- and mineral-producing areas to the south. It nestles in an intermountain valley created by the San Pedro River. Although the original streets were designed in a grid on a 160-acre plat, the town grew haphazardly.

Today Benson is emerging as a suburb of Tucson. Surrounded by natural beauty, the immediate area offers a wealth of things to see and do.

where to go

Amerind Foundation. Exit 318, south of I-10 in Texas Canyon between Benson and Willcox; (520) 586-3666; www.amerind.org. Take the Dragoon exit (318) on I-10 and continue east 1 mile to the Amerind Foundation turnoff, then turn left into the foundation.

This museum is a jewel. A privately funded center for archaeological field research, the center also houses a museum and art gallery dedicated to archaeological and ethnographical material on Indians from all the Americas. The gallery contains a superb collection of western, Native American, and American art.

Why a fine museum in the middle of the desert? The answer lies in the passions of one man, William Shirley Fulton, a Connecticut industrialist. Fulton purchased this property, 65

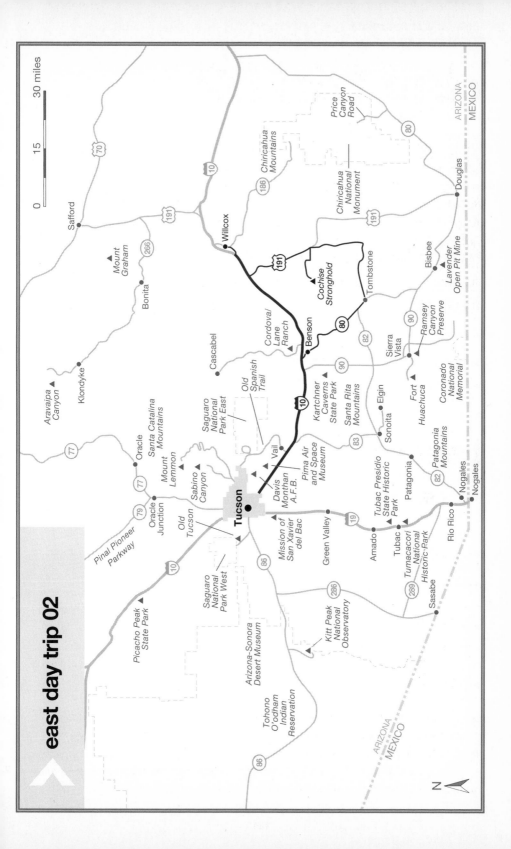

east day trip 02

Tucson

0   15   30 miles

N

ARIZONA
MEXICO

Safford

70

191

266

Mount
Graham

Bonita

Klondyke

Aravaipa
Canyon

77

Oracle

77

Santa Catalina
Mountains

Mount
Lemmon

79

Oracle
Junction

Pinal Pioneer
Parkway

10

Picacho Peak
State Park

Saguaro National
Park West

Arizona-Sonora
Desert Museum

Tohono
O'odham
Indian
Reservation

86

Sabino
Canyon

Old
Tucson

Saguaro
National
Park East

Old Spanish
Trail

Cascabel

Cordoval
Lane Ranch

10

Willcox

191

Chiricahua
Mountains

186

10

Price
Canyon
Road

80

Chiricahua
National
Monument

191

Douglas

Cochise
Stronghold

191

Benson

80

Tombstone

Bisbee

Lavender
Open Pit Mine

82

Sierra
Vista

90

Ramsey
Canyon
Preserve

Kartchner
Caverns
State Park

Santa Rita
Mountains

Elgin

Sonoita

90

83

Fort
Huachuca

Coronado
National
Memorial

Patagonia
Mountains

Patagonia

82

Nogales

Nogales

Rio Rico

Vail

Davis
Monthan
A.F.B.

Pima Air
and Space
Museum

Mission of
San Xavier
del Bac

Green Valley

86

Kitt Peak
National
Observatory

286

Sasabe

289

Amado

Tubac

Tubac Presidio
State Historic
Park

Tumacacori
National
Historic Park

19

ARIZONA
MEXICO

miles east of Tucson, in the early 1930s and became intensely involved in Native American cultures. As he began to acquire a sizable collection of diverse artifacts, Fulton hired noted architect H. M. Starkweather to design and build a permanent home for his important collection. Starkweather visualized the Spanish Colonial Revival–style structure as an eloquent contrast to the massive natural boulders of this part of Arizona.

Until recently, the Amerind Foundation (the name is a contraction of the words American Indian) concentrated more on research than outreach. However, the Amerind has redirected its focus to make its impressive collection of artifacts, arts, and crafts more accessible to visitors. The site includes a picnic area, museum, store, and cultural weekends. Open Tues through Sun. Closed major holidays. Fee.

Cascabel Clayworks. Twenty-four miles north of Benson on Pomerene Road; (520) 212-CLAY. Expect to travel on a dirt road for many miles to reach this community of artists. Handmade clay works are fashioned in a unique setting with shade trees, the San Pedro River, and a backdrop of gold cliffs.

Singing Wind Book Shop. 700 West Singing Wind Rd.; (520) 586-2425. Two and one-quarter miles north of Benson on Ocotillo Road. Turn right (east) on Singing Wind Road. If the gate is closed, open it and go on in, or give them a call. You'll find a white ranch house nestled in a scene straight out of a Western film. This renowned bookshop contains a complete collection of books about the Southwest and western Americana as well as an amazing assortment of books on nearly any subject. Plan to spend quality time browsing through the many rooms. Open daily.

San Pedro Valley Arts and Historical Society. 242 South San Pedro; (520) 586-3070. In 1983 the San Pedro Valley Arts and Historical Society purchased a building that had been boarded up for nearly 50 years. After renovating it, the society opened a museum/gallery that features changing exhibits and a permanent display. There's also a gift shop that features handcrafted items, ceramics, and paintings by local artisans. Free, but donations are appreciated. Open Tues through Sat.

Texas Canyon. Located 14 miles east of Benson on I-10. This is a lovely natural area with spectacular rock formations. You can picnic here, hike, or simply enjoy the views of nature as the master sculptor.

willcox

From Benson, follow I-10 east 36 miles to Willcox. This small Arizona community was settled in 1880 as a construction camp for the Southern Pacific Railroad. When the track went down, Willcox sprang to life. It quickly became a focal point in Cochise County for cattle shipping and still holds that position. Some of the largest cattle ranches in the state are located in the broad, grassy valleys in this area.

Often called the "Gateway to the Chiricahua Wonderland," Willcox is rich with Native American lore. Here the U.S. Cavalry battled the Chiricahua Apaches. Many sites commemorate various skirmishes. This is the country of Cochise, the legendary Apache chief who stalked and struck deep in the valleys and then faded back into the shadowy mountains. This land was holy to all Apaches. The Apache chief Geronimo wrote: "There is no place equal to that of Arizona. I want to spend my last days there and be buried among those mountains."

If you pay a visit to the Old Willcox Cemetery, southeast of town, you'll see where Warren Earp, brother of the famous frontier marshal Wyatt Earp, is buried. For more information about other points of interest, drop by the Willcox Chamber of Commerce, 1500 North Circle I Rd.; (520) 384-2272; www.willcoxchamber.com.

where to go

Apple orchards and pistachio groves. Follow Fort Grant Road northwest 20 miles from town to arrive at these private orchards and nut groves. Willcox is a major apple-producing area and, in season, hosts popular U-Pick-Em days. Call the chamber of commerce at (520) 384-2272 for dates and times.

Apple Annie's Orchards. 2081 West Hardy Rd.; Apple Annie's Produce & Pumpkins. 6405 Williams. (520) 384-2084; www.appleannies.com.

The Cochise Information Center. 1500 North Circle I Rd.; (520) 384-2272. Stop for information about this area and tour the museum. You may also want to stroll around Heritage Park, on the grounds of the center, where you'll see a replica of a mining display.

go east for adventure

Birders know this area because of the annual migration of sandhill cranes. There's a whole festival, Wings Over Willcox, that celebrates the arrival of these large white birds. I was fortunate enough to visit the Willcox Playa when the cranes were in residence and witnessed as hundreds—it felt and looked like thousands—of cranes rose in the air en masse and flew over my head. If you attend this festival, come with binoculars and a camera, and prepare to be awed. When you think that these cranes migrate here from Russia, their arrival is truly mind-blowing, especially when you remember that many Arizonans have never discovered this part of the state. Another reason to make the trip is for the U-pick operation at Apple Annie's Orchards. The farm store run by Annie and her husband is stocked with homemade apple bread, pies, cider, butter, and other locally grown treats.

Chiricahua Regional Museum. 127 East Maley. The museum features exhibits on the area's history, including Apache Indians, Geronimo, the Butterfield Stage Line, ranching, farming, mining, and railroad displays. There is an impressive bust of Cochise. Take time to read some of his sayings, and you'll get an insight into the mind of this unusual man. Call the Cochise Information Center at (520) 384-2272 for hours.

Cochise Stronghold. Follow I-10 west about 8 miles from Willcox. Take US 191 south about 17 miles. About a mile before you get to the community of Sunsites, there is an unnamed graded road that heads west. Look for the sign indicating that this is the road to Cochise Stronghold. Take this road west for 10 miles until it ends at the parking lot and campgrounds.

Cochise Stronghold is the area of the Dragoon Mountains that served as home, headquarters, and safe haven for Apache chief Cochise. Cochise was a fierce leader, on par with Geronimo and Mangas Coloradas. As you drive into the mountains, more than one writer has noted a "presence" that seems to linger over the landscape. Somewhere in this tangle of rocks and canyons, towers and domes, and manzanita shrubs lay the bones of Cochise. Even in death, he remains a controversial character.

One legend says that when Cochise died in 1874, his braves buried him in full regalia. They lowered his body into a deep crevice along with his horse, dog, and rifle. According to another story, his men, fearing vandalism by white men, buried their chief on a grassy mesa and then ran their horses back and forth to mask the grave site. In any event, although the exact location of Cochise's body is unknown, his spirit is everywhere.

As you enter the area of the stronghold, you'll see a Forest Service campground. A good hiking trail into the Dragoon Mountains begins here. If you decide to explore this region, remember that the area is not commercially developed. You won't find any souvenir shops or cafes at the end of your journey, which takes about 4 hours. If you're prepared for a rugged walk, park at the campground and follow the well-marked 3-mile trail. Some of the climb is steep, but eventually you'll arrive at an open area where you can gaze over a 40-mile vista. This point on the trail is designated as the heart of the stronghold. As you stand there, surrounded by the cliffs and sculpted spires, it's easy to imagine Apache bands moving in and out of the shadows.

When you start down, you'll need to watch your footing because the path is steep. Around the 2-mile mark, turn to see towering above the walnut and sycamore trees an almost overpowering view of Cochise Stronghold. It's the same scene that greeted Gen. O. O. Howard as he marched into the stronghold in 1872 carrying a flag of truce. As a result of Howard's trek, Cochise agreed to end the hostilities at last.

No doubt General Howard had other things on his mind than the scenery, but, as you leave the stronghold, take one last, lingering look at this Apache sanctum. Don't be surprised if you have the distinct feeling that the great Chief Cochise is looking back at you.

A word of caution: This area has no amenities other than picnic tables—not even a telephone.

Stout's Cider Mill. Located at I-10, exit 340; (520) 384-3696; www.cidermill.com. This is the only cider mill on I-10 from the East Coast to the West. The apple pies are stuffed to overflowing and are superb. The cider is delicious. Even if you're not hungry, the place is fun for browsing. Open daily.

Walking tour. The Willcox Chamber of Commerce has published a historical walking tour of the area that gives you insight into this old western town.

where to stay

Mule Shoe Ranch Preserve. 6502 North Mule Shoe Ranch Rd.; (520) 507-5229. Exit 340 from I-10. From Bisbee Avenue (next to the shopping center), go to Airport Road. Turn right and continue for 30 miles on a washboard road. This ranch is owned and operated by the Nature Conservancy and sprawls over 48,500 acres of the Sonoran and Chihuahuan Deserts. There are 7 permanently flowing streams that make this a wonderful riparian habitat. The small stone cabin and 4 casitas are comfortable and were recently rebuilt. All have kitchenettes; some have claw-foot tubs and even corrals. They are available from Sept to May. $$.

day trip 03

east

>>> **a hidden world deep inside a mountain:**
kartchner caverns state park

kartchner caverns state park

Kartchner Caverns State Park has one of the finest examples of caves found anywhere in the world. It is located 160 miles southeast of Phoenix and about 50 miles southeast of Tucson. From I-10, take exit 302 and travel south for 9 miles on AZ 90. It is 19 miles north of Sierra Vista.

This is definitely worth a special day trip, as there is much to see and do here. However, you must make a reservation to see the cave. Don't expect to show up on a whim and be able to get inside. What makes this day trip so special is that Kartchner Caverns is a wet, alive cave that is continuing to form. It is extremely unusual for nonspelunkers to have the opportunity to visit such a vast, living underground formation.

Kartchner Caverns, an absolutely magnificent limestone cave, was discovered in the Whetstone Mountains by accident. Amateur spelunkers, Randy Tufts and Gary Tenen, found a sinkhole into the cave while on a hike in 1974. Fortunately for all of us, these two young men swore themselves to secrecy about their amazing find until they could be sure that the cave would be protected.

Establishing protection for the cave took more than 14 years. Not until 1988 was the director of the Arizona State Parks system, able to crawl into the hole to see the cave first-hand. Then it took until November 1999 to open even a portion of this amazing wet cave to the general public. Happily, everyone involved in this unique project pledged from the

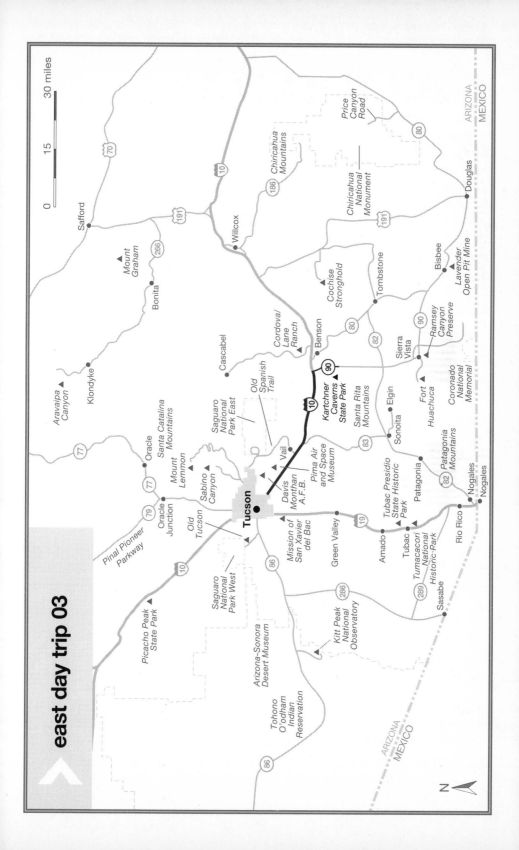

0   15   30 miles

Safford

70

191

266

Mount
Graham

Bonita

Klondyke

Aravaipa
Canyon

77

Santa Catalina
Mountains

Oracle

77

Mount
Lemmon

Sabino
Canyon

Oracle
Junction

79

Pinal Pioneer
Parkway

10

Picacho Peak
State Park

Saguaro
National
Park West

Old
Tucson

Saguaro
National
Park East

Cascabel

Old Spanish
Trail

Cordoval
Lane Ranch

Willcox

10

186

Chiricahua
Mountains

Price Canyon
Road

80

Chiricahua
National
Monument

191

Cochise
Stronghold

Tombstone

Bisbee

Lavender
Open Pit Mine

Douglas

ARIZONA
MEXICO

Benson

80

82

Sierra
Vista

90

Ramsey
Canyon
Preserve

Fort
Huachuca

Coronado
National
Memorial

90

10

Kartchner
Caverns
State Park

Santa Rita
Mountains

Elgin

Sonoita

83

Vail

Davis
Monthan
A.F.B.

Pima Air
and Space
Museum

Tucson

Mission of
San Xavier
del Bac

Green Valley

86

Amado

19

Tubac

Tubac Presidio
State Historic
Park

Tumacacori
National
Historic Park

Patagonia

Patagonia
Mountains

82

Nogales

Nogales

Rio Rico

289

Sasabe

286

Kitt Peak
National
Observatory

Arizona-Sonora
Desert Museum

Tohono
O'odham
Indian
Reservation

86

ARIZONA
MEXICO

N

start to protect the cave so its "live" status would not be negatively impacted. The result is a project that, under the protection of the Arizona State Park system, does a spectacular job of protecting the cave while, at the same time, making it accessible to those who want to experience its wonders. Note that the park occasionally closes certain tours to perform scientific work.

Technically, Kartchner Caverns was formed by underground water cutting through Escabrosa limestone over eons. Water, mixing with mineral deposits, formed the sculptural and colorful formations. Although the formations within the cave are breathtaking, the size and scope of the project deserves equal attention. The state of Arizona has poured $34 million into this project to develop it aesthetically and ecologically, and it is not done yet. Cave experts maintain that Kartchner Caverns established new standards for how caves should be developed.

The surveyed portion of the cavern is 2⁴⁄₁₀ miles long, but the park includes a 23,000-square-foot Discovery Center that explains the geography and natural history of this unique underground feature and the story of the caverns. Plan ample time to peruse the Discovery Center because the exhibits are definitely worthwhile. Your entire park experience will take a minimum of 3 hours and includes the tour of the cave, walk through the visitor center's exhibits, perusal of the gift shop, and enjoyment of the outdoor scenery, including a hummingbird garden and hiking trails. The Rotunda cave tour lasts about an hour and includes a tram trip to the cave entrance and a 45-minute underground tour. The Big Room tour lasts 1 hour and 45 minutes.

Because this is a wet desert cave, be prepared for almost 100 percent humidity inside the underground chambers. The temperature is 68 degrees just below the surface.

a remarkable story; an amazing living cave

Kartchner Caverns is one of the finest examples of a living cave in the world. You can tour the rooms and combine this day trip with another activity, but because Kartchner Caverns is so unusual, I recommend that you spend the better part of the day here, enjoying the tour and the exhibits. The cave is remarkable for its beauty and size, but so is the story of how it was discovered and how the secret was kept for years until the state was certain that the cave would be protected. I had the pleasure of touring the cave with the director of Arizona State Parks on the day that the team that worked inside the cave was showing off the completed project to their families. We could feel the love and pride from these workers. Many were former miners who created the special amenities that make it possible to enjoy the cave today without damaging its fragile ecosystem.

An elaborate tunnel and door-lock system assures that the environment of the cave is not affected by visitors entering or leaving.

Once inside the air locks, visitors follow 1,800 feet of hand-poured concrete trails to see the wonders of this underground labyrinth, such as the longest "soda straw" formation in the United States (21 feet, 2 inches) and the most massive column in Arizona, Kubla Khan, which measures 58 feet. The two main galleries are both the size of football fields and contain extraordinary formations. From April to September, the cave is a maternity ward for about 1,000 female *Myotis velifer* bats that roost here.

After stepping through the second air lock, visitors are greeted by a chamber with walls climbing almost 4 stories to a ceiling that is dotted with stalactites. All rooms in this cavern have stood untouched for thousands of years.

As you walk through the cave, pay attention to how visitors are accommodated in this unique environment. Construction inside the caverns was done almost totally by hand, by a devoted crew of local workers (many of whom had worked in mines previously) who care deeply about the success of this project.

Reservations are a must. All tours are guided by a park ranger and trained volunteers, and tours run approximately every 15 to 20 minutes. The rules of the cavern must be obeyed. These include no touching or breaking of formations; no coin tossing; and no flash photography, tripods, or video cameras. No food, drink, gum, or tobacco products are allowed inside. No strollers, walkers, backpacks, or pets (except assist dogs) are permitted, and, of course, no littering is tolerated.

Reservations can be booked up to 1 year in advance and cancelled 15 minutes prior to tour departure time. Cost of the underground trek varies, depending on tour and time of year. Open daily except Christmas. Offers 63 camping and RV sites. Big Room open from Oct 15 through Apr 15. Fee. For reservations or additional information, call (520) 586-2283 or visit www.azstateparks.com/Parks/KACA/index.html.

San Pedro Valley Observatory. 1311 South Astronomers Rd. (888) 455-6934; www .arizona-observatory.com. Formerly SkyWatcher's Inn and the Astronomer's Inn, this facility is now available only for astronomy purposes and no longer operates as a B&B. Founded in 1990 by Dr. Eduardo Vega and Max Bray, the San Pedro Valley Observatory attracts amateur astronomers from all over the nation. Recently updated with the latest in astrophotography and astronomical equipment, the observatory hosts many events that are open to the public. Rental packages available for families, astronomers of all levels of experience and serious researchers. Fee.

where to stay

Sonoita and Sierra Vista have some good and convenient choices of accommodations,. See Day Trip 01 Southeast from Tucson and Day Trip 01 South from Tucson for additional recommendations.

day trip 04

east

>>> **rocks, spires, and magical spaces:**
chiricahua national monument

chiricahua national monument

From Tucson, follow I-10 east to Willcox. At the junction of AZ 186, turn south and follow this road about 20 miles to the Chiricahua National Monument. If you pick up this trip at Safford, take US 191 south to I-10, head west to AZ 186, and follow it to the park. After paying the entrance fee, proceed to the visitor center. The exhibits graphically describe both the man-made and natural history of this mountainous area. You may pick up pamphlets or buy guidebooks that describe the various trails. If you take the time to go through the visitor center first, you'll appreciate this region of the country much more.

Described as "a wonderland of balanced rocks, volcanic spires, and grotesquely eroded cliffs," Chiricahua National Monument was established in 1924. Endlessly mysterious, this is an ever-changing landscape. One moment shadows caress the spires that rise nearly 200 feet into the air; the next, light plays hide-and-seek with chiseled rocks that stand silently shoulder to shoulder.

Plan this day trip when you have lots of time and energy. If you want advance information, write Chiricahua National Monument, 13063 East Bonita Canyon Rd., Willcox 85643. Twenty-four campsites open year-round. (520) 824-3560, ext. 302; www.nps.gov/chir.

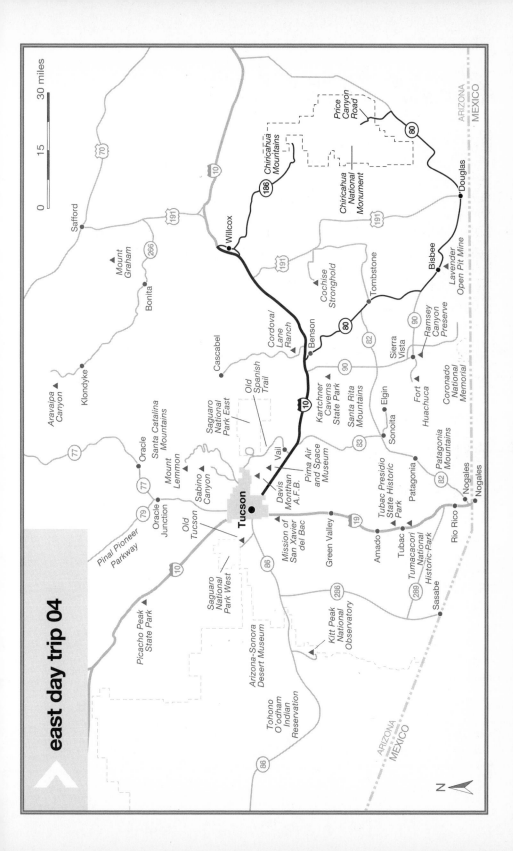

N

30 miles

15

0

ARIZONA
MEXICO

ARIZONA
MEXICO

70

Safford

266

Mount
Graham

Bonita

10

191

Willcox

191

186

Chiricahua
Mountains

Chiricahua
National
Monument

Price
Canyon
Road

80

Douglas

191

Cochise
Stronghold

Bisbee

Lavender
Open Pit Mine

77

Aravaipa
Canyon

Klondyke

Cascabel

Cordoval
Lane
Ranch

Benson

Tombstone

80

82

Sierra
Vista

90

Ramsey
Canyon
Preserve

Oracle

Santa Catalina
Mountains

Saguaro
National
Park East

Old Spanish
Trail

10

Kartchner
Caverns
State Park

90

Fort
Huachuca

Coronado
National
Memorial

Mount
Lemmon

Sabino
Canyon

Vail

Santa Rita
Mountains

Elgin

Sonoita

Patagonia
Mountains

77

Davis
Monthan
A.F.B.

Pima Air
and Space
Museum

33

79

Oracle
Junction

Old
Tucson

Tucson

Mission of
San Xavier
del Bac

Green Valley

19

Tubac Presidio
State Historic
Park

Patagonia

82

Pinal Pioneer
Parkway

86

Amado

Tubac

Nogales

Nogales

10

Saguaro
National
Park West

Tumacacori
National
Historic Park

Rio Rico

Picacho Peak
State Park

286

289

Arizona-Sonora
Desert Museum

Kitt Peak
National
Observatory

Sasabe

Tohono
O'odham
Indian
Reservation

86

what to do

To see this sprawling park from the comfort of your car, follow Massai Point Drive, a 6½-mile paved road that leads up Bonita Canyon to Massai Point. From the top you'll get a good view of Sulphur Springs Valley to the west and San Simon Valley to the east. The Massai Point Exhibit Building is a worthwhile stop, for it offers more information on the natural history of the area.

However, you'll experience the sense of the Chiricahuas more if you travel on foot. There are 18 miles of trails to choose from. If you plan to hike for more than an hour, take water with you. Whether you decide on a 20-minute stroll or a 2½-hour hike, you're sure to succumb to the strange beauty of this rocky place. Let your imagination fly—and you may even sense the spirit of Geronimo lurking in the shadows.

From here you can retrace your steps, heading north on AZ 186 to Willcox and then going west on I-10 back to Tucson.

where to stay

Price Canyon Ranch. South of Chiracahua Mountain National Monument and north of Douglas. From Tucson, follow I-10 east to Benson; exit at SR 80 to Douglas. At Pan American Avenue, go left on the Truck Route on SR 80 to mile marker 400. Follow the dirt road west for about 7½ miles past the fork. The ranch is at the end of the road. (800) 727-0065 or (520) 558-2383;www.pricecanyon.com.

experience the "chiricahuas" any way you like

Going to the "Chiricahuas," as we Arizonans say, is an inspiring experience. Hikers can spend hours or days following the web of trails, and birders can sit and fill their lists. Hiking can be as challenging or as relaxing as you wish. While some of the trails require a serious time and energy commitment, others are easy loop trails that also provide you with expansive views of the rock formations. If your idea of good scenery is watching it go by from your car window, you are also in for a treat. The paved roads through this national monument lead to extraordinary views. Don't think of this as only a winter destination. Because the elevation is higher in southeastern Arizona, temperatures are more moderate, so it's fine to visit this park in spring and even summer. While you're here, see Faraway Ranch, the historic homestead that is within the park. It was both a cattle and working guest ranch and gives you an appreciation for how people lived in this remote and rural part of the state.

A true working guest ranch, Price Canyon is tiny—just 10 rooms. But these are elegant western-style rooms. Two horseback rides are offered daily, and cattle drives take place monthly. Since the ranch sits at 5,400 feet, the climate is much cooler than Tucson or Phoenix. Open Aug 15 through Dec 1 and Feb 15 through June 1. The ranch does not have a liquor license but allows guests to bring their own beverages. Three home-cooked meals are included in the price. A 2-night stay is required, except during the months of Oct and Apr when a minimum stay of 3 nights is required. $$$.

day trip 05

east

>>> **cactus to aspens and an unforgettable canyon:**
safford
worth more time: aravaipa canyon

safford

From Tucson, head east on I-10 to its junction with US 191. Go north on US 191 about 34 miles to Safford.

Dwarfed by towering Mount Graham, which rises 10,713 feet above it, Safford has grown as an agricultural and copper mining community. Like many small Arizona towns, this Graham County community offers the casual visitor more outdoor than indoor activities.

Graham County was organized in 1881, but its history dates back to the Anasazi Indians, an ancient people who inhabited the area around the time of Christ. The Anasazi were followed by the Hohokams, farmers who disappeared in the 13th century, and finally by the Apaches, who were nomadic, fierce fighters. Although Coronado visited this area in 1540, it wasn't until tiny Camp Goodwin was established in 1864 that Caucasians made their presence known in this area. Not surprisingly, the Apaches were not about to give up this land easily, and they battled to keep their territory. The last of the Apache chieftains, Geronimo, finally surrendered in 1888.

As you drive through the sculpted countryside, with its broad valleys and secluded canyons, you will be enthralled by the strange, twisted beauty and may understand why the Apaches believed this landscape was worth fighting for.

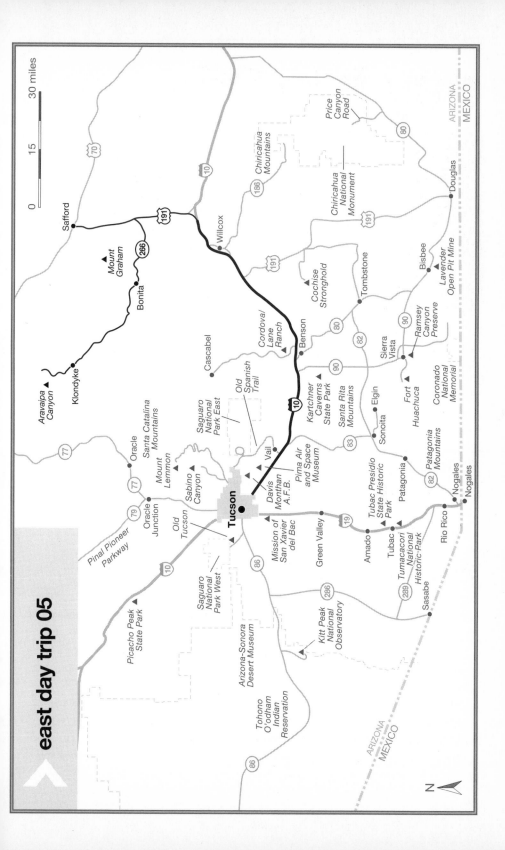

where to go

Mount Graham. About 9 miles south of Safford, off US 191, you will see AZ 266, or Swift Trail. Turn right and follow this road for a spectacular journey to the summit of Mount Graham. Like the drive to Mount Lemmon, this takes you through 5 of the 7 ecological zones of western North America. You'll begin in desert cactus and end in mountainous aspen.

When you see a sharp right-hand turn leading to Marijilda Canyon, don't take it. This road is not recommended for passenger cars. (As you travel around Arizona, *always* obey a sign that says NOT RECOMMENDED FOR PASSENGER CAR OR SEDAN TRAVEL. These roads can go from rough to impassable fast.) Instead, continue on Swift Trail. The first 22 miles are paved, but then the road becomes well-maintained gravel. With its many switchbacks, you'll need about 2 hours to make it to the top. As you traverse the 36 miles to the summit, you'll pass campgrounds—complete with showers—and picnic grounds. Pull off at the scenic turnouts to drink in the views.

Although the drive is worth the trip, Mount Graham has 9 major trails to hike on, once you ascend. Dutch Henry Trail originates at Ladybug Saddle; Ash Creek Trail begins at the summer-home area of Columbine, at 9,500 feet. You can pick up Grant Goudy Ridge Trail at Soldier Creek Campground. Try the Round-the-Mountain Trail, which covers 14 miles and touches on some of the most popular features of the area, or High Peak Trail, which originates a short distance southeast of Columbine, at 9,600 feet. In addition, you can hike on Clark Peak Trail in the Taylor Pass and West Peak area, Bear Canyon Trail, Snake Trail, and Arcadia Trail. Pick up information and trail guides at the Graham County Chamber of Commerce, 1111 Thatcher Blvd.; (928) 428-2511; www.graham-chamber.com.

worth more time:

aravaipa canyon

You *must* contact the Bureau of Land Management (BLM) before making a trek into this jewel of a wilderness area, and there is a fee. Write to the Bureau of Land Management, 1906 West Thatcher Blvd., Safford 85546; call (928) 348-4400; or visit www.az.blm.gov.

To get to Aravaipa Canyon from Safford, take US 191 south to AZ 266. Follow AZ 266 west to Bonita, and then pick up the secondary road to the village of Klondyke. Follow this road to the canyon entrance. Park your vehicle and proceed on foot.

Aravaipa is located in the Galiuro Mountains, and the creek supports an abundance of wildlife. More than 230 species of birds have been recorded here, including some rare black- and zone-tailed hawks and yellow warblers. To protect the wildlife, only 50 people per day are permitted to hike on the trail, and permits should be obtained in advance. It is always important to ask about the condition of the canyon in terms of weather.

This canyon is *not* for the casual hiker. Aravaipa is designated as a wilderness area; it is not a picnic ground. The area covers 4,044 acres and offers hikers and backpackers a relaxing-to-challenging experience. Bring water and a trail map (which you receive when you contact the BLM), even if you plan to spend only a few hours in this desert splendor.

Today Aravaipa is such a tranquil place that it's difficult to remember its violent history. The confluence of Aravaipa Creek and the San Pedro River, however, was the original site of Camp Grant (now Fort Grant). Although the U.S. Army swore that the Aravaipa Indians had not been responsible for raiding the white settlements, both the white men and the Papago (now Tohono O'odham) Indians were unconvinced. In 1872 a group of Tucson citizens and Papagos approached the Aravaipa Reservation and, before the sun rose, massacred 85 men, women, and children.

As you hike in the canyon, you'll be flanked by cliffs rising 700 feet or more on either side of you. In some areas you must squeeze through narrow stone hallways. If you choose to follow Aravaipa Creek, plan on having wet shoes at times. You'll be wise to move quietly and carry a good camera to catch much of the endangered wildlife on film. Bighorn sheep take refuge here, and the largest number of native fish in any stream in the state populate the water. Aravaipa is also a birder's paradise.

While hikers wax eloquent about an autumn backpacking trip into Aravaipa Canyon, enthusiasts insist it's ideal any time of year.

a magical canyon and memorable getaway

It takes a little time to get here, but it is definitely worth the time and effort. This canyon is a wonderland of riparian beauty, and Aravaipa Farms is one of the state's most delightful treasures. My husband and I spent a weekend in early July at Aravaipa Farms, not considered the optimal time to visit since the summers are warm in this part of the state. After taking a stroll around the property, admiring the fruit orchards and enjoying a gourmet (translate that as huge and delicious) lunch, we decided to take a quick nap before hiking farther afield. After almost an hour, we were awakened by the sounds of a summer thunderstorm. Thunder rolled and rain beat down on the tin roof of our cozy, delightfully appointed casita. We gave ourselves permission to sleep just a little bit longer, ensuring the perfect start to our getaway weekend. What is truly magical is that these two very different ecological destinations—Mount Graham and Aravaipa Canyon—are in such close proximity, so you can enjoy them both.

To return to Tucson after such a full day, follow US 191 south to I-10 and head west back to the "Old Pueblo." Or you can go on to Chiricahua National Monument (Day Trip 04 East from Tucson).

where to stay

Aravaipa Farms. (520) 357-6901; www.aravaipafarms.com. From Tucson take AZ 77 north toward Winkelman. Exit the route about 10 miles south of Winkelman at mile marker 124. Follow the dirt road for 8 miles and be prepared to cross a flowing creek to reach this B&B. It is 2 hours southeast of Phoenix and 1 hour north of Tucson, just outside Winkelman. Carol Steele, a former Phoenix culinary star, is the hostess of this charming and gourmet B&B, which features just 5 cottages located on a 300-acre fruit orchard. The unique furniture is made on the premises, as are the birdhouses that hang everywhere. The daily rate includes 3 great meals prepared by your hostess. Two- and three-course dinners are memorable and are served at 7 p.m. On weekends a 2-night minimum stay is required, but during the week, guests may book a single night. During the fruit season, guests can pick apricots, peaches, and pears in the Aravaipa orchard. There's a nominal fee to pick fruit by the pound, so you can carry it home with you. Open Wed through Sat. $$$; no credit cards accepted.

southeast

>>>

day trip 01

southeast

the good, bad, and real history of the old west:
tombstone, bisbee, sierra vista,
coronado national memorial,
fort huachuca

Although this day trip can be done in 1 day, you may prefer this as a more leisurely 2-day excursion. Plan to arrive in Tombstone by midmorning and reach Bisbee by suppertime. Stay overnight in Bisbee, and then drive on to Sierra Vista, Fort Huachuca, and back to Tucson the following day.

Should you decide to cover this portion of southern Arizona in 1 day, know at the outset that you can't see everything described here. Choose carefully among the attractions. There is so much to see that if you aren't careful, you'll arrive home in the wee hours of the morning, overtired and overflowing with images and memories.

tombstone

Begin in familiar territory by taking I-10 east to Benson. At AZ 80, head south to Tombstone. Here's where all your western fantasies will come true. This is "The Town Too Tough to Die." It's where Ed Schieffelin went prospecting in 1878 for silver, warned that all he would find in this Apache-infested land was his tombstone. Instead, he found one of the richest silver strikes in the country.

Tombstone, for all its touristy atmosphere, is no false-front, made-up western town. This is the *real* thing, and it has emerged in recent years as a fun and fascinating destination.

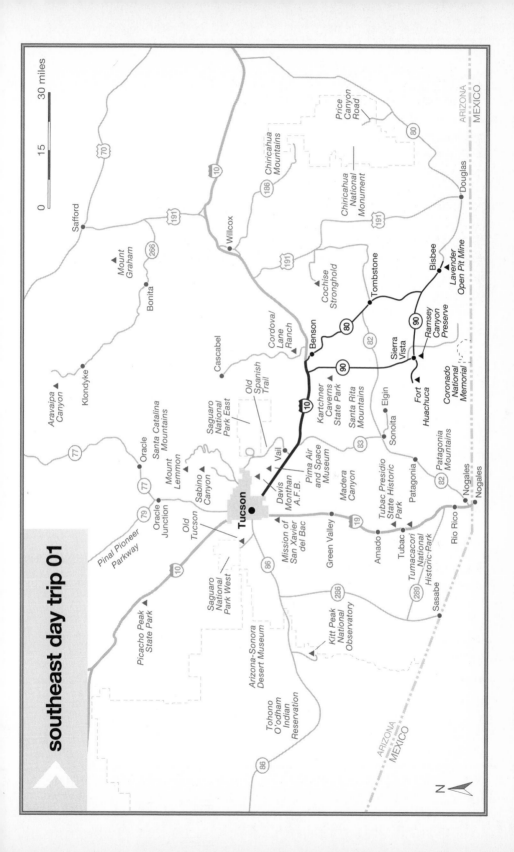

southeast day trip 01

N

30 miles
15
0

Once it boasted a population of about 10,000 wild and respectable souls. Today the community caters to tourists, but all the legends are alive and well here. As you walk along the dusty streets, you'll see the O.K. Corral, the Bird Cage Theatre, the Crystal Palace, and other historic sites. Tombstone is the Wild West preserved at its raunchiest and best. It personifies the frontier experience in those wild days before the turn of the 20th century.

What was it like to live here? George Parsons, an early settler, noted in his diary in 1880 that "a man will go to the devil pretty fast in Tombstone. Faro, whiskey, and bad women will beat anyone." And Wyatt Earp once commented, "We had no YMCAs."

As you come into town on AZ 80, you'll hit Fremont Street. Park anywhere. Since the entire town is a living museum, you'll want to see this National Historic Site on foot. And save time to shop. The wooden sidewalks are faced by as fine an array of shops as one can find in urban settings. Tombstone has definitely discovered fine boutiques.

Begin with a liberal dose of history. Stop at the **Tombstone Epitaph,** 9 South 5th St., and pick up a map describing the points of interest.

Take a moment to familiarize yourself with the town. Most of what you'll want to tour lies within a few main streets. The sites are concentrated in a square framed by Fremont and Toughnut Streets to the north and south, and 3rd and 5th Avenues on the west and east.

Since most of the attractions have an entrance fee, you may prefer to stop in at the O.K. Corral or Tombstone Historama and buy a combination ticket rather than pay separately for each. The combination ticket saves you a little money and a lot more time waiting to buy other tickets.

For more information before you go, write the Tombstone Tourism Association, 9 South 5th St., Tombstone 85638, for a map and a brochure. (520) 457-2211; www.tomb stoneaz.com.

where to go

Tombstone Courthouse. On the corner of Toughnut and 3rd Streets; (520) 457-3311. This elegant structure was built in 1882 for the then-amazing sum of $43,000. It served as the Cochise County Courthouse until 1929, when the county seat was moved to Bisbee. Two floors of exhibits await visitors. There's a ghoulish side trip out the side door to see the hangman's platform, a room devoted to cattlemen, another to lawyers, and rooms full of costumes, jewelry, and china. This is a good first stop to get you in the mood for the 1880s.

Tombstone Historama. Allen Street between 3rd and 4th Streets, next to the O.K. Corral; (520) 457-3456. Enter this bright, airy building and slide back into time thanks to this unique, informative electronic presentation of Tombstone's history. You'll be seated in a small theater to watch an excellent mini sound-and-light production and will gain an understanding of the forces that shaped this tough little town. Fee.

O.K. Corral. Allen Street between 3rd and 4th Streets; (520) 457-3456. This is where it all happened, where history was made that bloody, dusty October day in 1881 when the Earp brothers and Doc Holliday faced off against the Clanton and McLaury brothers. You'll see the lifelike figures positioned as they stood in the dust that fateful day, and you'll marvel that a major gunfight was staged in such a small space. Even non–western history buffs will be strongly affected by this site. Live shows daily 9 a.m. to 5 p.m. Fee.

Bird Cage Theatre. On the corner of Allen and 6th Streets; (520) 457-3421 or (800) 457-3423; www.tombstoneaz.net. Here tired miners bragged of strikes yet to come. Gamblers and gunmen cavorted. The law kept order, and pretty young girls charmed them all. Preserved as it was in the 1880s, this theater was the gathering place for Tombstone citizens looking for fun. There's less glamour than you might expect, but remember that in the 1880s, this place was "it." Open daily 8 a.m. to 6 p.m. except Christmas. Fee.

Rose Tree Inn Museum. On the corner of 4th and Toughnut Streets; (520) 457-3326. The world's largest rose bush, which grew from one slip sent to a Scottish bride living in Tombstone, spreads for more than 8,500 square feet. Inside the museum, antique furnishings give visitors a glimpse of how people lived in Tombstone more than a century ago. Open daily 9 a.m. to 5 p.m. Fee.

Crystal Palace Saloon. Allen and 5th Streets; (520) 457-3611. While the Bird Cage Theatre was bawdy, the Crystal Palace was more refined. Here the elite and not-so-elite gathered for food and drink. You can belly up to the bar and eat and drink (both soft drinks and alcohol) in the carefully preserved interior. Come for good food, atmosphere, and loud, vintage 1890s saloon music. $ at the bar.

vintage clothing and lasting memories

I don't know any other place in Arizona where townspeople dress in 1800s attire and shops still sell clothing styles that were worn in that era. Each time I visit I get a thrill out of going into the Bird Cage Theatre, the Crystal Palace Saloon, and Big Nose Kate's, knowing how much history clings to these old saloons. But I also adore Bisbee with its quirky residents (they seem to have landed from the 1960s), narrow, twisted streets, and shops. My favorite Bisbee experience is the underground mining tour, which is great for kids as well as adults. We took our grandchildren on it. We all dressed in mining slickers and donned our helmets with headlamps, and rode through the mine on the train. Later, our then-5-year-old granddaughter wrote an essay about our trip for her class. She wrote that she liked the trip and learned about copper, but what she liked most was that she was with her grandparents! I cannot think of a better reason than this for a parent or grandparent to take day trips in Arizona.

Tombstone Epitaph. On 5th Street near Fremont Street; (520) 457-2211. Visit the original newspaper building where people continue to publish the famous *Tombstone Epitaph*. Purchase a subscription for $20 and keep up on Tombstone once you are home. Open daily 9:30 a.m. to 5 p.m.

Boot Hill. You pass the sign to Boot Hill as you come into town on AZ 80. You can stop either on the way in or on your way out of town to discover the many infamous gunslingers who are buried at Boot Hill. Read the epitaphs, as they are wonderfully cryptic and humorous. Open daily. Donations suggested.

Tombstone has many other museums and points of interest. Depending upon your time and enthusiasm, spend a full day or just a few hours to get the flavor of this bawdy, rugged place.

where to eat

Longhorn Restaurant. 501 East Allen St.; (520) 457-3405. Come for breakfast, lunch, or dinner and feast on Mexican and American food. Ask about the lunch special; it's always good. $$.

where to stay

Tombstone has joined the 21st century (or maybe it's just returned to the 1880s) by attracting several bed-and-breakfasts. All are close to town and convenient. The following two are my favorites. More B&Bs can be found by contacting the Tombstone Chamber of Commerce, P.O. Box 995, Tombstone 85638; (888) 457-3929; www.tombstone.org.

Buford House. At 2nd and Safford Streets; (520) 457-3969 or (800) 273-6762. This 1880 two-story haunted adobe residence is registered as a National Historic Landmark. The house has 5 rooms and serves full breakfast. Nonsmoking only. $.

Marie's. At 4th and Safford Streets; (520) 457-3831; www.mariesbandb.com. A 1906 Victorian adobe home that is 1 block from the Historic District, it offers 2 rooms and serves full breakfast. $–$$.

bisbee

Continue south about 25 miles on AZ 80 to Bisbee. Just 6 miles north of the Mexican border, this charming community is famous for its mountainous setting; steep, winding streets; and a crazy patchwork of architectural building styles. You'll enter town on AZ 80 through Mule Pass Tunnel. A third of a mile long, it is Arizona's longest tunnel. As you get near town, watch for the Bisbee business loop, which will be on your right. Follow it to Old Bisbee, and you'll wind up on Main Street.

Bisbee has been described by the late Arizona writer Joseph Stocker as a "larger and newer version of Jerome." (See Day Trip 02 North from Phoenix.) Like Jerome, Bisbee began as a mining town. During its heyday, this was the place to stop between New Orleans and San Francisco. Millions of tons of copper, gold, and silver were pulled from the Mule Mountains, which surround the town. Until the late 1880s, Bisbee offered every cultural, culinary, and sporting diversion found in any major American city.

The Phelps Dodge Corporation closed its copper operations in Bisbee in the mid-1970s, but instead of dying, the community determined to survive as a tourism center of southeastern Arizona. During the late 1960s and 1970s, hippies heard about the community and flocked here in droves, attracted by the temperate climate and inexpensive housing. Today most of the hippie culture has vanished, but some artists, poets, and artisans remain in residence. Thanks to a strong dose of community spirit, Bisbee is succeeding as a tourist center, and visitors appreciate the blend of historical charm and modern-day convenience the town offers.

Bisbee is quite small, with a population of less than 10,000, but it supports a lively cultural scene. Classical concerts are presented at the Bisbee Women's Club. There are gallery openings by local artists, poetry readings, dinner theater, even melodramas. Most weekends the town hums with activities. Antiques shops are everywhere.

The unique blend of Victorian and 1930s art deco images have inspired many creative people who have come to work here. The late world-renowned Arizona artist Ted DeGrazia once lived in Bisbee and managed the now-restored Lyric Theatre.

You'll want to wander around "Old Bisbee," as it's called. Don't be deceived by the sleepy facade. This isn't a living museum like Tombstone. Rather, this is a very much alive community populated with Bisbee boosters. You'll enjoy touring the old residential sections where turn-of-the-20th-century homes are squeezed onto narrow, steep streets wedged into equally narrow, scenic canyons. The result is an intriguing web of tangled mountain roads and architecturally interesting structures.

If possible, do take a complete walking tour of downtown. Stop in at the chamber of commerce, 1 Main St., and pick up a brochure (520-432-5421; www.bisbeearizona.com). Even if your time is limited, plan to walk around some of Bisbee's historic district to savor its past. If you aren't up to a strenuous stroll, take a bus tour of Old Bisbee and the hilly residential neighborhood known as the Warren area. Each tour lasts approximately 1½ hours and allows you plenty of time to take pictures. Fee. For information regarding hours of departure, call (520) 432-2071.

where to go

Queen Mine and Lavender Open Pit Tours. 478 Dart Ave.; for information about tour times, call (520) 432-2071 or visit www.cityofbisbee.com. To get to the Queen Mine building, drive or walk immediately south of Old Bisbee's business district off the AZ 80 interchange. Underground mine tours leave daily at scheduled hours. As you explore the mine with your guide, you'll hear about George Warren, who, having celebrated with a few too many on the Fourth of July, bragged that he could outrun a horse and rider. In a burst of inebriated pluck, he bet his mining claim, the Copper Queen Mine, on the race. He ran and lost. Eventually his claim panned out, ultimately worth more than $40 million. Today George Warren's biggest claim to fame is that he was the model for the man who stands with his shovel in the center of the Arizona State Seal.

During this educational tour, you'll learn how Bisbee miners coaxed minerals from the mountains. Much of the original mining equipment stands in place. Although you walk into the Copper Queen, you'll ride out on small train cars. Bring a sweater. The mine remains a chilly 47 degrees Fahrenheit. Tours run daily. Fee.

Lavender Open Pit. (520) 432-2071. Drive to a viewpoint on AZ 80 that is ¾ mile beyond the Queen Mine building to see the open pit, or take a guided tour that leaves from the Queen Mine building every day at noon. As you gaze into this huge bowl scooped out of the landscape, you'll marvel at how humans ever carved such an immense niche in the earth. Although the Lavender Open Pit shimmers with color, the name comes from a mine manager, Harry Lavender. Fee.

Brewery Gulch. 13–17 Brewery Ave. Also known as the Muhlheim Block, this street shoots dramatically uphill or downhill (depending upon your vantage point) from Howell Avenue. Completed in 1905, Brewery Gulch was once home to the Bisbee Stock Exchange, brothels, restaurants, lodging facilities, and saloons. It emits old echoes of wilder days when gamblers and miners traipsed up Brewery for excitement. Today visitors can poke through shops and art galleries along this narrow street.

Bisbee Mining and Historical Museum, a Smithsonian Affiliate. In front of the Copper Queen Hotel; for information call (520) 432-7071; www.bisbeemuseum.org. The permanent exhibition opened in September 1991 and combines mural-size photography, artifacts, minerals, and hands-on displays. The mineral collection is small but select and features a variety of copper-related materials, such as azurite, that can be found in the area. A one-hour visit will explain the political, economic, and labor history of this mining camp turned cosmopolitan town. The World War I labor section describes how Arizona cleaned up prostitution and gambling so it could join the Union. A rare faro table illustrates gambling; prostitution is left largely to the imagination.

A poignant exhibit tackles discrimination. Through a mirror device, visitors' faces are superimposed on heads of minorities. The question asked is: Does it make a difference?

The museum's award-winning exhibit, "Digging In," tells the story of Bisbee's mineral heritage and challenges long-held perceptions about this industry and its cultural and economic impacts. This museum is part of the Smithsonian Institution's Affiliations Program, a prestigious honor. The museum is located in a historic structure built in 1897. Fee.

Old Phelps Dodge General Office Building. 5 Copper Queen Plaza; (520) 432-7071. This structure was completed in 1895 and was designed as the general offices of the copper company. A National Historic Landmark, the Old Phelps Dodge building is located in Bisbee's "Grassy Park." It is now the Bisbee Mining and Historical Museum. Here you can see early mining equipment and a diorama that depicts a mining operation. In another setting, such a display may not excite you, but it springs to life in Bisbee. Open daily. Fee.

Covenant Presbyterian Church. 19 Howell Ave.; (520) 432-4327. Next to the Copper Queen Hotel, this imposing European-style church was built in 1903. At the time it was built, a 579-pipe organ was installed. Over the years the organ has been enlarged, and it remains in excellent condition. Best days to visit are Mon, Wed, and Sun. Free.

where to stay

Like Tombstone, Bisbee has several good to great bed-and-breakfast inns, making this a fine place to spend the night in southern Arizona. Here are some suggestions:

The Bisbee Inn. 45 OK St.; (888) 432-5131; www.bisbeeinn.com. This old hotel has been renovated to bring back a feeling of Bisbee at its heyday. Not as luxurious as the Copper Queen, it is nevertheless a good choice for travelers who want to experience life in the Old West. Originally built in 1916 as a miner's hotel, the Bisbee Inn offers 20 guest rooms. *A special note:* The original name of the hotel was "La More," which leaves little of its history to the imagination. $$.

Copper Queen Hotel. 11 Howell Ave,; (520) 432-2216; www.copperqueen.com. This famous hotel was built by the Copper Queen Mining Company (later Phelps Dodge Corporation) shortly after the turn of the 20th century, when Bisbee was the largest mining town in the world. It is Arizona's oldest hotel—it has been run continuously as a hotel since it opened. The owners have restored most of the rooms to their former glory, making this a good choice for travelers. The rooms are large, and each one is different. Some bathtubs come with feet attached; wallpapers are period restoration. Although the lobby still feels dark and old, the renovated rooms are bright and cheery. The Copper Queen may not be quite as quaint as you may hope it to be, but it is authentic. When you sleep here, you are in good company. Theodore Roosevelt stayed at the Copper Queen, as did Gen. John J. Pershing when he was on his way to Mexico to catch up with Pancho Villa.

The dining room at the Copper Queen is recommended. The fare is sophisticated and well prepared. Have breakfast, lunch, or dinner here. Dine outdoors at the patio cafe or sit inside in the historic, restored dining room. $$.

Letson Loft Hotel. 26 Main St.; (520) 432-3210; www.letsonlofthotel.com. The most upscale property in town is located on the second floor of the Letson Block Building and features 8 individually designed, spacious guest rooms, each with a queen-size bed and fine linens. Guests rave about the service and ambience. Continental breakfast is complimentary and features Old Bisbee Roasters coffee and fresh-baked pastries. In-room massage may be arranged. $$.

The Oliver House. 26 Soule; (520) 432-1900 or (877) 832-1900. This B&B has 14 units. The house, in the heart of town, was supposedly haunted. A continental breakfast is served; king-size beds and suites are available. $$.

School House Inn. 818 Tombstone Canyon; (800) 537-4333; www.virtualcities.com/ons /az/b/azb4501.htm. Nine units (nonsmoking) are available in a 1918 schoolhouse. A full breakfast is served, and there are private baths. $–$$.

sierra vista

From Bisbee, backtrack 9 miles north on AZ 80 and follow AZ 90 west 20 miles to Sierra Vista. Perched at an elevation of 4,623 feet, this fast-growing city is nestled on the slopes of the Huachuca Mountains. Surrounded on all sides by mountain ranges and never-ending views of the San Pedro Valley, the climate is as awesome as the scenery. Sierra Vista ranks as one of the three most temperate regions in the nation, and its cool summers and moderate winters make this city increasingly popular with newcomers and tourists.

With an abundance of outdoor pleasures nearby (everything from hiking trails to ghost towns and a mountain lake), Sierra Vista has become an important southern Arizona town. In the past, its biggest claim to fame was nearby Fort Huachuca. While the economy remains closely tied to the military installation, Sierra Vista is establishing itself as a manufacturing, wholesale, and retail center.

where to go

The Nature Conservancy's Ramsey Canyon Preserve. Located 6 miles south of Sierra Vista on AZ 92 (turn right on Ramsey Canyon Road); (520) 378-2785; http://nature .org/wherewework/northamerica/states/arizona/preserves/art1973.html. Turn right onto Ramsey Canyon Road and drive 3½ miles to the preserve. This 380-acre preserve, owned and managed by the Nature Conservancy, is sheltered in a deep gorge in the Huachuca Mountains. It's a favorite place for birders and others who are interested in learning more about this unique, fragile environment.

Ramsey Canyon is located at an ecological crossroads, where habitats and species from the Sierra Madres of Mexico, the Rocky Mountains, and the Sonoran and Chihuahuan Deserts all can be found. The preserve is a haven for one of the largest arrays of plant and animal species of any preserve in the United States. About 170 species of birds, 45 species of mammals, and 20 species of reptiles and amphibians have been found in the canyon. Some, like the lemon lily, are found in few other places on Earth.

Ramsey Canyon continues to be the center of the Conservancy's upper San Pedro River program and is an eloquent testimony to the landscape-scale partnership-based work the Conservancy does.

The nature trail opens a window to a world populated by a great variety of birds, reptiles, and other animals. Guided nature walks are held every Tues, Thurs, and Sat at 9 a.m. from Mar through Oct. A visitor center, bookstore, gift shop, and nature reference library are on the grounds.

When you plan a trip here, remember that not every type of bird can be seen at the canyon during all times of the year. Ramsey Canyon is known as a hummingbird sanctuary, but these delicate creatures are in residence only from Apr through early Sept. During the winter, they migrate south to Mexico.

Because of the comparatively small size and ecological fragility of the area, certain rules are strictly enforced. Pets, picnicking, and smoking are not allowed anywhere on the preserve. Parking is extremely limited. There are only 23 parking spaces available on a first-come, first-served basis. RVs and campers cannot be accommodated. Visitor hours are strictly enforced. For information write the Nature Conservancy's Ramsey Canyon Preserve, Ramsey Canyon Road, Hereford 85615. Fee.

San Pedro Riparian National Conservation Area. (520) 439-6400; www.blm.gov/az/st /en/prog/blm_special_areas/ncarea/sprnca.html. The information center, San Pedro House, is 8 miles east of Sierra Vista on AZ 90. This 46,000-acre area stretches 43 miles from the Mexican border near Palominos to about 3 miles south of St. David. It includes one of the most significant broadleaf riparian ecosystems in Arizona and perhaps the entire Southwest. More than 360 species of birds, 82 species of mammals, and 41 species of reptiles and amphibians may be seen here. This is a wonderland for hikers, birders, and nature lovers.

where to stay

Casa de San Pedro. 8933 South Yell Lane, Hereford; (520) 366-1300 or (888) 257-2050; www.bedandbirds.com. From Sierra Vista, take AZ 90 Business Loop to Buffalo Soldier Trail to AZ 92 in Sierra Vista. Travel south on AZ 92 for 18½ miles to Palominos Road. Turn north on Palominos Road for 2 miles to Waters Road. Turn east on Waters Road for 1 mile. This charming bed-and-breakfast is backed by the San Pedro riparian area and is situated on 10 acres that border the San Pedro River. Cottonwood and willow along the river provide a verdant habitat for a variety of wildlife—more than 330 species of birds, 82 species of mammals, and 47 species of reptiles and amphibians. A birders' paradise, this special B&B is an ideal getaway for any traveler seeking peace and relaxation. Built in territorial style around a courtyard and fountain, this property has 10 guest rooms with private baths. All are well appointed. A comfortable great room invites lounging and reading, and superb breakfasts are served in the sunny dining room. The facility is superb. A list of special events from lectures to hikes is available, along with a pool, spa, and Internet access. $$.

Ramsey Canyon Inn. Next to Ramsey Canyon Preserve; (520) 378-3010; www.ramsey canyoninn.com. This B&B is a great alternative for couples or nature lovers who crave ambience. There are 6 rooms and 3 apartments, all lovingly decorated with antiques. Guests enjoy herb teas, fresh-brewed coffee, and a variety of gourmet breakfasts. Order a fluffy omelet, German apple pancake, or the specialty, Dutch babies. Or sample fresh-fruit cobblers before heading out to hike. All pies and cobblers are prepared daily. The small lodge has a beautiful living area with large fireplace. All rooms have private baths. $$$.

coronado national memorial

Located 20 miles south of Sierra Vista off AZ 92, Coronado National Memorial salutes the Spanish explorer Francisco Vasquez de Coronado, who searched for the Seven Cities of Cibola looking for gold.

From Sierra Vista, head south on AZ 92. Turn west onto Montezuma Canyon Road and continue for 5 miles until you come to the visitor center and museum. The road is paved for just about a mile west of the visitor center, and then it becomes a mountainous gravel path that leads to Montezuma Pass, a narrow passageway over the Huachuca Mountains. Park and pick up the hiking trail of your choice. From the pass, you can gaze west over the San Rafael Valley and Patagonia Mountains toward Nogales (see Day Trip 03 South of Tucson).

The Coronado National Memorial is the name given to this entire area and includes both natural and manufactured historical features. There is no plaque or statue commemorating Coronado's adventures. Instead, hiking trails lace the 4,976 acres that are home to a variety of birds, animals, and plants.

Told that cities existed where streets were paved with gold, Coronado arrived in Mexico in 1535. On February 23, 1540, he headed north with 336 Spanish soldiers and four priests to search for treasure. Instead of finding golden cities, Coronado found mud houses—adobe pueblo—inhabited by Native Americans. Pushing on, he ultimately came upon Hopi Indian villages in northeastern Arizona. Driven by the promise of gold, he continued to search past Acoma and onward to the upper Pecos River. Finally, discredited and disheartened, Coronado admitted defeat and died in relative obscurity. Although he never found gold, Coronado did change the course of Southwestern history. The Spaniards left behind horses that helped the Native Americans dominate the plains and mountains, and they introduced the Catholic religion to the region. Historians agree that the Coronado expedition formed the basis for contemporary Hispanic-American culture.

If you have a car that can go over miles of dirt road—and you have the time—the trip over Montezuma Pass is well worth the effort. It is perhaps the most outstanding physical feature in this memorial. The pass is located at an elevation of 6,575 feet, and once at the top, visitors are treated to sweeping views of the San Rafael Valley to the west and the San Pedro River Valley to the east. The road has steep grades and tight switchbacks, and the top of the pass serves as a parking area for hikers who are exploring the memorial's trails. Standing at the top of Montezuma Pass is a living lesson in the geography and history of this area. You can easily imagine how it must have been when Coronado discovered this place and determined to conquer it. A picnic area near the visitor center is open from dawn to dusk. At the top of the pass is an excellent national park plaque that describes the sweeping vista. The road continues to Sonoita—the scenery is spectacular, but the going will be slow. Or turn around and return to the visitor center.

The Coronado National Memorial is well known for the variety of birds that live in the area. The Park Service reports that more than 140 species have been recorded, including 50 resident birds. Open daily. Free. (520) 366-5515; www.nps.gov/coro.

fort huachuca

From the Coronado National Memorial, return to Sierra Vista on AZ 92, then drive west for 4 miles to Fort Huachuca. To get to the main gate, follow AZ 90 south to where it intersects with Squier Avenue. The main gate is on the corner of Squier Avenue and AZ 90.

This 73,000-acre installation lies within the boundaries of Cochise and Santa Cruz Counties and is closely tied to the history of Arizona. Now the largest employer in southern Arizona, Fort Huachuca was established in 1877 as a base for American soldiers during the Native American wars of the 1870s and 1880s. Fresh running water, high ground, and shade trees convinced the army that this was a wise location for a fort. When Geronimo surrendered and the Native American hostilities ended, Fort Huachuca was kept active to guard against problems around the Mexican border.

Many well-known units were stationed here, but the most famous is the "Buffalo Soldiers," the Tenth Cavalry Division of African-American fighters who accompanied General Pershing when he chased Pancho Villa into Mexico in 1916.

Closed down after World War II, Fort Huachuca was later reactivated, and in 1953 became the home of the U.S. Army Electronic Proving Ground. Again, its physical setting saved the fort, because the mild, dry climate and open spaces made it a natural for the electronics field. Today the base buzzes as a center for intelligence and worldwide communications. For information regarding the base, write: Headquarters, Fort Huachuca, Attn: ATZS-TAM, Fort Huachuca 85613; (520) 533-3638.

Fort Huachuca Historical Museum. Corner of Boyd and Grierson Streets, overlooking the Brown Parade Field; (520) 533-5736; http://huachuca-www.army.mil/history /museum.htm. The museum is housed on the historic Old Post, where almost all of the original buildings are still in use. Opened in 1960, the museum tells the story of Fort Huachuca and of southwestern Arizona. It showcases military memorabilia from the 1800s to the present. Because Arizona history is closely tied to the military, the exhibits will help you understand events leading up to this young territory becoming the 48th state. There's ample parking, and a gift shop features items and books related to the Southwest. Open daily except major holidays. Free.

To return to Tucson from Fort Huachuca, drive north on AZ 90 to I-10, then west on I-10 to Tucson.

south

day trip 01

south

>>> **vines and wines and a natural sanctuary:**
sonoita, patagonia

This day trip can also be done from Phoenix if you don't mind adding an extra 2 hours driving time each way. If you do it from Tucson, it's an easy hour or less to Sonoita and Patagonia.

From Tucson, take the scenic drive southeast on I-10 toward Nogales. Go south on AZ 83 for 27 miles to Sonoita. The route takes you through magnificent country studded with cactus, beveled with foothills, and ringed with wide, open valleys. As the road climbs toward Sonoita, the landscape grows more lush—the area is nurtured by Sonoita Creek. Even during the summer, when the rest of the Arizona desert is bleached to a coarse yellow, the high grasses here retain their green tint.

If you decide to stay overnight in Tombstone (see Day Trip 01 Southeast of Tucson), you can start this day trip by heading south the next morning. Follow AZ 80 north of Tombstone to AZ 82, continue west on AZ 82 to Sonoita, and then go south on AZ 82 to Patagonia and Nogales. You can return to Tucson by driving north on I-19, stopping at Tumacacori and Tubac on your way back. This makes a pleasantly packed 2- or 3-day minivacation. Spend the first night in Bisbee, the second in Tombstone, and arrive in Tucson the third evening.

If you make this trip in a single day from Tucson, plan on a long, full day to travel to the Mexican border and return to the Old Pueblo. Visitors have always liked seeing Mexico at least once while in Arizona although, as of this writing, Arizona's anti-immigration stance has cast a pall over this experience. What makes this trip easier than most Mexican vacations is that you don't drive across the border. You'll park in Nogales, Arizona, and walk across the

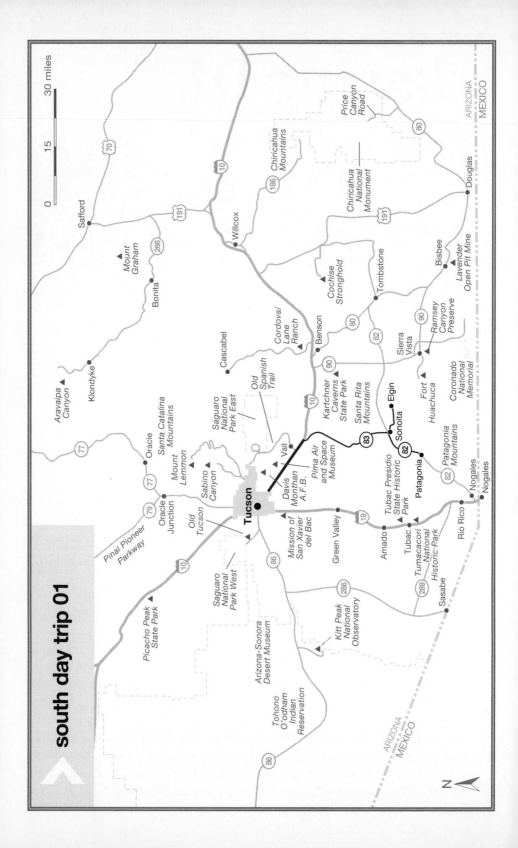

south day trip 01

a day trip for wine lovers

Southern Arizona has always owned the wine country experience for the state. It's only in recent years that competition has arisen from the Verde Valley and Sedona. We started visiting Arizona vineyards more than 30 years ago when the wine industry here was small and still new. Now there are serious tasting rooms to visit and prize-winning wines to sip. It's fun to see how the vines and the industry continue to grow and mature. If you are based in Tucson, this is an easy day trip to enjoy, but from Phoenix we prefer to do this as an overnight so we can spend some time in the high desert, not to mention sampling the wines.

international line into Nogales, Mexico. If you decide to leave Arizona and enter the state of Sonora, Mexico, you'll feel worlds away from the United States. Despite all the bad press, Arizona's border towns are usually safe as long as you stay on the main streets. You must bring your proof of citizenship or passport so that you can reenter the United States.

sonoita

Sonoita is a very old community that dates to around 1699. Originally it was the site of a Vista, a mission that only occasionally received personal visits by Spanish padres.

According to Arizona historian Marshall Trimble, the modern-day town of Sonoita owes its existence to the Benson-to-Nogales railroad line, which was built in 1882. Today this community is still on the transportation "line" for visitors who take what locals call "the back way"—the scenic and more interesting noninterstate route—to Nogales.

More than a place along the way, Sonoita is coming into its own as the site of Arizona's flourishing wine industry. And now with new parts of Kartchner Caverns continually opening (see Day Trip 03 East from Tucson), visitors have even more reason to visit this tiny Arizona town. For more information visit www.sonoitaaz.com.

where to go

Callaghan Vineyards. I-10 east to AZ 83 south, to AZ 82 east and south to Elgin; (520) 455-5322; www.callaghanvineyards.com. The vineyard is located on Elgin Road, 5 miles south of town. Owned by Kent Callaghan, the wines produced are considered outstanding. Established in 1991, this is a family-owned winery that produces a variety of blends. Open Fri through Sun, the winery offers tastings. Among the wines made here are barrel-fermented Sauvignon Blanc, Zinfandel, Cabernet Sauvignon, and the Buena Suerta Cuvée (a blend of Merlot, Cabernet Franc, and Cabernet Sauvignon). Mourvedre, Petit Verdo, and Viognier production began in 1998.

Dos Cabezas Wineworks. (520) 455-5141; www.doscabezaswinery.com. Another very rustic family-owned winery, Dos Cabezas concentrates on making a variety of good wines rather than showcasing the winery to tourists. Those who call in advance can set up an appointment to tour and taste. Its primary focus is on Chardonnay, Viognier, Sauvignon Blanc, Pinot Gris, and Riesling, but it also has Sangiovese and Petite Syrah "resting comfortably in oak barrels." The actual winery is located in Willcox, about 1½ hours from Sonoita, in the Kansas Settlement area of that town. You need to call for directions, because the owners say that visitors cannot find them without a compass.

Sonoita Vineyards. On Elgin Canelo Road, 12 miles southeast of town and 3 miles south of Elgin; (520) 455-5893; www.sonoitavineyards.com. Take the delightful tour through the winery and sample some excellent wines being made in southern Arizona. In the past decade or so, Arizona has experienced a growth of wineries, as its climate and soil are similar to that found in the Napa Valley area around San Francisco and the great wine country of France.

Sonoita Vineyards was selected for the 1989 Inaugural Food and Wine Gala for President George H. W. Bush. The winery is situated in rolling hills and is surrounded by grape arbors with the Huachuca Mountains clearly visible in the not-far-off distance.

Sonoita Vineyards makes private reserve Cabernet Sauvignon, Pinot Noir, Fume Blanc, Cuvee Sonoita, Sonora Blanca, Sonora Rossa, Arizona Sunset, and Cochise County Colombard. Wines are available for purchase and sampling. Tour requires a fee but includes wine tasting.

The Chapel of Santa Maria. Located in the village of Elgin. The chapel is overseen by the Monks of the Vine, a Wine Brotherhood of vintners. The Santa Fe–style chapel is a non-denominational shrine. Local legend is that vines planted around the shrine are thought to come from cuttings from the earliest conquistador cultivars. In April the Blessing of the Vine Festival is held, with music, processions, and food and wine tastings.

Village of Elgin Winery. Within walking distance from the Chapel of Santa Maria in Elgin; (520) 455-9309; www.elginwines.com. Located 4½ miles from upper Elgin Road. The winery is located in an old brown hay barn and is the only winery in Arizona to stomp its grapes. The winery accents small-lot red and white wines ranging from single varietals such as Pinot Noir, Cabernet Sauvignon, and Colombard to blended varieties and clarets. Open daily from 10 a.m. to 5 p.m.

where to eat

The Steak Out Restaurant and Saloon. Next door to the Sonoita Inn, at the crossroads of AZ 82 and AZ 83; (520) 455-5205; www.sonoitainn.com. The Steak Out serves mesquite-broiled steaks, seafood, ribs, and chicken, and the menu touts their "famous" margaritas. Built on the site of a famous western restaurant that burned to the ground, the new restaurant re-creates the 50-year-old historic landmark building. The Steak Out is owned and operated by the owners of the Sonoita Inn, who also operate and own the country store, deli, and gas station on the property. $$

where to stay

Sonoita Inn. At the crossroads of AZ 82 and AZ 83, 3243 Hwy. 82; (520) 455-5935; www.sonoitainn.com. This upscale country lodge was designed by local owner Margaret Charmichael, who owned the famous race horse Secretariat. The lodge is a tribute to that thoroughbred, who won the Kentucky Derby, the Preakness, and the Belmont in 1973. Photographs, press clippings, and other memorabilia are displayed in the lobby of the lodge.

Opened in 1998, the inn features 8 rooms downstairs and 10 rooms upstairs. Each room is named for a ranch in the Sonoita area as a tribute to the families who have operated those ranches for centuries. Guests will find photos and bibliographical accounts of the ranches and the families in the hallways.

Your overnight lodging fee includes deluxe continental breakfast in the morning and wine and cheese in the evening. Although the outside of the inn appears plain, inside you'll find a homey and comfortable atmosphere, with every well-appointed room decorated in a western theme. Located just 30 miles from Mexico and close to Kartchner Caverns, the Sonoita Inn offers a welcome alternative to look-alike motel rooms. $$

patagonia

Patagonia is a picturesque town that lies in a narrow valley bounded by the Santa Rita Mountains to the north and the Patagonias to the south. The mountains and the town were named after the now-closed Patagonia Silver Mine, which operated there in 1858. Also known as the Mowry Mine after Sylvester Mowry purchased it in the 1850s, it produced more than $1.5 million worth of ore during its heyday. By the early 1900s the veins were too diminished to merit any more activity.

Today Patagonia has some of the finest quarter-horse and cattle ranches in the Southwest. It is known throughout the state for its inviting location and, thanks to the higher elevation, slightly cooler temperatures.

In recent years Patagonia has become its own tourist destination. There are several excellent arts-and-crafts galleries to peruse, and good hiking. in the Patagonia–Sonoita Creek Sanctuary, which is a birder's paradise.

There are only two main streets in town, McKeown and AZ 82. You can't get lost in "downtown" Patagonia. For more information visit www.patagoniaaz.com.

where to eat

Velvet Elvis Pizza Company. 292 Naugle Ave,; (520) 394-2102; www.velvetelvispizza .com. Gourmet pizza is served at this local favorite that is a "find" for tourists. $–$$

where to go

Mesquite Grove Gallery. 373 McKeown Ave.; (520) 394-2358. Owner Nancy Merwin and manager Regina Medley have assembled a special array of art, most by local artists. You'll find sculpture, needlework, jewelry, wood, and dozens of other kinds of artwork all crafted with high style and talent. The prices are excellent, and the work is uniformly fine.

The Patagonia–Sonoita Creek Preserve. South of Patagonia on AZ 82 between Patagonia and Nogales; (520) 394-2400; www.nature.org/wherewework/northamerica/states /arizona/preserves/art1972.html. As you enter Patagonia on AZ 82, watch for the Stage Stop Inn and the Patagonia Market. Turn right onto 3rd Avenue. You may want to stop at the filling station in town to use the restrooms since there are no facilities at the sanctuary. Continue south on 3rd Avenue to Pennsylvania Avenue and turn east onto Pennsylvania. Follow the road across a small creek and watch for signs that say NATURE CONSERVANCY. (The conservancy operates the sanctuary.) Look for Gate 2, which will be on your left. Turn in and drive to the Information Center. All visitors must register at an entrance gate.

Birders and naturalists flock to this 312-acre preserve. Located in a narrow floodplain, the sanctuary features a majestic stand of cottonwood trees interspersed with Arizona walnut and velvet ash. Avid birders from all over the world know that this is the place to see more than 200 species.

To protect the fragile character of the sanctuary, rules are strictly enforced. Pets are not allowed on the grounds. There is no picnicking or camping, fires are prohibited, and motorized vehicles are not allowed on trails within the conservancy. This is especially lovely to visit in the spring and fall. Free.

where to stay

Circle Z Ranch. (520) 394-2525 or (888) 854-2525; www.circlez.com. Write P.O. Box 194, Patagonia 85624, or call for directions. A dude ranch, Circle Z, open Nov 1 through May 15, requires a 3-day stay in season. There are rooms, suites, and cottages for 40 guests. The ranch is located in the rolling grasslands just north of the Mexican border. It is known worldwide for birding. $$$.

The Duquesne House. 357 Duquesne St.; (520) 394-2732; www.theduquesnehouse .com. This B&B is almost directly across the street from Cady Hall and was once miners' apartments. The charming adobe building has been renovated with love and attention to detail. Call for reservations. $$; no credit cards accepted.

day trip 02

south

>>> **celestial wonders to wonderful hiking:**
amado, green valley, madera canyon

From Tucson, follow I-19 south toward Nogales, Arizona, and Nogales, Sonora, Mexico. This day trip is devoted to manufactured wonders of the high-tech world. Because of the time involved for the tours, if you want to cover both sights, I recommend going first to Amado and Whipple Observatory and then seeing the Titan Missile Museum on the way back to Tucson. This is not recommended for young children, but older children and teenagers will enjoy it.

amado

Follow I-56 to exit 56 (Canoa). Then follow directions to the observatory.

Fred Lawrence Whipple Observatory. (520) 670-5707; http://cfa-www.harvard.edu/flwo. From exit 56, turn left and drive under the freeway to the frontage road on the east. Turn right and drive south 3 miles to Elephant Head Road. Turn left and drive east. Follow the signs to Mount Hopkins Road for about 7 miles to reach the observatory office.

Operated by the Smithsonian Institution, Whipple Observatory sits atop Mount Hopkins, the second-highest peak in Arizona. It commands a heavenly panorama north beyond Tucson and south into Sonora, Mexico, over hundreds of miles of saguaro-studded Coronado National Forest, desert floor, and rolling mountain ranges.

Visitors take a daylong tour that describes a brief history of astronomical time and includes visits to the computer laboratories, massive telescopes, optical arrays, and celestial mirrors.

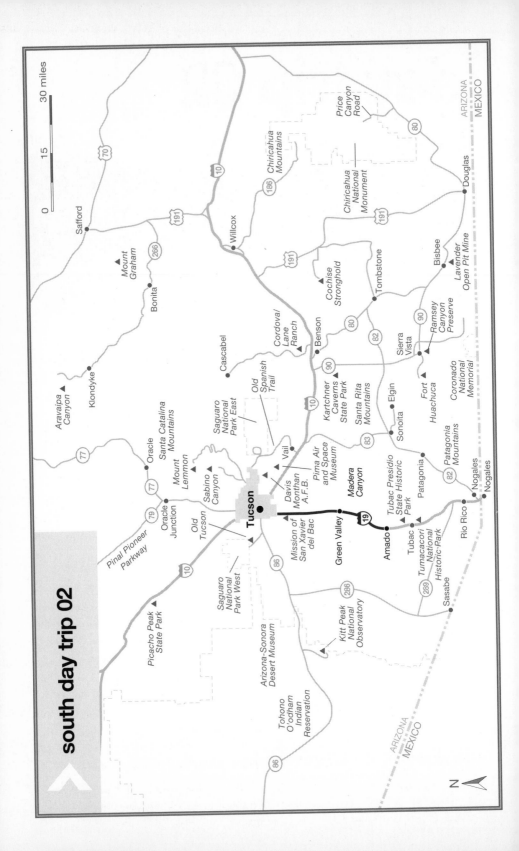

south day trip 02

> ## astronomical importance
>
> *I was surprised some years ago to discover a world-famous facility right here in southern Arizona. Astronomers from all over the world always knew about it. They sign up months in advance for time on the telescope for their individual projects. If by chance "their" night is cloudy or rainy, they have to get back in line and wait their turn all over again. It is mind-boggling to think that some of the most important work in the astronomical world happens right here at the top of Mount Hopkins, and visitors can see where it takes place.*

From the visitor center, everyone boards a bus for the 45-minute climb to the top of the mountain and the observatories. The bus travels through various Arizona life zones, from desert to high chaparral to pine forest. The first stop is at 7,600 feet, for a tour of 48-inch and 60-inch telescopes and a gamma-ray optical reflector. After lunch (you bring it; it's not provided), there's a short, steep ride to the 8,550-foot summit, where the Multiple Mirror Telescope (MMT) stands. You learn that the building rotates slowly so the "eyes" can track the stars. Computers synchronize the entire operation. With its 276-inch mirror, the MMT claims to be the largest single-mirror telescope in North America.

Whipple Observatory Visitor Center is open year-round, Mon through Fri. Observatory tours are available March through Thanksgiving only. The tour is 6 hours long, from 9 a.m. to 3 p.m. Reservations are required. Bring your own lunch. Fee.

From Whipple Observatory, head back to Tucson via I-19 to Green Valley. This is less than a 20-minute drive, and you can still make the last tour(4 p.m.) at the missile museum.

green valley

Pima Air Museum's Titan Missile Museum. (520) 625-4759 or (520) 625-7736. From I-19 south, take exit 69. Go west ⅒ mile past La Cañada. Turn right. This is the only intercontinental ballistic missile complex in the world that is open to the public. This museum is dedicated as a memorial to all loyal Americans who served their country so valiantly in peace and in war. Guided, hour-long tours are available through the complex and the silo starting at 9 a.m. The museum is open daily except Christmas. The last tour starts at 4 p.m. *NOTE:* High heels cannot be worn at this museum. Fee.

madera canyon

From I-19 south, follow the signs to Madera Canyon. This wooded riparian island in the sky offers an excellent choice of well-marked hiking trails. Trails range from moderate to difficult, and the Nature Trail and Amphitheater Trail are both good choices for beginners. Madera Canyon, with its abundance of trees and a running creek, is especially gorgeous in fall and spring. Madera Canyon is an outstanding "find" for birders! For information about trails and the park, call Santa Rita Lodge at (520) 625-8746; www.maderacanyon.net. Free, but donation suggested.

where to stay

Rex Ranch. 131 Amado Montosa Rd.; (520) 398-2914; www.rexranch.com. Located 30 minutes south of Tucson, the ranch is also 30 minutes from Mexico. Some years ago this property was a small and rustic B&B. Over time, it has expanded to include a fine-dining room, Cantina Romantica, and a full-service spa. The dining room serves dinner, European gourmet cuisine with Southwest flair Wed through Sun. $$–$$$.

The spa, Cielo Health Spa, offers a full range of therapies to pamper the body and soul. What hasn't changed is the pink hacienda ambience of this historic property and the magnificent views of the high chaparral desert that surrounds it. Available to individuals and to groups, Rex Ranch has 30 adobe casitas, each individually furnished with unusual antiques and collectibles from around the world. $$–$$$.

day trip 03

south

spanish history and sensational shopping:
tubac; tumacacori national historic park; nogales, arizona, u.s.; nogales, sonora, mexico; sasabe

This day is filled with arts and crafts and great shopping. It's not recommended for non-shoppers, but anyone with even a passing interest in local art and native culture will find it very enjoyable. This trip can be combined with seeing the Titan Missile Museum (Day Trip 02 South from Tucson). Be aware that while there is much being written about the dangers of travelling to Mexico, my experience is that this danger is highly exaggerated. Nevertheless, you should pay attention when driving near the border. The drive to Nogales, Arizona is easy, with a divided highway much of the way signed in kilometers, a reminder of when the U.S. government considered moving to the metric system. Americans can park on the U.S. side and walk across the border. Carry proof of citizenship if you plan to visit Mexico so you can re-enter the United States.

tubac

From Tucson, follow I-19 south for 45 miles to Tubac. According to archaeologists and anthropologists, the Santa Cruz River area has been home to many different people for perhaps 10,000 years. It is likely that the prehistoric Hohokam tribe lived here between AD 300 and AD 1400 to 1500. The Ootam (Pima and Tohono O'odham) arrived here in the 1500s.

The Spaniards came in the 1600s, led by Father Kino, who explored Arizona beginning in 1691. In 1821 the area belonged to Mexico, which won it along with its independence.

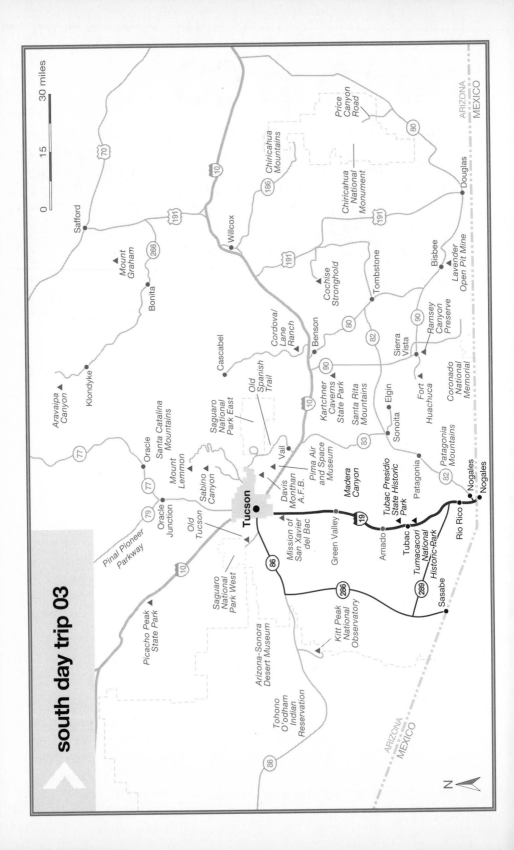

south day trip 03

30 miles
0   15

Since 1853, when the Gadsden Purchase was signed, Tubac has been part of the United States.

Tubac claims to be the first European settlement in Arizona, and it housed the state's first newspaper and state park. It also had the first schoolhouse. In 1751 the Pima Indians swept through Tubac, burning and murdering to defend their homeland. They were defeated, and the Spanish established a garrison, the Tubac Presidio, to defend the missions and the Spanish settlers. The presidio was moved to Tucson in 1776, leaving the town open to Apache attacks. The area quieted, and R. Toribio de Otero applied for and got a land grant in 1789.

When the United States took possession with the Gadsden Purchase of 1853, Tubac was a ghost town. But when ancient mines were discovered and minerals unearthed, it became a favorite spot for prospectors, miners, and journalists.

The Tubac Presidio State Historic Park, Arizona's first, was established in 1959, and the museum opened in 1964.

Tubac is a center of arts and crafts for southern Arizona, touted as the place where "art and history meet." For once, hype is not far from the truth, because Tubac is a unique artistic community.

In 1948 Dale Nichols opened an art school here and over the years potters, painters, and designers of batik, gold, silver, and wood have all "discovered" Tubac. Today more than

reminiscent of old spain

One of the best things about living in Arizona is that when you travel a couple of hours in any direction, not only experience a change in climate, but find yourself in a different culture. This is particularly true in southern Arizona. The point was driven home when my husband and I did a bicycling trip through southern Spain. We were struck by the lasting impact of the Spanish Empire on the southern part of our state. To a history buff, this may sound obvious, but to those of us who live in Arizona, the history of the Spanish explorers, while taught in school, is not truly understood or appreciated by most of us. Not only is the geography of Arizona similar to southern Spain (especially if you include the Sea of Cortez in your sweep of landscape as the Spanish did), but the architecture, customs, and atmosphere of Old Spain remain remarkably intact in this stretch of Arizona. It's one of the reasons why I love it here. Another reason is the great shopping in Tubac and Nogales. From Tucson it is an easy "hop" to Tubac, but it's also quite doable from Phoenix. If you are starting from Flagstaff, I recommend that you drive either to Phoenix or Tucson first, or you'll spend all your time in the car with no time to explore the wonders of Old Spain, Arizona-style.

80 galleries, shops, and studios are located here. Tubac sponsors many festivals. Check with the chamber of commerce, (520) 398-2704, for dates. Two festivals are scheduled in December: the Fiesta—Annual Intercultural Fiesta—and Fiesta Navidad, when the village is lit by luminarias. The Tubac Art Festival is held in February, and the Artwalk is scheduled for early March. www.tubacaz.com.

where to go

The Presidio Museum and Ruins. Tubac Presidio State Historic Park; (520) 398-2252; www.pr.state.az.us/Parks/TUPR/history.html. As you continue on Tubac Road past the business area, it becomes Wilson Road after it crosses Burruel Street. Then, as it curves toward the presidio, it is called Presidio Drive.

The Presidio Museum offers a glimpse into life in a Spanish fort around 1750. An underground exhibit includes some of the original wall and floor. Because of budget cuts, this state park is currently open Thurs through Mon. Fee.

where to eat

Elvira's Mexican Restaurant. 2201 East Frontage Rd., Tubac; (520) 398-9421. Relocated from its original place in Nogales, Sonora, Mexico, Elvira's has recreated its look in its new digs. Same great food and stylish ambience. $–$$.

Wisdom's Café. 1931 East Frontage Rd.; 2 miles south of Tubac and 1,500 feet north of Tumacacori Mission; (520) 398-2397; www.wisdomscafe.com. A landmark cafe for more than 60 years, the specialty here is Mexican food prepared by the family/owners using the freshest of ingredients. Their signature is fruit *burros* made with your choice of fruit, rolled in a crispy burrito, and topped with cinnamon and sugar. This fun and funky cafe is decorated with family heirlooms. So you don't miss out a minute on shopping, there's even a gift shop that sells lots of stuff. $–$$.

where to stay (and eat)

Amado Territory Inn. 3001 East Frontage Rd.; (520) 398-8684 or (888) 398-8684; www .amado-territory-inn.com. Off I-19, exit 48 (Amado exit). This charming nine-room ranch-style B&B is located on 17 acres. The inn is not historic. All rooms have private baths, patios, and balconies. The inn serves excellent home-cooked breakfasts, mystery dinners, and high teas. Rates include full breakfast and happy hour. $$.

Rio Rico Resort and Country Club. (800) 288-4746;. Eight miles south of Tubac on Camino Caralampi in Rio Rico, this AAA Four Diamond resort features a championship Robert Trent golf course, tennis, horseback riding, swimming, and fine dining. $$.

The Tubac Golf Resort and Restaurant. P.O. Box 1297, Tubac 85646 (just north of the village); (800) 848-7893; www.tubacgolfresort.com. When you take the Tubac exit off I-19, continue north on Frontage Road for 2½ miles. The public is welcome at the club restaurant, which offers the most relaxing place to eat between Tucson and Nogales. The menu is mostly American, although some south-of-the-border dishes are included.

This picturesque, small resort sports a golf course and hotel accommodations surrounded by patio homes. Book a room by the day or week, or for the entire season. Reservations are suggested in the summer and necessary during the rest of the year. $$–$$$.

Tubac Secret Garden Inn. 13 Placita de Anza; (520) 398-9371 or (888) 398-9371; www .tubacsecretgarden.com. This B&B is a Spanish Colonial home located on 3 private acres in Tubac's historic zone. A 2-night minimum is requested. $$; no credit cards accepted.

where to shop

Gift shops, arts and crafts galleries, and boutiques are clustered within an area bounded by Tubac Road and Camino Otero, Calle Baca, and Presidio Drive. Here you find many one-of-a-kind items created by local residents. Most shops are open Mon through Sat, and many have Sun hours as well. Ask for a free illustrated map of the area at any store.

Tubac Center of the Arts. Plaza Road (there are no street addresses in Tubac); (520) 398-2371; www.tubacarts.org. As you head toward Tubac on Frontage Road, Plaza Road intersects with Frontage. You're welcome to browse during the season, Sept through May. This is the home of the Santa Cruz Valley Art Association, which showcases a variety of styles and types of art by local painters, sculptors, and craftspersons. Open daily except holidays, Sept through May. Donations are suggested.

tumacacori national historic park

From Tubac, continue south on I-19 for 3 miles to Tumacacori National Historic Park.

The Tumacacori mission is a national treasure that rises from the desert floor like a half-finished cathedral. Built by the Franciscans around 1800, this church was a functioning religious center for 5 years. Then the Franciscans were expelled, and the church was abandoned. Unattended, the mission was gutted repeatedly by Apaches and fortune hunters.

In 1929 the National Park Service restored it to its former, if unfinished, glory. Visitors can take a self-guided tour and see a scale model of how Tumacacori might have looked around 1820. If you call ahead, arrange a guided tour. Open daily except Thanksgiving and Christmas. For information write Tumacacori National Historical Park, P.O. Box 67, Tumacacori 85640. Fee. (520) 398-2341; www.nps.gov/tuma.

nogales, arizona, u.s.

Back on I-19, continue to Nogales, Arizona, which is just over the border from Nogales, Sonora, Mexico. Notice the colors of the houses on the Mexican side and how different the two cities look, even from a distance. As you continue into town, you'll be in the heart of Nogales, Arizona, where AZ 89 and AZ 82 join I-19.

The community on this side is a bustling place complete with a good manufacturing and retail base.

what to do

Crawford Street Historic District. (520) 287-8685; www.nogaleschamber.com. It is possible to tour the historic homes that still stand on Crawford Street as reminders of when Nogales was one of the most important cities in the state and the border was less of an impediment to traffic. There was even a saloon here that straddled the border, with one door in Mexico and one in the United States. Home tours may be scheduled through the Nogales Chamber of Commerce.

where to stay

Hacienda Corona de Guevavi Bed and Breakfast. 348 South River Rd.; (520) 287-6503 or (888) 287-6502; www.haciendacorona.com. From Tucson, take I-19 south to the Ruby Road exit (number 12). Turn left and follow Ruby to Frontera. Turn right, and then turn left at the stop sign. You are now on South River Road. Follow that road for about 1½ miles to the Guevavi Ranch gate on the left. Turn left through the gate, head straight across the Santa Cruz River, and go up the dirt road, passing a yellow barn on your right. This delightful and elegant B&B is located on 36 acres of the historic Guevavi Ranch. Be sure to admire the murals painted by Mexican muralist and bullfighter Salvador Corona. Corona painted them in 1942 and 1955. This ranch was a favorite hideaway for John Wayne, and the innkeepers have lovingly restored it. A breakfast bar serves early risers, and a full breakfast is served from 7 to 10 a.m. The social hour here is delightful. Trail rides are available, limited to 2 guests at a time. $$

nogales, sonora, mexico

Nogales, Sonora, projects a south-of-the-border feeling, even though you're only a few feet into Mexico. The *mañana* atmosphere prevails, and the more you compare the two cities, the more you'll realize how far away Arizona seems once you step across the international line. This is Old Mexico, with bullfights, fiestas, and streets lined with small shops.

The border is always teeming with cars and trucks that are jammed with people and packages. Some of the guards will check every package thoroughly, so allow enough time to get across the border on the return trip.

It's recommended that you park your car on the Arizona side and do not attempt to drive into Mexico. Obey signs, and don't park illegally. Parking is usually available by the railroad tracks on the Arizona side, and you can proceed across the border on foot. Carry proof of citizenship. Should you decide to drive into Mexico, take out Mexican automobile insurance first, since most U.S. insurance doesn't cover you in foreign countries. You can buy Mexican car insurance by the day in Tucson or in Nogales, Arizona, at several agencies.

where to go

In Mexico, walk up any of the main streets in Nogales and browse. You'll find good shops on Elias Calles, Lopez Mateos, and Obregon Avenues and on Hidalgo Street. Think of the shopping area as a long rectangle bounded by Elias Calles Avenue and Hidalgo Street, stretching from the border to Andonegui Street. Look for good buys on pottery, baskets, leather, wrought iron, and Mexican silver. You can also find lovely embroidered clothing as well as linens and crystal. Remember, this is Mexico, and you are expected to bargain. Take your time and look around. You'll find the shop owners friendly and happy to make your trip worthwhile.

When you buy in Nogales, you'll deal in U.S. dollars. When you return to the United States, you must verbally declare your U.S. citizenship and purchases. You are allowed to bring back up to $400 of merchandise duty free, including 1 quart of liquor and 1 carton of cigarettes per adult.

La Roca. 91 Elias St. After you cross the border, turn left and cross over the railroad tracks. Continue 2 blocks, turn right onto Elias Street, and walk 2 more blocks to La Roca, an elegant, enclosed shopping center that resembles a large, pinkish-red, adobe-style hotel. Inside you'll find more expensive items than on the main shopping streets. Most shopkeepers here accept credit cards. You'll encounter some rough sidewalks and high curbs en route to La Roca, so be careful where you walk.

where to eat

La Roca. 91 Elias St.; 2-0760 (in Mexico) or 011-52-631-20760 (from the United States). Mexican food is an obvious specialty here. The upstairs dining room offers margaritas and nachos, as well as complete lunches and dinners. $–$$.

sasabe

Rancho de la Osa. P.O. Box 1, Sasabe 85633, Attn: Veronica; (800) 872-6240; www .ranchodelaosa.com. From Tucson, follow I-19 south to AZ 86 or Ajo Way. Turn west (right) for 24 miles to Robles Junction, which is AZ 286. Turn south (left) for 44 miles. At the sign for Sasabe, turn right for 1½ miles to the ranch. *NOTE:* If you reach the Mexican border, you have gone 1 mile too far.

The only and best reason to go to Sasabe is to visit the historic Rancho de la Osa. The ranch dates back to 1730. Lovingly restored, the small guest ranch has been refurbished with Mexican antiques and wonderfully eclectic art so it is now an authentic Southwest experience. Rooms have private entrances and wood-burning fireplaces.

This intimate ranch is set amid magnificent desert wilderness and offers lots of bird-watching opportunities. The ranch has always been a favorite with Tucsonians who wanted a true getaway destination. The owners have replaced the old ultrarustic experience with one that is much more guest oriented.

The best option is to make the trip and plan to stay a few days or a week or more. The ambience is the best in all of southern Arizona, and the food is equally outstanding. While the horses are gentle, the riding is challenging because of the mountain landscape. However, the staff at the ranch provide enough instruction for guests to feel comfortable after a few days. All meals are included. $$$.

southwest

day trip 01

southwest

>>> **starry days and nights:**
kitt peak and
kitt peak national observatory

kitt peak and kitt peak national observatory

From Tucson, pick up AZ 86 (Ajo Highway) and follow it southwest for 37 miles. At the junction of AZ 386, turn left (the only way you can) and begin the 12²⁄₁₀-mile climb to Kitt Peak. Although this is an excellent road, it twists and winds around the mountain, giving passengers sometimes breathtaking views of sheer drop-offs and broad valleys.

The Kitt Peak National Observatory is located on top of Kitt Peak in the Quinlan Mountains and is on the Tohono O'odham Indian Reservation. At an elevation of 6,882 feet, this giant eye-in-the-sky houses the largest concentration of facilities for stellar and solar research in the world. Founded in 1958, it operates 3 major nighttime telescopes and hosts a consortium that operates nineteen optical telescopes and 2 radio telescopes. The primary mission of Kitt Peak National Observatory is optical astronomical research.

Scientists from all over the world regularly visit Kitt Peak. Although the astronomy center employs more than 50 people, only the necessary support staff live on the mountaintop. The rest make the daily round-trip trek to the summit. There is plenty for the public to see here. You can spend an hour or a full day, depending upon your interest in astronomy.

If you visit during the day, stop first at the visitor center. Pick up an illustrated brochure

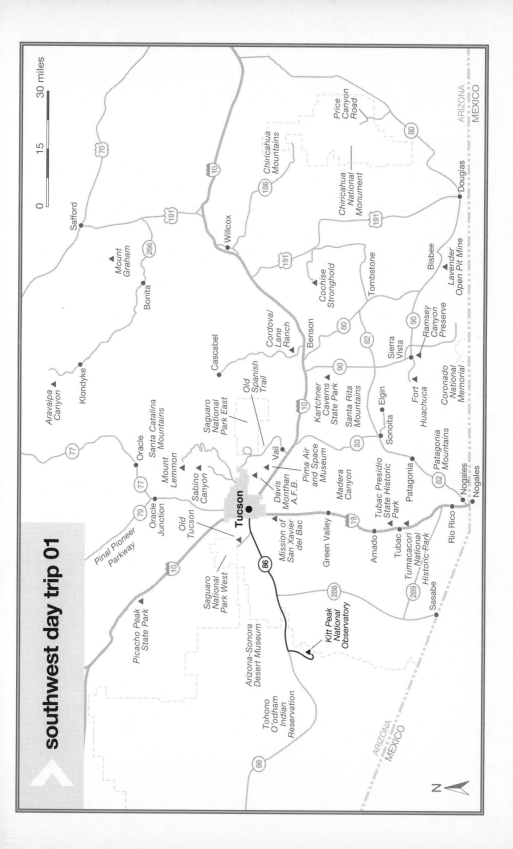

southwest day trip 01

kitt peak by night

See Kitt Peak at night to fully grasp the magnitude of this amazing array of equipment. We called ahead to book the night tour and were given explicit instructions to arrive by 6 p.m. The drive up took us about 30 minutes. After an introduction to the program, we were given box dinners and divided into groups. During the next 3 hours, we were bused to different observatories where we looked through powerful telescopes. They were amazing, but I also loved learning to read a star chart. The sky was blanketed with the brightest stars and planets I had ever seen, and with help I did find a number of constellations. Equally unforgettable was the drive down the mountain, which is done sans headlights, following a lead car, so as not to disturb the dark night sky.

for a self-guided walk, or join one of the regularly scheduled tours that begin here. You also will find exhibits and models to study, films to watch, and even an occasional daytime observing program. The nighttime observing program is offered 7 nights a week except during July and August.

There is also an excellent exhibit about the Tohono O'odham people, whose ancestors were the Hohokam, and a fine display of baskets made by Tohono O'odham weavers. Baskets are for sale.

As you walk out of the visitor center, look out over Altar Valley. Some 18 miles to the southwest you will see Sells, headquarters of the Tohono O'odham tribe. Due south, there is a dome-shaped mountain peak called Baboquivari, the traditional home of the Tohono O'odham Indian god I-I'toy.

While at the Kitt Peak National Observatory, you'll want to see the McMath-Pierce Solar Telescope, which is the largest solar telescope in the world. It is always aligned with the celestial North Pole at Tucson's latitude, and the entire structure that houses it is encased in copper. Coolants are piped through the scope's outer casing, or "skin," as it is called, to ensure that this sensitive instrument is maintained at a uniform temperature.

Another fascinating device to see is the Nicholas U. Mayall Four-Meter Telescope, the nation's second-largest optical instrument. It allows astronomers to study objects 6 million times fainter than the dimmest star visible with the naked eye.

Only candy and soft drinks are sold on Kitt Peak, so if you decide to make a day of it, pack a picnic lunch. Follow the signs to the picnic area, complete with a ramada and table.

Since it's usually about 15 degrees cooler at the top of the mountain than in Tucson, take a jacket or sweater. Free, but donations are suggested. For more information, including arrangements for group tours, visit the website www.noao.edu, or call (520) 318-8726.

west >>>

day trip 01

west

>>> **white dove to desert wonderland:**
mission of san xavier del bac, old tucson,
arizona-sonora desert museum, saguaro
national park (west)

It would be a shame to try to put all these experiences into a single day trip as you need time to enjoy each attraction. For starters, you travel through one of the most majestic forests of saguaro cacti you'll ever see. You can spend a full day of glitz and glamour combined with a liberal dose of science and education and unparalleled natural beauty. I recommend visiting each of these attractions in separate half-day trips and spending a few hours or an entire day seeing each one of them. If you decide to take in all four at once, be ready for a long, full day—not because the distances are great but because there's so much to see at each destination.

mission of san xavier del bac

Pick up I-19 and head south for this 9-mile trip through Tucson and South Tucson to San Xavier (Ha-veer) del Bac. At Valencia Road, turn west and enter the district of San Xavier on the Tohono O'odham Indian Reservation. Small houses and broad, tilled fields stretch in all directions.

In the distance, you will see the White Dove (as it's called) rise dramatically from the desert floor. Dazzling white, San Xavier shimmers like a bird caught between the brown-beige land and indigo sky. With its imposing dome and lofty parapets and towers, the mission contrasts brilliantly against the violet of the nearby mountains. You'll quickly see why it has been called the finest example of mission architecture in the United States.

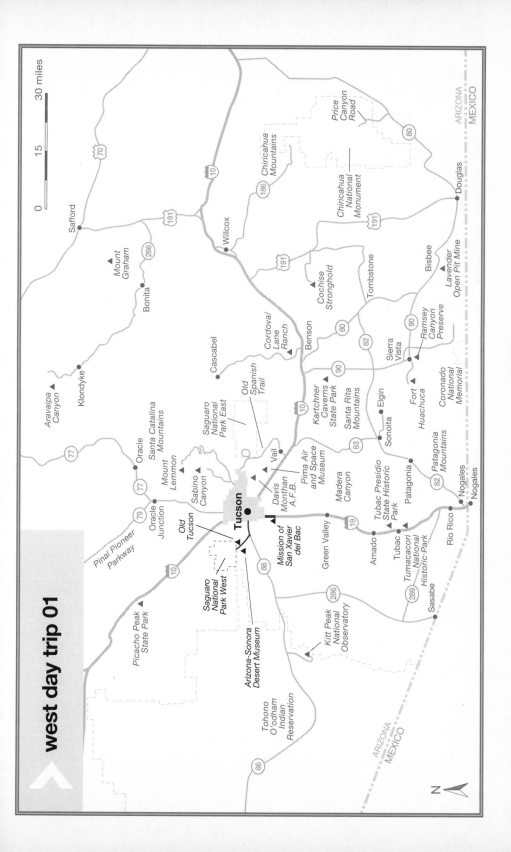

west day trip 01

Turn south at Mission Road and follow it to the church. Constructed over a period of 14 years, from 1783 to 1797, San Xavier is a graceful blend of Moorish, Byzantine, and late Mexican Renaissance styles. Mass is celebrated every morning and in 3 services on Sunday. A vital, living mission, this church is used regularly by the nearby Tohono O'odham and San Xavier Indians. (The vast Tohono O'odham reservation is just west of the San Xavier land.)

Stand outside and contemplate the structure. The entire building is a series of domes and arches, and every surface is intricately adorned. Notice that wood was used only in the door and window frames. Look carefully to see a cat and a mouse carved into the facade of the building, one in each tower. Legend has it that if the cat ever catches the mouse, the world will end.

Walk inside. As your eyes become accustomed to the interior of the church, you'll see that, thanks to a cleaning project undertaken by Italian restorers and local residents, the mission is alive with vibrant color once again. A profusion of statues and paintings give this mission a warm, lived-in feeling.

Father Kino, a Jesuit padre widely revered in this area, visited this site in 1692. The padre laid the foundations for the first church, which was 2 miles north of the current mission, and named it San Xavier in honor of his chosen patron, St. Francis Xavier, who was the illustrious Jesuit "Apostle of the Indies." The reclining statue to your left, as you face the main altar, is St. Francis Xavier.

To many people in the Southwest, this image of St. Francis Xavier has become a place of pilgrimage. If possible, plan to sit a while inside the church and experience the special ambience. A taped narrative provides an educational commentary about the mission.

magical southern arizona journey

It is very hard to choose one day trip over another but, if you have time for only one trip to southern Arizona, follow this route. It's a magical journey no matter how many times you experience it. The Arizona-Sonora Desert Museum is our number-one excursion for family and friends who visit Tucson. We recommend that you couple it with a visit to San Xavier del Bac, known as the White Dove of the Desert, to complete the experience. A few years ago, I had the pleasure of visiting San Xavier on a Sunday morning when the local residents come to worship. What had always seemed like a museum suddenly became a living church. The residents of this reservation welcome strangers who wish to attend their services so long as visitors are respectful. While the mission is always a magnificent sight, it is at its very best when it is filled with worshippers.

Outside once again, visit the mortuary chapel, and then climb the hill east of the mission to see the replica of the grotto in Lourdes, France. Be sure to pick up a brochure as you enter the church for a more detailed explanation of the history of San Xavier del Bac. Free, although donations are accepted. (520) 294-2624; www.sanxaviermission.org.

old tucson

Old Tucson. 201 South Kinney Rd.; (520) 883-0100; www.oldtucson.com. From San Xavier, travel north on Mission Road to Ajo Road (AZ 86). Take Ajo Road west to Kinney Road. Follow Kinney north to Old Tucson.

If you are coming from Tucson rather than from San Xavier, drive west on Speedway Boulevard to where it joins Anklam Road and becomes Gates Pass Road. As you continue west, you'll climb quickly into the foothills of the Tucson Mountains. Soon you'll be engulfed by the desert. As you get near Gates Pass, the road will twist and dip and climb until even the sky seems filled with mountains and saguaros. Once you are over the mountaintop, you'll gently descend into the valley. Watch for Kinney Road to your left. You'll turn south on Kinney and follow that a few miles to Old Tucson. If you are driving a large motor home or towing a trailer, take the Ajo Road–Kinney Road route and avoid Gates Pass.

Old Tucson is great fun for the entire family. This complete frontier town is peopled with characters who perform stunts, do trick riding, and have shootouts. Visitors like to get a part in a saloon musical or appear in a Western film shoot. Youngsters and oldsters will get a kick out of the almost-real gunfights. There are movie sets to ogle and a narrow-gauge railroad that takes you around the grounds. Enjoy amusement park rides, climb aboard a stagecoach, or take a tour behind a sound stage. Naturally, it's a little bit fake, but after all, Old Tucson never pretended to be authentic.

Old Tucson serves up plenty of good western grub—mesquite-broiled steaks and barbecue and authentic Mexican dishes. There are lots of places to shop here, including stores filled with western wear, movie memorabilia, and gifts.

Built originally in 1939 as a set for the epic movie *Arizona,* this location continues to attract crowds. Cinematographers and tourists love the place. Since *Arizona,* more than 100 other movies, television shows, and national commercials have used Old Tucson as a setting. Fee.

arizona-sonora desert museum

The museum is on Kinney Road. From Old Tucson, head north on Kinney Road. Continue on Kinney as it bends northwest and follow the signs to the entrance of the Arizona-Sonora Desert Museum (520-883-2702; www.desertmuseum.org).

If you think of museums as stodgy places you visit when it rains, think again. This one has a well-defined mission: to tell the story of life in the Sonoran Desert and of all the creatures who call this region home. An exciting combination of a zoo, an aquarium, and a botanical garden, this one-of-a-kind place defies a simple definition.

Look carefully. You'll see samples of nearly everything that crawls, runs, climbs, flies, or slithers in the desert, as well as a wondrous display of plants indigenous to this special environment. Some are gorgeous; others, almost grotesque. If you've ever wondered what a boojum tree looks like, this is the place to see one.

Stroll along manicured garden paths to see well-designed, educational exhibits. With the addition of the Earth Sciences Center, the Desert Museum has created an exhibit that mimics the underworld. Through an ingenious display, it opens this little-seen place to visitors. There's even an imitation limestone cave where stalactites and stalagmites "grow."

Another section of the Earth Sciences Center transports you back billions of years to the time when the desert began. Thanks to films, photographs, and maps, this exhibit enables you to understand how this part of the world was formed.

In the earth-science cave, you can follow a loop trail for 75 feet. There is also a mineral exhibit that covers almost every known mineral on Earth, from large crystals to ones so tiny they can only be seen through the microscopes provided.

Before you leave the museum grounds, be sure to browse through the gift shop, which is filled with various arts, crafts, and scientific displays.

Can you see why I believe that if you have time to see only one museum in southern Arizona, this is the place to visit. In the summer arrive early so you can observe the creatures when they are most active. (Like all smart residents of the desert, they siesta in the afternoon.) No pets allowed. Open daily. Fee.

where to eat

Octillo Café. Arizona-Sonora Desert Museum; (520) 883-5705. This fine dining restaurant is open for lunch from Dec to Apr, and for dinner Sat nights in June, July, and Aug. Cuisine is Arizona-Sonora regional made with the freshest ingredients. Call for hours, as opening and closing dates for lunch service vary, depending upon the weather.

saguaro national park (west)

This is the western (Tucson Mountain) park of Saguaro National Park (see Day Trip 01 East from Tucson for information on the eastern Rincon unit). There are two areas that make up Saguaro National Park: One lies to the east of Tucson, and the other to the west. Both are worth your time.

As you leave the Arizona-Sonora Desert Museum, continue northwest on Kinney Road to the Red Hills Information Center in the Tucson Mountain section of the Saguaro National Park. Pick up a map at the information center, or sightsee from your car by taking the Bajado Loop drive. To do this, continue on Kinney Road until it becomes Golden Gate Road. Follow this road until you see Hohokam Road to your right. Take Hohokam Road south back to where it meets Kinney.

In a recent poll of Arizona's most visited sites, Saguaro National Park (East and West) ranked just behind the Grand Canyon in popularity. While traffic can be slow over Gates Pass, the area is so vast that visitors who choose to get out of the car and hike can always be assured of plenty of "getaway" space.

If you aren't walked out from Old Tucson and the Desert Museum, there are several good hiking trails, some of which lead to the 1,429-foot-high **Wasson Peak.**

This western section of Saguaro National Park is slightly smaller than the eastern Rincon Mountain area. However, the 21,078 acres contain an unusually dense and vigorous saguaro forest. The cacti, coupled with dramatic foothills and mountain views, make this a favorite photographic and relaxation stop. Although firewood and water are not available in the park, you will find picnic areas, scenic overlooks, and restrooms. At the end of a long day, you may be happy to just drive through and save the hiking for another time. Fee. For more information call the Tucson Mountain District Visitor Center at (520) 733-5158; www .nps.gov/sagu.

From Saguaro National Park, it's an easy trip south on Kinney to either Gates Pass Road or Ajo Road to Tucson.

northwest

day trip 01

northwest

>>>
capital city, capital fun!:
phoenix

phoenix

From Tucson, follow I-10 northwest to Phoenix. This is an easy freeway drive that takes a little over 2 hours, depending upon traffic.

Contemporary Phoenix, which is the 5th-largest city in the nation, cherishes its desert, water supply, sunshine, and famous leisure lifestyle. A fine climate translates into the good life. With 3,177,016 acres of city, state, and county parks; federal lands; and freshwater lakes within 1 hour's drive, play's the thing in Phoenix. Outdoor sports are de rigueur here. People jog, climb, swim, and bike all year long. Everyone who stays comes to appreciate the natural setting. Those who didn't know a maple from an oak tree when they lived "back East" move to Phoenix and become connoisseurs of cactus.

In the old legend, the phoenix bird spread her wings and rose from the ashes. For the last few decades, the contemporary version starred its own legendary "bird"—the construction crane. In the last half of the 20th century, Phoenix consistently was one of the fastest-growing cities and metropolitan areas in the country.

But the downturn in the economy impacted the city, which has been dependent upon the construction industry. While development on the far edges has slowed to a crawl, urban infill has increased, especially as new buildings were constructed for the downtown Arizona State University (ASU) campus and students arrived. The happy result is that the city is evolving with a more vibrant downtown that includes a community of avant-garde artists.

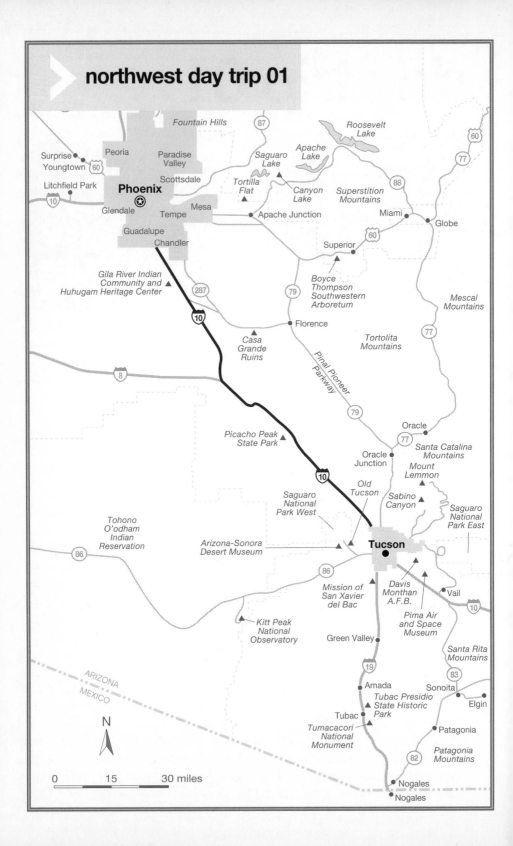

northwest day trip 01

Their art is celebrated on "First Fridays" of every month. Downtown galleries stay open in the evening, and the streets come alive with an art fair and exhibitions. Many galleries are located around 7th Street and Roosevelt; others are found along Grand Avenue. The art is fun and sometimes fabulous. Crowds are younger and a bit rowdier than what you see at the Scottsdale ArtWalk, but it is definitely a "scene."

Phoenix residents and visitors have long enjoyed their plethora of mountain parks. The 16,000-acre South Mountain Park is the largest municipally owned facility in the world. Piestewa Peak, the Phoenix Mountain Preserve, and North Mountain Parks each provide many more thousands of recreational acres.

Yet with all its emphasis on the big and the new, Phoenix is equally proud of its beginnings. A former mayor spearheaded the move to restore and dedicate a special section of downtown as Heritage Square. A stretch of freeway that leads to Sky Harbor Airport, called the Hohokam, is painted with designs derived from ancient Native American symbols.

As you approach Phoenix, don't be put off by its size. It's an easy town to get around. Washington Street runs east and west and is the zero ("0"), or starting point, for all north and south addresses. Central Avenue runs north and south and is the starting point ("0") for east and west addresses. East of Central, the roads are labeled as streets, while west of Central they are called avenues. Keep this in mind, and you won't find yourself at 35th Avenue looking for a number that is on 35th Street.

Stop first at the Downtown Phoenix Visitor Information Center, 125 North 2nd St., Suite 120 (across from the main entrance of the Hyatt Regency Phoenix); call (877) CALLPHX; or visit www.visitphoenix.com. Here you can inquire about accommodations, attractions, special events, and dining, and pick up brochures that describe these in more detail.

where to go

The following is a sample of what Phoenix has in store for visitors. For a more complete listing, read the brochures from the Downtown Phoenix Visitor Information Center.

The Old State Capitol Museum. 1700 West Washington St.; (602) 926-3620; www.lib.az .us/museum. Pick up Washington in downtown Phoenix and follow it directly west to the capitol building. There is ample free parking in 2 large lots on the east side of 17th Avenue. When you park and turn toward the west, you'll be facing the old capitol building with its copper dome. Inside is a museum that features an exhibit of territorial and Arizona history and government. You can take either a self-guided or guided tour. This is a recommended trip for people who have a strong interest in the state. Open Mon through Fri. Free.

Arizona Mining & Mineral Museum. 1502 West Washington; (602) 771-1600; www .admmr.state.az.us. With the restoration of the old El Zaribah Shrine near the Arizona capitol at 15th Avenue and Washington, the Arizona Mining & Mineral Museum acquired a shining new gem in a lustrous old/new setting. Outside, the blue and white structure has been restored to vintage 1922 elegance. Inside, more than 3,000 minerals collected from Arizona

> # a desert city ringed by mountain peaks
>
> *If you've lived in Phoenix a long time as I have, the sight of trains running down-*
> *town still is a surprise. Phoenix's Light Rail system has been years coming, and*
> *it is just the start of what will be a comprehensive system. But even this limited*
> *system has proven very popular. The main artery for the light rail runs along*
> *Central Avenue, past Chase Field and the U.S. Airways Arena. It is convenient*
> *to downtown attractions like Phoenix Symphony Hall and the Herberger Theater.*
> *When the Phoenix Suns or Arizona Diamondbacks are playing in town, trains are*
> *jammed with usually happy sports fans. A connection to Sky Harbor Airport is*
> *under construction. For now, buses connect from the rail station to the airport.*
> **One hint:** *Take time to look around the station while you wait for the train. Each*
> *station incorporates a work of art. The art is fun and even informative and makes*
> *the few minutes wait go by fast.*

and the world are on display. (The collection includes more than 9,000 pieces.) Rock hounds of all ages will find much to marvel at here, and friendly lapidary club volunteers are on-site to answer questions. Be sure to visit the separate Governor Rose Mofford room at the museum. The former governor has loaned the collection of artifacts and gifts she acquired from her more than 4 decades of public service. There is also a 250,000-pound scoop bucket, 13-foot-high tire, and a fulgarite display. Fee.

Heritage and Science Park. At 6th Street and Monroe Street; (602) 262-5071; www.phoenix .gov/parks/heritage.html. In this area, you'll find the best of the old and, with hotels and the convention center looming nearby, the most dazzling of the new that symbolize contemporary Phoenix. The centerpiece of Heritage and Science Square is the **Rosson House,** a restored home built in 1894. With its spires and turrets, it casts a benevolent shadow on downtown. Surrounded by other houses, including the **Silva House, Stevens House,** and **Stevens-Haugsten House,** and topped off with the airy **Lath House,** Heritage and Science Park has become a favorite gathering place for residents and tourists.

As you walk through this charming block of homes, you'll be transported to a gracious time when people slept on open sleeping porches to survive the desert summer and ladies fanned themselves and sipped cool lemonade. A fee is charged to tour the Rosson House, but the others are free of charge.

Arizona Doll and Toy Museum. 602 East Adams; (602) 253-9337; www.azcama.com /museums/doll_toy.html. Children and adults will enjoy this constantly changing scenario of dolls and toys from the past and present. An authentic 1912 schoolroom features antique dolls as the "students." Closed Mon. Fee.

Arizona Science Center. 600 East Washington St.; (602) 716-2000; www.azscience.org. Located in Heritage and Science Park. The museum is the work of famous Albuquerque architect Antoine Predock and is one of the city's points of civic pride. Inside find an array of hands-on exhibits geared for preschool to junior high students explaining the natural and manufactured world—from health to astronomy, technology to weather. The museum is organized around thoughtful topics such as "Communication" or "All About Me" and contains colorful exhibits on all floors. In addition, there are classrooms in the adjoining building as well as a lunch cafe. This is a favorite destination for families, but it is also appealing to adults with or without kids. Another plus is the museum gift shop, Amazing Atom. Visit the Dorrance Planetarium, the first public planetarium in Phoenix, and enjoy the full-size theater that shows IWERKS films. Visitors to the Arizona Science Center can select which programs they want to see and pay for those separately (e.g., museum exhibits, the planetarium, or IWERKS). Open daily. Fee.

The Civic Plaza. 111 North 3rd St. From the Rosson House, you can walk west to the Civic Plaza, which contains the **Phoenix Civic Plaza Convention Center** and **Symphony Hall.** Both are focal points for business and entertainment for the entire valley. The redesigned convention center can host the world's largest conventions, and top-name talent is booked into Symphony Hall throughout the year. Parking is available under the Civic Plaza complex. For more information on the convention center, call (602) 262-6225 or (800) 282-4842, or visit www.phoenix.gov/phxplaza.html. To inquire about events at Symphony Hall, call (602) 495-1999 or visit www.phoenixsymphony.org.

The Phoenix Art Museum. 1625 North Central Ave, on the corner of Central Avenue and McDowell Road; (602) 257-1222 (prerecorded information line); www.phxart.org. Long known for its fine collections of both Asian and Mexican art, the museum also is home to an impressive collection of western American art. Each Oct the Cowboy Artists of America ride into Phoenix to hold their annual show and sale at this facility. The museum's permanent collection concentrates on 18th- and 19th-century American and European art and sculpture. There is a distinguished collection of exquisitely detailed Thorne Miniature Rooms, and the museum is home to the Arizona Costume Institute, which affords the facility an elegant display of period clothing.

In addition to the museum's own collection, visitors can view fine traveling exhibitions scheduled throughout the year. Tours led by museum docents are available by special arrangement. The museum shop is a good place to find unusual gift items and art books. Closed Mon. Fee.

The Heard Museum. 2301 North Central Ave.; (602) 252-8848; www.heard.org. Considered one of the finest anthropological museums in the world, the Heard has an impressive permanent collection, an inspiring audiovisual exhibit, and important traveling shows. All of this excitement is encased in a lovely building that faces Central Avenue and preserves the hacienda building style that shows off old Phoenix at its best.

While at the Heard Museum, visit the **Kachina Gallery,** which holds a dazzling display of nearly 1,000 kachina dolls. These hand-carved, hand-painted wooden figurines represent various Hopi religious spirits. You can trace the progression of this important art form from old, crudely carved figures to today's slick, sophisticated statues collectors vie for. Be sure to spend time in the museum's art galleries as well, where different artists are showcased. On your way out, browse through the spacious gift shop. Here you can find fine works by both established and undiscovered Native American artists. After visiting the Heard Museum, you'll know why this facility is the pride of the entire Southwest.

If you have more time, take a guided docent tour of the museum. The volunteer docents are extremely knowledgeable and will add to your enjoyment of the museum. The Heard also has a cafe that serves excellent light meals. Open daily. Fee.

Phoenix Mountains. The southern trailhead is at a small parking lot at the northeast corner of 32nd Street and Lincoln Drive in Phoenix. Or park at the north trailhead at Fortieth Street, just south of Shea Boulevard. The Quartz Ridge trail is a semistrenuous 2½-mile (one way) trail that leads to the top of this ridge. The climb ascends from 1,300 to 1,800 feet. By comparison with Piestawa Peak summit trail, the Quartz Ridge trail is practically deserted. It is easy to follow and can be completed in an hour, round-trip. The trailhead off Shea Boulevard has restroom facilities, water, a covered ramada for a quick picnic, and room for parking about 70 cars. Leashed pets are allowed. Plastic "poop" bags are available at the trailhead, and hikers are expected to use them and clean up after their pets. Free.

Piestewa Peak at Phoenix Mountain Park. 2701 East Squaw Peak Dr.; (602) 261-8318; www.phoenix.gov/parks. Head east on Lincoln Drive to Squaw Peak Drive. Turn left at the light. For a quick desert experience in the heart of the urban scene, park and hike. You can join the crowds who religiously trek up and down the well-marked trail to the summit. The park has many ramadas, shelters that offer shady areas for picnicking. Water and restrooms are available.

The trail to the summit is 1²⁄₁₀ miles and is an excellent aerobic exercise as well as a fine social activity. Parking spaces can be scarce. The hike up starts at 1,400 feet and climbs to 2,600 feet. There are also excellent trails that circle around Piestewa Peak. While these don't offer the strenuous climb, they have the advantage of being more peaceful ways to experience the park. Free.

South Mountain Park. 10919 South Central Ave,; (602) 262-7393; www.phoenix.gov/parks. Take Central Avenue south to the far end of town, a 15- to 20-minute drive beyond downtown Phoenix. Eventually Central Avenue will curve to the west, and you'll approach the park. This 16,000-plus-acre mountain range was a gift to the city of Phoenix in the 1920s by a group of farsighted Phoenix boosters, including Clare Boothe Luce and Elizabeth Arden. It is the largest municipal park in the country. The environmental center is a special treat for visitors of all ages. As you enter the park, the ranger at the stone gatehouse will ask you not to bring any glass containers or alcoholic beverages.

Take a scenic drive up to a mountaintop for a thrilling look down at Phoenix, or park your car and walk along the trails. There are many opportunities here for serious biking, walking, or hiking. Picnic facilities and restrooms are plentiful. Fourth Sunday of the month is "Silent Sunday". No motorized vehicles. Free.

Mystery Castle. 800 East Mineral Rd.; (602) 268-1581. Located next to South Mountain Park, Baseline Road to 7th Street. Turn east (left) on Mineral Road. The road dead-ends in the parking lot. Mystery Castle is a home created out of "found objects" by Boyce Gulley, who disappeared into the Arizona desert when he was diagnosed with tuberculosis. Gulley spent the last 15 years of his life creating an 18-room mansion out of native stone, adobe, chunks of petroglyphs, and automobile parts. His wife and child inherited the castle after he died in 1945. His daughter passed away in November, 2010, but the castle remains open to the public. Open Oct to mid-June, Thurs through Sun. Fee.

Nina Mason Pulliam Rio Salado Audubon Center. 3131 South Central Ave,; (602) 468-6470; http://az.audubon.org/Center_RioSalado.html. This wonderful nature center is located in the heart of the city's Rio Salado Habitat Restoration Area. The 600-acre park is less than 2 miles from downtown but is home to over 200 species of birds and other wildlife. An interpretive loop trail connects to miles of hiking and riding trails. Apart from the birds, exhibits, tours, and riparian surroundings, the unique and beautiful "green" LEED Platinum-certified building itself is worth a visit. Closed Mon. Free.

within the papago salado

Arizona Historical Society Museum. 1300 North College Ave.; (480) 929-0292; www .arizonahistoricalsociety.org. This museum is located at the crossroads of 68th Street (called College after it crosses McKellips) and Curry. Housed in an impressive structure, this contemporary history museum features exhibits on agriculture, tourism, mining, World War II, and other aspects of Arizona's diverse history. A large outdoor replica of Roosevelt Dam describes how this structure was made and the importance it plays in Arizona life.

The permanent exhibits are varied. Start with the "people" who represent those groups who settled the state. Inside are historic rooms, films, and outstanding photographs. Go upstairs to enjoy the "Fair." The main agricultural exhibit is designed to teach children about the important contribution of agriculture. Kids can have a lot of fun answering the questions posed, and so can grown-ups! Among the many exhibits are ones depicting the impact of water on the desert, the importance of agriculture to Arizona, and an exhibit devoted to "Wallace and Ladmo, the TV Series," which was a popular Phoenix area show. Fee.

Arizona Military Museum. 5636 East McDowell Rd. in the National Guard Complex; (602) 267-2676; www.az.ngb.army.mil/museum/museum.htm. Enter through the main gate of Papago Park Military Reservation. This museum houses the weapons, uniforms, photographs, maps, etc., of Arizona's military history, dating from the 16th through 20th centuries. The building served as a prisoner-of-war camp during World War II. Open Sat and Sun only. Free.

Desert Botanical Garden. 1201 North Galvin Pkwy. (next to the Phoenix Zoo in Papago Park); (480) 941-1225; www.dbg.org. The Desert Botanical Garden presents a living museum of desert plant life and is one of the nation's only informal science centers dedicated to the desert, desert plants, ecology, and conservation. Here are more than 10,000 plants and 3,500 different species of cacti, succulents, trees and flowers, and attendant wildlife. Be sure to admire Dale Chihuly's desert-inspired glass sculpture at the entrance. This massive agave-inspired work was created for the DBG when it hosted an outdoor exhibit of Chihuly's glass. Adults and children should experience the exhibit entitled "Plants and People of the Sonoran Desert." Gardeners will enjoy the Demonstration Garden and the Desert House, which demonstrates how technology that is currently available can produce an environmentally pleasing home. There is also a shop that sells books and gifts on the grounds.

The Desert Discovery Trail follows a brick-paved path and leads to all trailheads and facilities. It will take you to the dramatic, new Cactus Galleries. The Plants & People of the Sonoran Desert Trail is a ⅓-mile, hands-on trail that illustrates how Sonoran Desert plants have been used by people for centuries to provide food, fiber, and shelter. The Sonoran Desert Nature Trail is a ¼-mile trail that is somewhat steep. It affords panoramas of the distant mountains as well as close-up views of the desert butte, which is the backdrop for this special garden. The 4th trail, the Center for Desert Living, showcases desert landscaping displays, vegetable gardens, herb gardens, and the Desert House exhibits. The 5th trail, Harriet K. Maxwell Wildflower Trail, is a ¼-mile trail highlighting wildflowers from the Sonoran Desert. Fee.

Hall of Flame. 6101 East Van Buren; (602) 275-3473; www.hallofflame.org. Turn south on Project Drive from Van Buren to see the world's largest display of firefighting equipment. More than 100 pieces are in this private collection, including hand-to-hand, horse-drawn, and mechanized firefighting equipment that dates from 1725. Open daily. Fee.

Papago Park. (602) 256-3220. This 1,200-acre desert island gets its red color from iron oxide–hematite. Formed 6 to 15 million years ago, this is a sedimentary formation and is among the oldest exposed rock found anywhere in the state. You can wander 13 miles of hiking and biking trails, fish the Urban Fishing Waters, climb to Hole-in-the-Rock, or play golf at the public course within the park. Full picnic facilities are available. Free.

Papago Park, Tempe. Curry Road and College Avenue; (480) 350-5200. This 296-acre park is contiguous with the Phoenix Papago Park. In addition to natural desert and picnic facilities, there is a softball field, an area to play Frisbee, a golf course, a lake/lagoon, a playground, and a nature trail. Free.

The Phoenix Zoo. 455 North Galvin Pkwy.; (602) 273-1341; www.phoenixzoo.org. Rated as one of the top 10 zoos in the country, this 125-acre zoo presents more than 1,400 animals, including 200 endangered species. Special exhibits not to be missed are the African Savanna, Arizona Trail, Sumatran tigers, and Tropical Flights. Even grown-ups will be wowed by the Phoenix Zoo, where giraffes gambol freely in a natural grassy setting framed by the Papago Buttes.

The Children's Zoo is self-contained. There are complete food and beverage facilities, a gift shop, and shaded picnic areas. Strollers and wheelchairs may be rented, and the Zoo Train offers a convenient way to cover the vast grounds. Open daily. Fee.

Pueblo Grande Museum and Archaeological Park. 4619 East Washington; (602) 495-0901; www.phoenix.gov/PARKS/pueblo.html. Art and architecture have ancient histories, as Pueblo Grande Museum and Cultural Park in east Phoenix reminds. This in-town Native American ruin is replete with platform mound and remnants of an ancient canal, as well as a small but charming museum of artifacts and art. The discovery of the ruin and subsequent park development prompted Phoenix to hire an archaeologist on city staff, the first city in the country to do so.

Occupied from AD 500 through AD 1450, Pueblo Grande was an important village that sported a ball court, homes, ceremonial mound, and canals. The canals and platform mound can be visited on the grounds. Permanent and rotating exhibits inside the museum describe the art and culture of the Hohokam and other prehistoric Native Americans. Closed Sun and Mon, May through Sept. Open daily Oct through Apr; Fee.

north phoenix

The Musical Instrument Museum. 4725 East Mayo Blvd; (480) 478-6000; www.themim .org. Located on the southwest corner of Mayo and Tatum Boulevards, this museum, which opened in 2010, is another reason to visit Phoenix. Its international collection contains musical instruments from every country in the world. Visitors see the instruments being played on flat-screen monitors located at each display and hear the music through headsets that pick up wireless "hotspots" at each exhibit, so as you walk in front of an exhibit, the music begins to play. This remarkable collection is organized by themes on the first floor and by geographic areas on the second floor. You visit ten major regions of the world: Africa, the Middle East, central Asia, south Asia, east Asia, Southeast Asia, Oceania, Latin America, United States/Canada, and Europe. MIM's goal is to acquire instruments that have been used for folk and tribal occasions wherever possible.

Everyone's favorite room is on the first floor, where instruments are available for playing. The museum's mission is to celebrate the similarities and differences of the world's cultures through music—a common language to us all. Engaging, interactive, and educational, the large facility is architecturally impressive and includes a theater where live performances are scheduled. Plan to spend at least a couple of hours here. Open daily. Fee.

where to eat

Phoenix offers every type of cuisine—from Mongolian and Mexican to Thai and elegant continental. Ask anyone in Phoenix to name a favorite dining spot, and you'll get a different answer. In the last few years, Phoenix has nurtured and attracted a variety of fine young chefs, making this a new town for "foodies" to explore. Here are a few local favorites:

Barrio Cafe. 2814 North 16th St.; (480) 636-0240; www.barriocafe.com. Chef/owner Silvana Salcido Esparaza, nominated for the James Beard Award in 2010, has created the ultimate upscale neighborhood haven for lovers of sophisticated Mexican cuisine. Guacamole made at the table is just one of the many standouts. Expect to wait for a table for dinner; the policy is no reservations. There's a tiny bar. Closed Mon. $$.

Biltmore Fashion Park. At 24th Street and Camelback. The upstairs of this outdoor shopping mall has some of Phoenix's best casual restaurants. These trendy restaurants serve food that is moderately priced, well presented, and, most importantly, good.

Los Dos Molinos. 8646 South Central Ave.; (602) 243-9113. Authentic Mexican fare—pronounce that very *hot*—served in a unique hacienda setting in south Phoenix. Very much worth the trip for those who love true Mexican food. Since there is usually a wait for seating, plan to visit the gallery on the grounds. See the other location in Mesa. Closed Sun and Mon. $–$$.

Pizzeria Bianco. 623 Adams St. (in Heritage Park); (602) 258-8300; www.pizzeriabianco .com. Considered by many the very best pizza in Arizona (and even the country), Chris Bianco's pizzeria has gotten the attention of national food writers. The pizza is fabulous, but know that there is always a wait. Reservations are taken only for parties of 6 to 10 people. Bar Bianco, next door, is where everyone goes to have a glass of wine or beer and wait it out for a table. Open Tues to Sat. $$.

Tarbell's. 3213 East Camelback Rd.; (602) 955-8100; www.tarbells.com. Local Chef Mark Tarbell is another chef star. Trained in Paris, he has cooked for celebrities and television audiences. His food features locally grown, organic products, and the bistro-style restaurant, with its outstanding wine cellar, is as unpretentious as the food is outstanding. Open for dinner every night. $$–$$$.

True Food Kitchen. 2502 East Camelback Rd. (in Biltmore Fashion Park); (602) 774-3488; www.truefoodkitchen.com. Arizona restaurateur Sam Fox teamed with Dr. Andrew Weil to create this delicious and unique dining experience that is based on Dr. Weil's anti-inflammatory diet and food pyramid. The result is a restaurant that offers elegantly prepared and beautifully served food that is actually good for you. Sam Fox is from Tucson, and his Fox Restaurants have taken Arizona by storm with their unique concepts; fabulous interior and exterior designs by local architect/designer, Cathy Hayes; and the many fine chefs. $$.

Vincent Guerithault on Camelback. 3930 East Camelback Rd.; (602) 224-0225. Vincent has joined the rare list of fine American chefs whose specialties feature native ingredients with superior and artistic presentation. One of Arizona's most outstanding restaurants, Vincent is open for lunch and dinner. The cozy Bistro, next to the restaurant, is also open for dinner. On Saturdays from October through the end of May enjoy the outdoor green market. Dinner reservations are suggested. The atmosphere is elegant yet relaxing; the food is outstanding. Closed Sun and Mon. $$$ for Vincent's On Camelback restaurant; $$ for Vincent's Bistro.

where to stay

Metropolitan Phoenix enjoys one of the world's finest collections of hotels and resorts. For a complete listing contact the Greater Phoenix Convention & Visitors Bureau, 400 East Van Buren St., Suite 600; (877) CALLPHX or (602) 254-6500; www.visitphoenix.com. But the following is one outstanding property that should not be missed.

Arizona Biltmore Resort & Spa. At 24th and Missouri Streets; (800) 950-2575; www .arizonabiltmore.com. The grand dame of Phoenix resorts, opened in 1929, the Arizona Biltmore should be on every visitor's list. Frank Lloyd Wright is not the architect of record for this historic property, but his fingerprints are everywhere—from the cement block to the prairie-type lines of the massive original hotel. Over the years, the hotel has been added onto, with more casitas, shops, and a conference center. But through the changes the structure has remained supremely elegant, a reminder of when gentlemen traveled with a dozen tuxedos and ladies with trunks full of dinner gowns to spend "the season" at this grand hotel. The restaurants are all superb. The wine room is particularly special. $$$.

>> part iii:
flagstaff

Most important when planning day trips that include Flagstaff, remember you are NOT in the desert. Flagstaff is more than a mile high, which means snow in winter and cool summer days. But with this city as your base (see Day Trip 05 North from Phoenix), the entire northern third of Arizona is open to you. You'll see wonders of the ancient world such as the Grand Canyon, the quiet beauty of lakes and forests, and remote Native American villages whose inhabitants live very much as their ancestors did hundreds of years ago.

If you're planning a visit during the fall, winter, or early spring, phone ahead to check the weather.

In summer, temperatures around Flagstaff remain moderate, with warm days and cool evenings. As you travel into the high desert areas of the northeast or to the far western border near California, you're back in the sizzling heat. Don't forget to carry water in your car.

The following trips are planned to include a maximum amount of sightseeing in a minimum of time. For northern Arizona, stretch your time limit for a day trip from 2 to 4 or even 5 driving hours one way. Many of these trips are better done in tandem—doing one trip one day and picking up the following trip the next day without heading back to Flagstaff. Combining trips cuts the driving distance and lets you maximize out-of-the-car time.

You can make each of these a separate overnight experience as long as you're prepared to go the distance to get back to Flagstaff.

One last piece of advice: This vast area has lots of open landscape. You won't find convenience stores at every corner so carry some food in the car, as well as water, soft drinks, or juice. Clean, well-equipped rest stops are often few and far between, so when you see a decent-looking gas station, stop if somebody needs to use a restroom and top off your tank if it's below half full. Forewarned, you shouldn't get caught in the wilds.

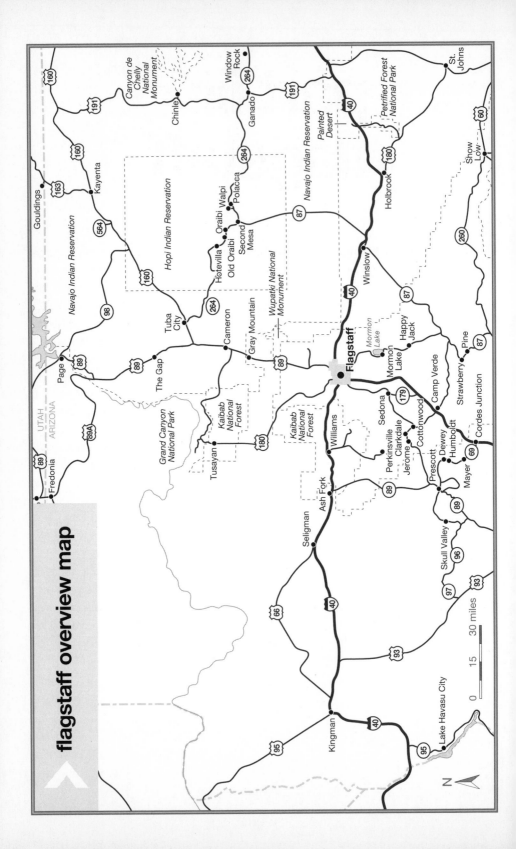

flagstaff overview map

north

>>>

day trip 01

north

incredible rocks and indian ruins:
sunset crater and
wupatki national monument

sunset crater and wupatki national monument

From Flagstaff, head north on this scenic drive to enjoy past treasures.

scenic drive

Volcanoes and Ruins Loop. The complete tour will take 2 to 3 hours and cover 70 miles. Drive 12 miles northeast on US 89 to the Sunset Crater–Wupatki turnoff. Turn east (right). It's about 36 miles around this road back to US 89 and then 22 miles back to Flagstaff. The road passes through the most recently active portion of the San Francisco volcano fields that surround the city. The last eruption occurred around AD 1250, but wounds heal slowly in an arid land, so much of the area looks as if it had been fuming and spurting just yesterday.

During this excursion, plan to stop at the visitor centers at both Sunset Crater and Wupatki.

Sunset Crater Volcano National Monument is a 1,000-foot-high historic cone. Here you will find strange rivers of lava that erupted 900 years ago that look as though they happened yesterday. There are many trails to hike along and explore; visitors, however, are asked to

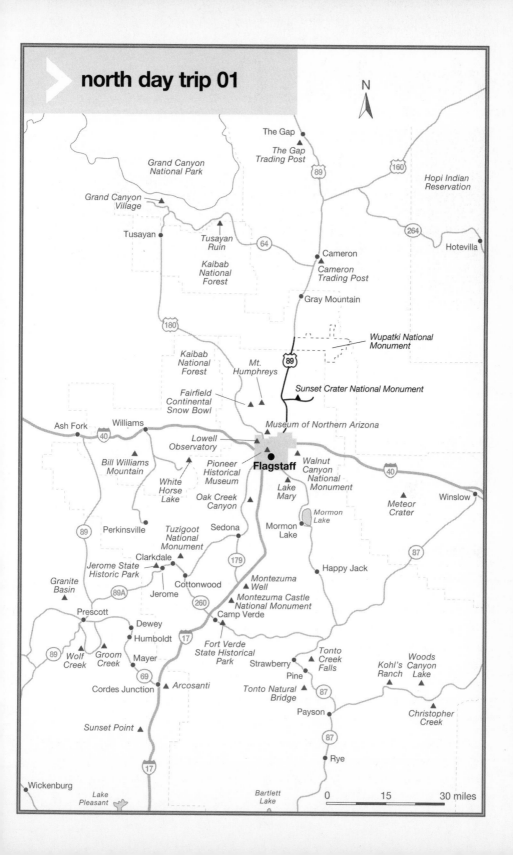

N

The Gap

The Gap
Trading Post

Grand Canyon
National Park

89

160

Hopi Indian
Reservation

Grand Canyon
Village

264

Tusayan

Tusayan
Ruin

64

Cameron

Hotevilla

Kaibab
National
Forest

Cameron
Trading Post

Gray Mountain

180

Wupatki National
Monument

Kaibab
National
Forest

Mt.
Humphreys

89

Fairfield
Continental
Snow Bowl

Sunset Crater National Monument

Ash Fork

Williams

Museum of Northern Arizona

40

Lowell
Observatory

Flagstaff

Walnut
Canyon
National
Monument

40

Bill Williams
Mountain

Pioneer
Historical
Museum

White
Horse
Lake

Oak Creek
Canyon

Lake
Mary

Meteor
Crater

Winslow

Perkinsville

89

Tuzigoot
National
Monument

Sedona

Mormon
Lake

Mormon
Lake

Clarkdale

179

Happy Jack

87

Jerome State
Historic Park

Granite
Basin

Cottonwood

89A

Jerome

260

Montezuma
Well

Montezuma Castle
National Monument

Prescott

Dewey

Camp Verde

Humboldt

17

Fort Verde
State Historical
Park

Tonto
Creek
Falls

Woods
Canyon
Lake

89

Wolf
Creek

Groom
Creek

Mayer

Strawberry

Kohl's
Ranch

69

Pine

Cordes Junction

Arcosanti

Tonto Natural
Bridge

87

Christopher
Creek

Payson

Sunset Point

87

Rye

Wickenburg

Lake
Pleasant

Bartlett
Lake

0   15   30 miles

geology and archaeology up close

This day trip takes you through the forests of northern Arizona and to one of our two remarkable craters. Combing these two attractions lets you time travel at supersonic speed. Sunset Crater was formed by a volcano—unlike Meteor Crater, which was formed by flying ice and rock. As you walk through the ruins of Wupatki, you can feel what it was like to be part of this ancient Pueblo culture. Whenever I amble through an Indian ruin, I cannot help but wonder what future generations will discover and think about our civilization. Will they see our shopping centers and sports arenas as centers for spiritual rituals? Then again, maybe that's not so far off.

stay on the trails and not forge their own. The lava flow is brittle and can be damaged easily. John Wesley Powell, who was the first man to successfully run the Colorado River, named Sunset Crater for the red-orange hue that is found near its peak. This is a strange and eerie landscape, but one that is well worth a visit. Fee. (928) 526-0502; www.nps.gov/sucr.

Wupatki National Monument. (928) 679-2365; www.nps.gov/wupa. These well-preserved Native American ruins are the remains of structures built by the ancient Pueblo Indians. These people were prosperous traders and farmers who left behind 35,000 acres of prehistoric ruins containing apartment houses, ball courts, and artifacts. The ball court is considered very rare by archaeological standards.

There is a park service station and interpretive center that explains the history and geology of the area. Self-guided trails make it easy to stroll among these structures and understand the significance of the sites. Fee.

From Wupatki, return to Flagstaff on US 89.

day trip 02

north

>>> **watery wonderland and ancient anasazi:**
page and glen canyon dam, marble
canyon, navajo national monument

page and glen canyon dam

From Flagstaff, go north on US 89 to Page and Lake Powell. You may want to plan to spend the night at Lake Powell before going on to the Navajo National Monument. You can also pick up Day Trip 01 Northeast from Flagstaff at Kayenta, or you can stay overnight in Page, then go on to Navajo National Monument the next morning and pick up Day Trip 01 Northeast from Flagstaff at Kayenta. Taking 2 days to see Lake Powell and Navajo National Monument allows ample time to explore, visit Page and Lake Powell, and tour Navajo National Monument. If you have only 1 day to cover this, you'll drive through Page, see Lake Powell from the shore, and take a fast trip to the Navajo National Monument. But cramming all this into 1 day will leave you hungry for more.

As you proceed north on US 89 from Flagstaff, you'll pass the tiny hamlet of **Gray Mountain**. Here you enter the vast expanse of the Navajo Indian Reservation. Summer travelers need to move their watches ahead 1 hour: While Arizona doesn't observe daylight saving time, the Navajo Nation does. This time change can be confusing and even frustrating if you aren't forewarned. You don't want to plan to arrive somewhere by 5 p.m. only to find that it's 6 p.m. and you've missed what you wanted to see.

Eight miles north of Gray Mountain on US 89, you'll see the **Cameron Trading Post**, the first of a number of Native American trading posts in this region. Cameron is actually a complex of buildings made of native stone and wood. Discover a treasure trove of

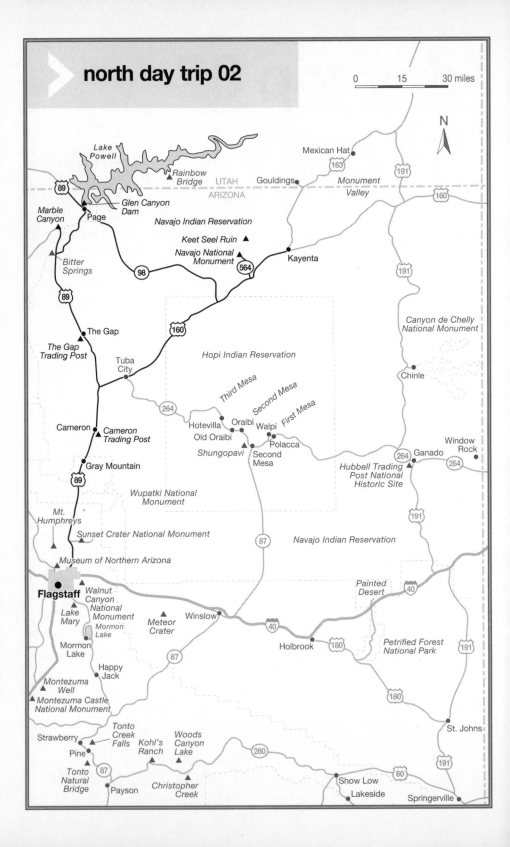

0   15   30 miles

N

Lake Powell

Mexican Hat

163

191

Rainbow Bridge   UTAH
Gouldings   Monument
ARIZONA   Valley

160

Glen Canyon Dam

Marble Canyon   Page

Navajo Indian Reservation

Keet Seel Ruin

Bitter Springs

Navajo National Monument   564   Kayenta

98

191

89

The Gap

160

Canyon de Chelly National Monument

The Gap Trading Post

Tuba City

Hopi Indian Reservation

Chinle

264

Third Mesa

Second Mesa

Cameron   Cameron Trading Post

Hotevilla   Oraibi   Walpi   First Mesa
Old Oraibi   Polacca
Shungopavi   Second Mesa

Window Rock

264   Ganado   264

89   Gray Mountain

Hubbell Trading Post National Historic Site

Wupatki National Monument

Mt. Humphreys

191

Sunset Crater National Monument

87   Navajo Indian Reservation

Museum of Northern Arizona

Flagstaff   Walnut Canyon National Monument

Painted Desert   40

Lake Mary   Mormon Lake

Meteor Crater   Winslow

40

Petrified Forest National Park

191

Mormon Lake

Holbrook   180

Happy Jack

87

Montezuma Well

180

Montezuma Castle National Monument

Strawberry   Tonto Creek Falls   Woods Canyon Lake

St. Johns

Pine   Kohl's Ranch

260

87   Tonto Natural Bridge   Christopher Creek

60

191

Payson   Show Low
Lakeside   Springerville

items—some exquisite, others tourist trinkets. There's also food service in a lovely, spacious dining room as well as some very nice overnight accommodations. Don't miss the display of Navajo weavings inside the trading post. The smaller gallery shop, next to the large trading post, has exquisite art, crafts, and jewelry.

After leaving Cameron, the highway crosses the Little Colorado River, one of the major tributaries of the Colorado River. Another 31 miles up the road you'll come to a second famous trading post, **The Gap**. Both Cameron and the Gap played important roles in opening the Arizona Territory. Trading posts helped to establish an economy that benefited both the white and Native American societies. To today's casual observer these places appear to be scenic tourist stops, but they aren't. Years ago, trading posts were lifelines for the Native Americans and traders who depended upon them. The Native Americans traded rugs, jewelry, and other handcrafted items for groceries and needed supplies. Occasionally, a Navajo man or woman would pawn a prized piece of jewelry for money, and the trader would keep the item until the owner could redeem it. Some owners never were able to get their heirlooms back, and "pawn jewelry," cherished by collectors, eventually was sold.

With a full day facing you, unless you need to stop, push on and explore these posts another day. Page and the wonders of Lake Powell await.

At Bitter Springs, US 89 bends east. Continue on US 89 to Page. Like all towns built to support generating plants, this community owes its life to power and glory—the power of Glen Canyon Dam and the glory of the Grand Canyon. The dam was built in the 1950s; the canyon has been under construction for millions and millions of years.

Glen Canyon Dam was constructed at a cost of $260 million, a hefty sum, especially when you consider that the cost to replace that plant today would be $800 million. It was October 15, 1956, when President Dwight D. Eisenhower pushed a button on his desk in the White House, 2,100 miles away, to set off the first blast. Four years later, on June 17, 1960, the last of 4,901,000 cubic yards of concrete was poured. The resulting dam, a 583-foot-high wall, holds back the second-largest manufactured lake in North America. (Lake Mead, also formed by the Colorado River, is the largest.) Glen Canyon conserves water from a 246,000-square-mile watershed, provides electricity for the Pacific Southwest and the Rocky Mountain areas, and gives Page a reason for being.

A small, friendly community dedicated to tourism and electricity, Page was first staked out as a temporary government construction camp in 1957. It was named for the first commissioner of the Reclamation Service established under President Theodore Roosevelt. Since then, the town has thrived. There is a busy airport, visitor center, museum, library, and 11 churches side by side on just one street. (Two other churches are located elsewhere in town.)

Near Page, US 89 climbs, and you'll get your first view of Glen Canyon Dam below. Behind it, the magical blue world of Lake Powell spreads out, improbably set into a rocky abyss of this far-eastern section of the Grand Canyon. Lake Powell is renowned throughout the world for its astonishing beauty, and no tourist yet has been disappointed by the views.

countless adventures (and a few complaints!)

As a committed environmentalist, I know that I'm not supposed to like the lake since Glen Canyon Dam doomed the wonders of Glen Canyon to a watery grave. But I am awestruck by the beauty of this enormous desert lake surrounded by sandstone cliffs. Our family has had countless adventures on Lake Powell over the years, including an unforgettable trip for a story I was writing for Arizona Highways *magazine. As luck would have it, it poured rain for 2 days. We had only an hour of sunshine to do the photo shoot we needed, and by then our children and their friends were not interested in getting into the cold lake. Our wonderful photographer cajoled them to no avail. Finally I took over and yelled at them in my sternest "mother voice": "Jump in the lake! What do you think this is? A vacation? We're doing a story here! Pretend you are having fun!" They did get in, we got our pictures, and we all had fun.*

Just outside of Page, visitors will often find Navajo artists selling their wares. It's fun to stop and browse and even shop. Often you can meet the artists, who are happy to describe their work to you. While it's fine to bargain with them, if you want to take a picture of the artists, always ask permission first. If you do take a photograph and don't purchase anything, it's good form to leave a "thank you" in the form of a tip.

where to go

Glen Canyon Dam and Carl Hayden Visitor Center. On US 89; (928) 608-6404; www .pagelakepowell.org; www.nps.gov/glca. This is a highly recommended stop. In the visitor center, an illustrated history depicts the construction and use of the dam. If you have time, watch the audiovisual program. If not, at least browse through the easy-to-follow displays, which reveal fascinating details about the dam. You can easily spend 30 minutes in the Carl Hayden Visitor Center. If you have time, take the guided tour of the generating plant given almost every hour. Visitors can also tour the dam on their own. The tour takes you from the crest of the dam down one of three elevators into the power plant, where you can see the inner workings of the turbines and understand how this dam delivers power to much of the western United States. Nearly an hour in length, the tour is not strenuous; you'll walk about ⅓ mile. It's a cool 50 degrees Fahrenheit down under, so bring a wrap. Free.

John Wesley Powell Memorial Museum. 6 North Lake Powell Blvd.; (928) 645-9496; www.powellmuseum.org. This is a small museum dedicated to Maj. John Wesley Powell, who not only explored the Colorado River but also wrote passionately and lyrically about it. In addition to presenting exhibits on Powell and his expeditions, the museum documents the story of Page and presents artifacts from ancient Anasazi-Hisatsinom culture through modern Native American history. A fluorescent mineral and rock display is also exhibited.

The Page Visitor Center/Museum. 644 North Navajo, Suite C; museum: 6 North Lake Powell Blvd.; (928) 645-2741; www.pagelakepowellchamber.org. Continue north on US 89 until you see a sign for the business district of Page. Follow the signs. Drive over the bridge and take Lake Shore Boulevard to the chamber of commerce and the visitor center and museum, all located in one building. Check with the visitor center for additional information on the area, and then take a quick trip through the museum, which is filled with artifacts and memorabilia commemorating John Wesley Powell and his expeditions.

Major Powell is acknowledged as the first explorer of the Colorado River and the Grand Canyon. A Civil War veteran, he lost his right arm at Shiloh before setting out on this expedition. The 35-year-old adventurer first conquered the Colorado in 1869, settling in at Green River, Wyoming. He went back in 1871 and did the trip again. Thanks to his meticulous personal journal, generations of "river rats" (people who run the rapids in the Grand Canyon) and canyon and river enthusiasts relive his experiences and can identify with his thought-provoking impressions. Free.

Wahweap Lodge and Marina. Four and a half miles from Glen Canyon Dam on US 89 northwest of Page. Turn right at the sign for the marina (the only way you can turn) onto a paved road that leads to Wahweap. One of four marinas on Lake Powell, Wahweap (pronounced Waa-weep) is the most accessible for tourists. Here you'll find overnight accommodations, fine dining, a gift shop, and a host of tours and adventures. Even if you don't plan to spend the night or eat at Wahweap, you'll want to stroll through the lodge to lose yourself in the views of the lake. Lake Powell is a complete recreational wonderland—the fishing is great, the views better, and the deep, cool, blue water and the out-of-the-way beaches are the best. Other lakes in Arizona may be closer to major cities or have more sandy beaches, but only Lake Powell, with its fjords and inlets, scallops and gulleys, wrapped in a golden desert sun, comes so close to perfection.

what to do

There's so much to do in this area that you can spend a week or an entire season at Lake Powell. In addition to the following listed trips, you can rent a personal watercraft with a top speed of 35 miles per hour. The Tigershark is easy to ride with a jet drive. While it is not inexpensive to rent, the thrills are worth it. All of the trips depart from Wahweap. Even if you can only squeeze in a 2-hour excursion, do so. You'll see the lake from the shore, but you can only experience its mystic setting when you're on it and surrounded by its sandy, sculpted mountains. To make reservations for boat tours or accommodations, or to inquire about all adventures in the area, call (888) 896-3829 or visit www.lakepowell.com.

For information about boat trips, call (800) 410-8302 or visit www.lakepowell.com. Tours leave from Wahweap Marina and are booked through Lake Powell Tours.

The *Canyon Princess.* Treat yourself to a dinner cruise on this elegant yacht. Fee.

Antelope Canyon Boat Tour. Cruise through Antelope Canyon and, on your return, see Glen Canyon Dam.

Canyon Adventures Boat Tour features a cruise to Navajo Canyon.

All-Day and Half-Day Rainbow Bridge Tour. The half-day involves a 5-hour trip; the all-day allows for more side-channel cruising. You'll depart in the early morning and follow the main channel of Lake Powell to Rainbow Bridge. This natural wonder literally fills the sky as you approach the docking area. You can read the dimensions, but the size of the stone arch will still astound you. The dome of the U.S. Capitol building could fit underneath it. After your boat docks, there's a short hike to get to the base of the bridge. Be sure to read the inspiring commemorative plaque.

Glen Canyon Dam was built over strong environmental objections. People grieved over the flooding of Glen Canyon, which John Wesley Powell considered one of the most beautiful areas in the Grand Canyon. They feared what traffic would do to fragile places like Rainbow Bridge. The dam did doom the canyon to a watery death, but the trade-off was Lake Powell, a shimmering body of water that dances between the intricate, spidery spires and rolling sandstone mountaintops. Neither the water nor the exposed desert canyon seems aware of the other's presence. You'll see the two worlds of lake and land meeting but not merging.

Since the dam was built and Lake Powell formed, more people see Rainbow Bridge each month than had ever seen it before the dam was built. But so far, visitors are considerate, and the area surrounding the bridge appears to be surviving well. Note that this tour involves a walk to the bridge.

Houseboating. Enjoy the water for a few days and nights or stay a week on a well-equipped, luxurious floating house. The best speeds for a houseboat are "slow" and "stopped," so wise houseboaters dock their boats at secluded coves early on and use a speedboat to water-ski and explore the thousands of skinny little canyons that lead from the main body of the lake. With 1,900 miles of shoreline to choose from, you can houseboat on Lake Powell repeatedly and never explore the same spot twice. Be prepared to get lost on Lake Powell. Most first-timers do, but keep reading your maps, and you'll come out fine. During the height of the summer season, you'll need to reserve a houseboat far in advance. This is an ideal family experience. For price information and availability, call Lake Powell Resorts and Marina at (888) 896-3829 or visit www.lakepowell.com. Fee.

Colorado River Float. Departs from the Page Museum, 6 Lake Powell Blvd. For would-be river runners who don't like whitewater craziness, a float trip provides the ideal alternative. You'll float for a day through the polished splendor of Marble Canyon, stop for lunch on the bank, and see ancient petroglyphs from the canyon floor. After the 15-mile float trip, you'll feel as if you've "done" the Colorado. This is great fun for families with young children and anyone who wants the see the Grand Canyon the most scenic way—from the bottom up. Fee. Inquire about float trips by calling Lake Powell Resorts and Marina at (888) 896-3829 or visiting www.lakepowell.com.

Page Loop Trail. Mountain bikers can have a blast on this 10-mile loop that is partly single-track and rough four-wheel-drive road. Beginning riders can complete the loop in about 2 hours, with an occasional dismount for the more difficult sections. Experienced riders can do it in about 1 hour. There's also a 3-hour ride that incorporates a detour to enjoy the slickrock. This is recommended for experienced riders only. The trail begins at the nature trail at the north end of Page near Lake View School. Free.

where to eat

The Dam Bar & Grille. 644 North Navajo; (928) 645-2161; www.damplaza.com. Trendy and fun by any standards, this restaurant is Page's most upscale spot. Find casual dining, a great bar, and wonderful historical photographs of when Glen Canyon Dam was constructed. Notice the etched glass "mural" that is dedicated to the water and power theme. This is a popular gathering spot for locals and visitors. $–$$.

Lake Powell Lodge. Wahweap Marina, Lake Powell; (928) 645-2433; www.lakepowell .com. The main dining room has a dazzling view of the lake. At night the room shimmers with elegance, and by day you can gaze out on the blue expanse. The specialty is prime rib, but the menu is varied and well prepared. Ask about the daily specials. $$.

where to stay

NOTE: In recent years, a number of excellent new hotels have been built that serve all price ranges.

The Quality Inn. 287 North Lake Powell Blvd., Page; (928) 645-8851 or (866) 645-8851; www.choicehotels.com/hotel/az214. This is right up the street from the Page Chamber of Commerce/visitor center/museum building. Although not on the lake, the motel units are quite nice. $$.

Lake Powell Resort. Wahweap Marina, Lake Powell; (928) 645-2433; www.lakepowell .com/lodging-food/lake-powell-resort.cfm. The rooms are large and spacious, but if you aren't on the ground floor, be prepared to tote your own luggage up the stairs. You can reserve rooms at the Lake Powell Motel, get a housekeeping unit, or rent space for a camper or RV through the central reservation service. While the views and locations are excellent, the rooms, while spacious, are basic "motel"—not exciting, but clean and comfortable. $$. Contact Lake Powell Resorts and Marina, Wahweap, at the number above for information and reservations.

marble canyon

Accommodations are limited in this area, but cabins are clean, and rooms are available at Marble Canyon Lodge and Cliffdwellers Lodge.

Navajo Bridge Interpretive Center. AZ 89A, 45 miles southwest of Page; (928) 355-2319; www.nps.gov/glca/historyculture/navajobridge.htm. The new bridge is one of only 7 land crossings over the Colorado River for 750 miles and was constructed in the late 1990s. It replaced the original structure that was built in the 1920; at that time, it was the highest steel arch bridge in the world. Prior to its construction, people and goods could only cross the Colorado River at Lee's Ferry. The interpretive center has exhibits and a bookstore, but the main reason to come here is to see the California condors. These enormous birds, which are being brought back from near extinction, are released in the nearby Vermillion Cliffs. They can often be seen hanging out at the old Navajo bridge.

navajo national monument

When you're ready to push on another 88 miles, leave Lake Powell and drive southeast on AZ 98 for 66 miles to US 160. At the junction, head northeast on US 160 toward Kayenta. Twelve miles farther, you'll see a sign for AZ 564. Turn left and follow it north for 9 miles.

This drive will take about 2 hours, during which time you'll cross the Navajo Indian Reservation, an often desolate landscape. Watch for the Navajo hogans—low, round houses that many Navajo families still use as homes. The hogan doorway will always face east, where the sun rises. When you reach AZ 564, you'll be on a paved road that leads to Navajo National Monument. This is a collection of 3 wonderfully preserved Native American ruins: all that is left of pre-Columbian communities known as Keet Seel, Betatakin (pronounced Be-tah-tah-kin), and Inscription House. Remote enough to be off the beaten tourist track and romantic, these ruins provide an unusually personal look into the past for travelers who have the stamina and time to go the distance.

As is recommended for all national parks and monuments, your first stop should be the visitor center. Here you'll get your bearings. Although this is called the Navajo National Monument, the name refers to its location on the Navajo Reservation. The remnants of dwellings are from the Anasazi civilization, a pre-Columbian people who inhabited this area around 1200 BC. The exhibits and the slide program at the center describe the life and items of the Anasazi. You'll learn about their homes and crops, and also get a quick lesson on the geology of this area. Free. For more information on Navajo National Monument, call (928) 672-2700 or visit www.nps.gov/nava.

where to go

Betatakin. (928) 672-2700. Guided tours of this Anasazi cliff dwelling are available through-out the year. Take an easy walk along Sandal Trail, which leads to an overlook of Betatakin. As you peer into this ruin, you'll sense that these people have left only momentarily and are due to return soon. During the season, June 1 to mid-Sept, there are 3 daily tours. After Sept, there is just 1 tour a day scheduled.

Betatakin means "house on a ledge," and this cluster of dwellings is literally set into a massive cavern in the canyon wall. The most accessible of the ruins here, Betatakin was constructed and abandoned in 2 generations between 1250 BC and 1300 BC. The 135 rooms constituted a total community. There's a kiva, or ceremonial chamber; granaries; and living quarters.

Discovered in 1909 by Byron Cummings, a pioneer archaeologist of the Southwest, and John Wetherill, a rancher and trader, Betatakin was made safe for exploration in 1917 by Neil M. Judd of the Smithsonian Institution. The 1-mile round-trip walk from the visitor center takes about an hour. Bring binoculars to see these dwellings from the vantage of the rim. Ranger-guided tours, which descend into the ruin, are limited to 20 people at a time because of the fragility of the area. These excursions take about 3 hours and involve some strenuous climbing. The canyon is 700 feet deep, equal to a 70-story building, and the altitude is 7,200 feet, which can be tiring for anyone, even those who are physically fit. Anyone with a heart condition should not attempt this climb. Free.

Keet Seel. Tucked away in a remote canyon 8 miles from the visitor center, Keet Seel is the largest cliff dwelling in the state and can be reached only on foot. It's a strenuous trip, but the journey is well worth the trouble for people who have adventurous hearts and strong legs. You must make arrangements for this trip with a ranger ahead of time, because visits to Keet Seel are limited to 20 tourists a day.

From Navajo National Monument you can head south on AZ 564 to US 160, then south on US 160 to US 89, and US 89 south back to Flagstaff. Or you can return to Page for the night.

northeast

>>>

day trip 01

northeast

john wayne country:
kayenta; monument valley, utah

kayenta

Kayenta is located 150 miles northeast of Flagstaff, and the trip takes about 3 hours. Go north on US 89 to its junction with US 160 and continue northeast on US 160 to Kayenta. This is a tiny town by American standards, but it is a major community on the Navajo reservation.

Be sure to visit the Shephard's Eyes Courtyard & Visitors Center (928-697-3368), located at the crossroads of US 160 and US 163, on the northwest corner. This is part museum and part gift shop, and is adjacent to the Hampton Inn. It is one of the newer enterprises of the Navajo Nation Department of Tourism. The arts and crafts and other objects displayed here for sale are authentic, and prices are reasonable. The purpose of these centers is to help the Navajo Nation support its own craftspeople and artists, and they are a visual statement of an aggressive program to help the Navajo Nation expand its economy through tourism.

In the evening, the outdoor amphitheater often features native dancing and performances. This is an excellent place to go if you are traveling with teens; it has a good coffee bar.

Kayenta is the jumping-off point for Monument Valley, your next destination. From Kayenta, turn north on US 163 to Monument Valley.

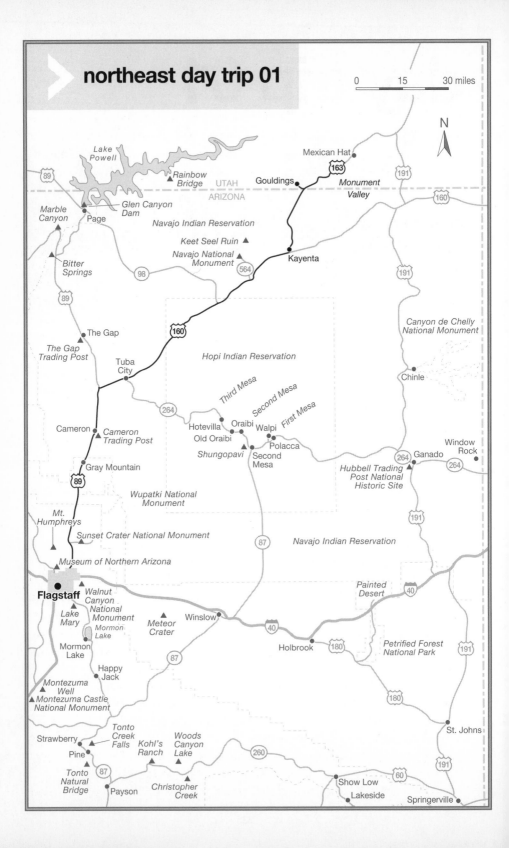

northeast day trip 01

0   15   30 miles

N

Lake Powell

Rainbow Bridge

89

UTAH
ARIZONA

Mexican Hat

163

Gouldings

Monument Valley

191

160

Marble Canyon

Glen Canyon Dam

Page

Navajo Indian Reservation

Keet Seel Ruin ▲

Navajo National Monument ▲

564

Kayenta

191

Bitter Springs ▲

89

98

160

Canyon de Chelly National Monument

The Gap ▲

The Gap Trading Post

Tuba City

Hopi Indian Reservation

Chinle

264

Third Mesa

Second Mesa

Cameron ▲ *Cameron Trading Post*

Hotevilla Oraibi Walpi *First Mesa*

Old Oraibi

Polacca

Shungopavi Second Mesa

Window Rock

264 Ganado 264

Hubbell Trading Post National Historic Site

Gray Mountain

89

Wupatki National Monument

191

Mt. Humphreys ▲

Sunset Crater National Monument ▲

87

Navajo Indian Reservation

Museum of Northern Arizona

Flagstaff ●

Walnut Canyon National Monument

Lake Mary

Mormon Lake

Painted Desert

40

Meteor Crater ▲

Winslow ●

40

Mormon Lake

Holbrook ● 180

Petrified Forest National Park

191

Happy Jack

87

Montezuma Well ▲

▲ Montezuma Castle National Monument

180

St. Johns ●

Strawberry

Tonto Creek Falls ▲

Kohl's Ranch

Woods Canyon Lake

260

Pine ●

87

Tonto Natural Bridge

Payson ●

Christopher Creek

60

Show Low ●

Lakeside ●

Springerville ●

where to eat

The Golden Sands Cafe. On US 163, 1 mile north of the Kayenta Holiday Inn; (928) 697-3684. Feast on the Golden Sands Navajo taco, a delectable combination of chili and Navajo fry bread. The place is a favorite of locals and tourists, and there is usually a collection of pickup trucks in the parking lot. The portions are huge, the prices are reasonable, and the atmosphere is authentic Navajo Indian Reservation. $–$$.

where to stay

Hampton Inn of Kayenta. US 160; (928) 697-3170; www.monumentvalleyonline.com. Approaching Monument Valley from Flagstaff, this property greets you before you get to the Tribal Park. It's near the junction of US 160 and US 163. Navajo owned, the inn is located in a three-story adobe-style building and contains 73 immaculate, charming rooms. The decor is contemporary Native American with a spacious and inviting lobby. The glowing fireplace invites guests to linger, but the wonders of Monument Valley are just outside your door. There is also a heated outdoor swimming pool.

The hotel gift shop is called the **Kayenta Trading Company**, and it contains a fine collection of jewelry, baskets, Native American arts and crafts, clothing, books, and more. The Navajo Cultural Center adjoins the hotel, where visitors can see the traditional ways of the Navajo people through exhibits and demonstrations. A great find and a wonderful place to spend the night. Full American breakfast is included. $$.

Holiday Inn, Kayenta. At the junction of US 160 and US 163; (928) 697-3221 or (800) HOLIDAY; www.holidayinnkayenta.com. You'll find clean, adequate accommodations. Nothing fancy, but considering the remote location, this Holiday Inn offers a surprisingly nice option for travelers. There's even a swimming pool. $$.

monument valley, utah

From Kayenta, take US 163 north approximately 20 miles. At a crossroads just over the Utah state line, bear right to the Monument Valley Visitor Center. If Salvador Dali had sculpted a landscape, this would be it. Stark spires rise abruptly from the sandy floor, and the rock formations appear to have been dropped onto the flat earth, as if some ancient people flew in from the stars, deposited their rocky cargo, and disappeared.

Monument Valley is not a national park but, rather, a Navajo Tribal park consisting of 29,816 acres owned and managed by the Navajo Tribal Council. The valley was made famous by John Wayne, who starred in many classic Westerns that were filmed here.

At the visitor center, you'll see a sign pointing to a 17-mile unpaved scenic loop through the park. You can pick up a brochure inside, which describes a self-guided tour. Along the way there are 11 numbered scenic stops. Although the signs say you can drive your car on this road, think twice before you do so. The road is narrow, rutted, and banked by deep

classic western setting

A lot of stealing goes on in the West. Las Vegas likes to claim that they have our Grand Canyon. But we act as if Monument Valley belongs to us when it is mostly in the state of Utah. Next to the Grand Canyon, Monument Valley is the most famous image associated with the Southwest, thanks to John Ford and his film Stagecoach. *Besides the incredible monuments, the overwhelming image of Monument Valley is sand. Once, when I was on assignment for* Arizona Highways *magazine, I dropped an expensive piece of jewelry on the ground and spent some frantic minutes sifting through deep sand to find it. I clearly remember looking up and seeing Spider Rock, which is a sacred rock for the Navajo, and hoping if there are spirits here, could they please look after me? There are, because they did.*

sands. In short, it isn't terrific. Most people prefer to take a guided Jeep tour, especially since many of the more spectacular rock formations can be seen only from off the road.

During the summer season, expect high daytime temperatures and long lines to get into the visitor center or the park, but know that it's well worth any inconvenience. Open year-round. Fee. (435) 727-5874/5870 or (435) 727-5875; www.navajonationparks.org/htm /monumentvalley.htm.

where to eat and stay

Gouldings. Six miles west of the visitor center, just over the Utah state line off US 163. As you approach Monument Valley, you'll see a cluster of reddish-colored buildings built into the cliff to your left. Gouldings Trading Post complex is a wonderful blend of nostalgia and convenience.

Meals are no longer served family-style here, because a modern restaurant has been built. While it is efficient, it is less charming than the old, small dining room. The food is adequate, the atmosphere is modern and clean, and the Native help is unfailingly pleasant and helpful.

Accommodations are clean and pleasant, and the views are spectacular. There is even a swimming pool—great after a day's drive in the sands of Monument Valley. $$. For reservations or information call (435) 727-3231 or visit www.gouldings.com.

From here you can retrace your steps to Flagstaff or pick up Day Trip 02 Northeast from Flagstaff. If you have the time, combining these trips can make a marvelous 4- to 7-day vacation. *One word of warning:* Always buy with caution. Not all items sold in the area are authentic. This is a problem that the Navajo Nation is well aware of and is trying to fix. Examine items carefully, and if you are not certain that a piece is authentic, don't purchase it. Save your money for reputable outlets, such as those sponsored by the Navajo Nation or galleries.

day trip 02

northeast

navajo country at its best:
tuba city, canyon de chelly national
monument, ganado and the
hubbell trading post
worth more time: window rock

tuba city

Tuba City is located at AZ 264 and US 160, 80 miles northeast of Flagstaff; it is the Navajo (or Diné) Nation's largest community. Located within the Painted Desert on the western side of the Navajo Nation, the Hopi town of Moenkopi lies directly to its southeast. If you are here during the summer, be aware that the Navajo Nation observes daylight savings time while Arizona does not. Three attractions will teach you a lot about Navajo culture and the Navajo Nation.

what to do

Explore Navajo Interactive Museum. Main Street and Moenave Road; (928) 283-5441; www.discovernavajo.com. This exhibit was originally produced for the 2002 Salt Lake City Winter Olympics and has been reassembled here as an interactive journey that takes visitors from the Creation Story to contemporary Navajoland. Traveling clockwise, you enter from the east and move to the south, west, and north; in each quadrant you are introduced to the land, language, history, culture, and ceremonial life of the Navajo. Within the 7,000-square-foot exhibit are Navajo hogans and many interactive exhibits. Open daily. Fee.

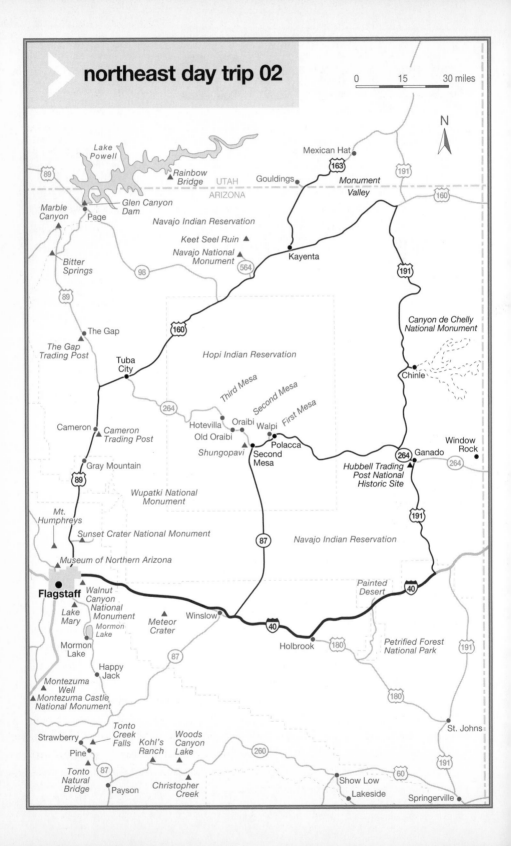

0 15 30 miles

N

Lake Powell

Rainbow Bridge

Mexican Hat

163

191

Gouldings

Monument Valley

89

160

Marble Canyon

Glen Canyon Dam

Page

UTAH

ARIZONA

Navajo Indian Reservation

Keet Seel Ruin

Navajo National Monument

564

Kayenta

191

Bitter Springs

98

Canyon de Chelly National Monument

89

The Gap

160

The Gap Trading Post

Tuba City

Hopi Indian Reservation

Chinle

264

Third Mesa

Second Mesa

Cameron

Cameron Trading Post

Hotevilla

Oraibi

Walpi

First Mesa

Old Oraibi

Polacca

Window Rock

Gray Mountain

Shungopavi

Second Mesa

264

Ganado

264

89

Hubbell Trading Post National Historic Site

Wupatki National Monument

191

Mt. Humphreys

87

Navajo Indian Reservation

Sunset Crater National Monument

Museum of Northern Arizona

Painted Desert

40

Flagstaff

Walnut Canyon National Monument

Winslow

Lake Mary

Meteor Crater

40

Mormon Lake

Petrified Forest National Park

Mormon Lake

Holbrook

180

191

87

Happy Jack

Montezuma Well

180

Montezuma Castle National Monument

St. Johns

Tonto Creek Falls

Woods Canyon Lake

Strawberry

Kohl's Ranch

260

Pine

87

Tonto Natural Bridge

Christopher Creek

60

191

Payson

Show Low

Lakeside

Springerville

Navajo Code Talkers Museum. Main Street and Moenave Road; (928) 810-8501. Next to Explore Navajo Interactive Museum, this exhibition tells about the "code talkers" who were instrumental in helping the Allied forces succeed in World War II by passing messages in Navajo and other native languages. See machinery and tools used in battle, victory stories, and a code-talker transcript. Open daily. Fee.

Tuba City Trading Post. Main Street and Moenave Road. Next to the Explore Navajo Interactive Museum, this historic trading post remains very much unchanged since it was established in 1906. Find authentic Indian arts and crafts here along with groceries and other supplies.

where to stay

Moenkopi Legacy Inn & Suites. At AZ 160 and AZ 264 on the Hopi Reservation; (928) 283-4500; www.experiencehopi.com. The first hotel to be built on the Hopi tribal land in more than 50 years, the Moenkopi Legacy Inn & Suites features a swimming pool, flat-screen TVs, meeting space, and a gallery in addition to 100 guest rooms. Display cases showcase Hopi art, and the TUUVI Café offers traditional American and Hopi food. The TUUVI Travel Center, located across the street, gives visitors information they need to explore the Hopi reservation. $$.

canyon de chelly national monument

Canyon de Chelly National Monument is approximately 135 miles southeast of Monument Valley on Indian Reservation Route 64. From Monument Valley, drive south on US 163 to Kayenta. At the junction of US 160 and US 163, drive east on US 160 about 40 miles to where US 160 meets US 191. Go south on US 191 for 75 miles to Chinle and the entrance to Canyon de Chelly (pronounced de Shay). To see Canyon de Chelly properly requires at least 1 overnight if you are coming from Monument Valley and 2 if Flagstaff is your base.

Canyon de Chelly is quite unlike Monument Valley. Where Monument Valley is stark and golden desert, Canyon de Chelly is pink and warm. It is one of the most appealing of Arizona's canyons. As you enter the canyon on Indian Reservation Route 64, you will see the visitor center directly ahead of you.

This park boasts towering sculpted rock formations, sheer and colorful cliffs, and picture-postcard scenery. It is inhabited both by modern-day Native Americans and memories of ancient ones. The Pueblo Indians, who vanished from this area around AD 1350, abandoned their dwellings forever. Their spirit infuses the ruins within the canyon walls. Hundreds of ancient communities, many of them poised on sandstone ledges within colorful caverns, give witness to the earlier vitality of this place.

The Navajos arrived in the area sometime before the 18th century. Even today, a small enclave of Navajo families live in modern dwellings on the canyon floor, tend sheep, and grow crops. Make sure you bring a light jacket or sweater for summer evenings if you visit from April through November. In the winter, you'll need to bundle up.

where to go

Self-guided tours. Pick up brochures that describe these tours at the Canyon de Chelly Visitor Center (928-674-5500; www.nps.gov/cach). When walking or driving on the rim, be sure to obey all signs. In places, it's a dizzying 400-foot drop onto the canyon floor.

The walk to White House Ruin is a pleasant hike along a well-marked path. The walk down takes less than an hour, but remember to add extra time to hike back up again. Wear tennis shoes and carry some water.

At the bottom you will cross the sandy wash that, in the winter and spring, can be running, so be prepared to get wet. Once across, you can gaze at this well-preserved ruin and imagine what it was like for these prehistoric people to live and farm in this incredible canyon.

Usually a Native jeweler is seen here, his blanket laden with rings, bracelets, and neck-laces that he's made. The prices are good, so if you see something that catches your eye, don't hesitate to buy it. It could be handmade.

As you drive around this canyon, remember that the best way to see Canyon de Chelly is outside of your car. Many trails beckon. Take advantage of them and enjoy the views. Pay attention to signs and respect the natural site.

Canyon de Chelly is a favorite spot for Native American entrepreneurs, who also sell their wares on the canyon rim. Again, buy with care, as not everything you'll see is authentic.

Guided Jeep tours. (800) 679-2473; www.tbirdlodge.com. To fully appreciate the geol-ogy, history, and anthropology of this exquisite canyon, take a guided half-day or full-day Jeep tour. Make arrangements at the Thunderbird Lodge. Unless you have an extensive interest in ancient Native American civilization, the half-day trip is your best bet; a full day could leave you exhausted. In summer, as you bounce along the canyon floor in an open Jeep, you may need the protection of sunscreen and a hat. You may even want to take a canteen or thermos with water. Open daily. Fee.

where to eat and stay

Best Western at Canyon de Chelly. (800) 327-0354; www.canyondechelly.com. As you enter Chinle, south on US 191, turn left at the intersection—the only one in town. Don't depend upon the road signs in this area. Often, if the road is under repair, the signs come down. (Take solace in the fact that Chinle is tiny, and you really cannot get lost.) $$$.

Thunderbird Lodge Motel. On US 191; (800) 679-2473; www.tbirdlodge.com. This historic lodge offers the most complete facilities in Navajoland. The rooms are clean and moderately priced, and the location, at the mouth of the canyon, is magnificent. You'll find a gift shop to browse through, and you can make arrangements for tours right at the lodge. The lodge, which was an original trading post, is a charming building, circa 1896. The menu selections for meals are limited, and food is served cafeteria-style. Know that the Navajo Nation does not serve alcoholic beverages and does not want visitors bringing them onto the reservation. Open daily during breakfast, lunch, and dinner hours. $–$$.

ganado and the hubbell trading post

Hubbell Trading Post National Historic Site. One mile west of Ganado; (928) 755-3475; www.nps.gov/archive/hutr/home.htm. Before returning to Flagstaff from Canyon de Chelly, you can continue south 30 miles on US 191 to the intersection of AZ 264, then 5 miles east to Ganado and the Hubbell Trading Post National Historic Site. A national treasure, the trading post is worth a visit.

The rug room at the Hubbell Trading Post rivals any museum collection in the world. If you're in the market for a Navajo rug, this is an ideal place to shop. The knowledgeable salespeople will be happy to tell you about the patterns and weavers. The only modern-day touch is that, along with the name of the weaver, you'll also occasionally find a Polaroid photograph of the weaver attached to the ticket. You also can browse through exquisite

time spent on the "rez"

The Navajo Nation, which is the size of the country of Ireland, stretches across 3 states: Arizona, New Mexico, and Utah. I had the privilege of working on a project to introduce visitors to the Navajo Nation during the 2002 Winter Olympics that were held in Salt Lake City. That exhibit is now reassembled in Tuba City for the enjoyment of visitors. It was fascinating to spend time on the reservation with my friend, who was then director of tourism for his nation. With Fred at my side I had the "shopping" tour of the Navajo Nation and came home at the end of the project with quite a few treasures—all obtained with what he said was the "Navajo price." We also attended the Navajo Nation Fair, the largest Native American fair in the country, which is held in September. I feel this is an acquired taste as it is not designed for the casual visitor. Both the parade and fair are huge draws for people who love crowds and confusion, and, if that's you, enjoy! If not, skip Window Rock during the first week of September.

jewelry, sandpaintings, books, and trinkets or even pick up food supplies if you plan to camp in the area. Groceries are sold in the front room.

John Lorenzo Hubbell was the dean of traders for the Navajos, and his trading post continues to act as a bridge between the Native American and Anglo worlds. In its heyday, the post offered a place for Navajos to socialize as well as to conduct business. VIPs of every culture who passed through northeastern Arizona during the late 1800s and early 1900s stopped here. The guest list includes presidents, generals, writers, scientists, and artists.

Today, business continues as usual in this elegant pocket of the state. The atmosphere hasn't changed; Navajos and tourists still come by to trade and talk.

Hubbell's career spanned critical years for the Navajos. When he came to the territory to open his trading post, the Native Americans were adjusting to life on a reservation and were attempting to cope with the restrictions placed on them by the U.S. government. Hubbell offered his friendship when great numbers of Navajo were struggling to free themselves from the confines of Fort Sumner in New Mexico. He sympathized with the Navajo and often spoke out on their behalf. When he died in 1930, one of Hubbell's Native friends eulogized him at the memorial service, saying:

You wear out your shoes, you buy another pair;
When the food is gone, you buy more;
You gather melons, and more will grow on the vine;
You grind your corn and make bread which you eat;
And next year you have plenty more corn.
But my friend Don Lorenzo is gone,
and none to take his place.

After browsing through the trading post, walk around the grounds to see the Hubbell home. Limited tours are available and are restricted to 4 tours per day. Free.

From Ganado, there are several ways to return to Flagstaff. The fastest route is US 191 south to I-40. Then head west on I-40 to Flagstaff. Another alternative is to take AZ 264 west to AZ 87, turn south on AZ 87, and then west on I-40 to Flagstaff. Get some sleep at Canyon de Chelly if you plan to head west on AZ 264 to Polacca for Day Trip 03 Northeast from Flagstaff after visiting Ganado.

worth more time:

window rock

Window Rock. The capital of the Navajo Nation, Window Rock is about 2 hours from Ganado and about 30 minutes from Gallup, New Mexico. From Hubbell, take US 191 south to AZ 264 and continue east to Window Rock. In Window Rock, visit the Navajo Nation Cultural Center, which includes a museum and indoor and outdoor theater, and, of course, Window Rock—the rock that gives this town its name.

where to stay

Navajoland Day's Inn. St. Michael's (located next to Window Rock); (928) 871-5690 or (800) 359-4827 (automated reservations service). This property in St. Michael's is an alternative to the Navajo Nation Capital. It is a bit newer than the Quality Inn (a mile or so up the hill) and has an indoor swimming pool, Jacuzzi, and fitness room. The rooms are clean and spacious. $$.

Quality Inn Navajo Nation Capital. AZ 264 and AZ 12; (928) 871-4108 or (800) 662-6189; www.qualityinnwindowrock.com. This well-equipped modern inn has good amenities, including a dining room that features some traditional Navajo dishes. The inn offers individual and family tours of the area. The gift shop is surprisingly inadequate for an inn that draws so much traffic, but the Navajo Nation Cultural Center is within walking distance, and you'll find a superb display of Navajo arts and crafts there. Prices are fair (don't expect bargains), but both the quantity and quality are good. $$.

day trip 03

northeast

>>> **the magic of the hopi mesas:**
first, second, and third mesas

first, second, and third mesas

This is a wonderful trip that shouldn't be rushed. Because of the great distances in this part of the state, visiting more remote areas means stretching your usual day-trip time limit.

As you plan, consider that the Hopi Reservation roads found in this sector are often narrow, 2-lane byways. You won't make fast time, so add another hour to your excursion limit.

You can begin the trip in Flagstaff by heading east on I-40 to Winslow and picking up the turnoff for AZ 87 north 3 miles east of there. Follow AZ 87 north for 65 miles to Second Mesa on the Hopi Indian Reservation, then turn right (east) for 7 miles and actually start at Polacca on First Mesa.

A better option might be to combine this trip with Day Trip 02, previously described. Time permitting, you will enjoy this journey more if you can begin it refreshed after a good night's sleep at Canyon de Chelly. After driving 30 miles south to Ganado and stopping at the Hubbell Trading Post (see Day Trip 02 Northeast from Flagstaff), head west on AZ 264 to Polacca.

If you look at a map, you'll see that the Hopi (pronounced Ho-pee) nation is plunked down in the middle of the vast Navajo Reservation. Although they live in close proximity, the Hopi and the Navajo couldn't be more different. Historically, the Hopi, whose ancestors are the Anasazi, have been pueblo dwellers—homebodies content to build permanent villages

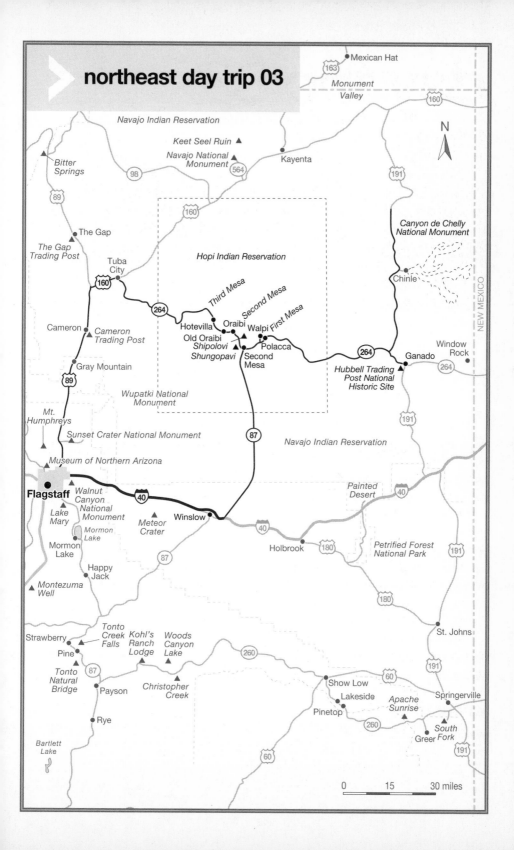

Mexican Hat
163
Monument
Valley
160

Navajo Indian Reservation

Keet Seel Ruin ▲
Navajo National
Monument
564
Kayenta

N

191

Bitter
Springs
98

89

Canyon de Chelly
National Monument

The Gap
The Gap
Trading Post

Tuba
City
160

Hopi Indian Reservation

160

Third Mesa
264

Chinle

NEW MEXICO

Cameron
Cameron
Trading Post

Hotevilla
Old Oraibi
Shipolovi
Shungopavi

Oraibi
Second Mesa
Walpi First Mesa

Polacca
Second
Mesa

Gray Mountain
89

Wupatki National
Monument

264
Ganado

Window
Rock
264

Hubbell Trading
Post National
Historic Site

191

Mt.
Humphreys

Sunset Crater National Monument

87

Navajo Indian Reservation

Museum of Northern Arizona

40

Flagstaff
Walnut
Canyon
National
Monument

Lake
Mary
Mormon
Lake
Mormon
Lake

Meteor
Crater

Winslow
40

Painted
Desert
40

Holbrook
180

Petrified Forest
National Park
191

Happy
Jack
87

Montezuma
Well

180

St. Johns

Strawberry
Tonto
Creek
Falls
Pine
Tonto
Natural
Bridge
87

Kohl's
Ranch
Lodge

Woods
Canyon
Lake
260

Payson

Christopher
Creek

Show Low
60
Lakeside
Pinetop
Apache
Sunrise
260

Springerville

Rye

South
Greer Fork
191

Bartlett
Lake

60

0   15   30 miles

charles loloma, famous hopi artist

The most famous Hopi artist was Charles Loloma, who is credited with bringing Indian jewelry into the world of fashion. Charles was a friend of Oscar de la Renta and traveled the world, but on Hopi, he was simply Charles, an active member of his clan who danced in a special annual ceremony with a rattlesnake in his mouth. I was fortunate to get to know this unforgettable gentleman and fly with him in his private airplane, which he kept at "Hopi International." One morning, as we flew over the landscape, he described the "cloud people" he was seeing. I turned his words into a poem for a story I was writing for Arizona Highways magazine. Even more than his artistry, I treasure the moments I sat quietly with Charles, eating freshly sliced watermelon and enjoying his special world.

and cement family ties. The Navajo, in contrast, were nomadic farmers and sheepherders. In fact, the word *hopi* means "the peaceful ones," and traditionally these people have led a peaceful, agrarian life.

The windswept mesas of the Hopi Reservation have long been a source of inspiration to the Hopi and non–Native Americans alike. As you drive through this reservation on AZ 264, you'll feel a subtle pull, the magic that makes life in the fast lane seem ridiculous. At first, the landscape seems barren, but look again. Everywhere you will see corn growing, even in the most improbable corners of backyards and in the rockiest soil. To the Hopi, corn represents life, and they cherish this food for its nutritional and spiritual values.

If this is your first trip to the Hopi Reservation, or Hopi, as it is more commonly called, you may wonder where the ancient villages are. Etched against the horizon, high on flattened mountaintops, the tiny pueblos jut against the sky like jack-o'-lantern teeth. Although the Hopi have lived here for hundreds of years, they do not intrude upon Mother Earth. They live gently and inconspicuously, coaxing life from this rocky soil they call their land.

All but one of the villages you may visit are located on or near the areas called First, Second, and Third Mesas. The names refer to the chronological shift of the Hopi population from AD 1500 to AD 1900. First the Hopi settled in Walpi (the area now known as First Mesa), and they gradually moved westward to Oraibi and Hotevilla.

where to go

Walpi, First Mesa. All the ancient villages are off the main roads, situated high atop the mesas. In the past, a mountaintop location protected the village from intruders.

As you drive through the reservation on AZ 264, you'll see signs pointing to Polacca, a Native American village. At Polacca, you'll spot a gravel road that leads north to Walpi.

(There are no names on the few streets that lead to these ancient villages.) The narrow road climbs and makes several sharp turns. Although the pueblo buildings may appear to be closing in on you, don't worry. This road is fine for passenger car travel. Once on top of the mesa, park. Proceed immediately to the visitor center. There you will be assigned to a guide. You'll see the ancient plaza, still used for ceremonials, with its kiva (underground ceremonial chamber) near the center. Walpi is an especially picturesque village that comes to life during important ceremonies.

Observe all the signs posted in the ancient villages that ask you not to take any photographs, make sketches, or make any sound recordings. Remember: When you are in Hopi (or any other reservation), you are a guest in another country.

When you leave First Mesa, continue west on AZ 264, and you'll see signs that lead to **Shipolovi** (Shi-pah-lo-vee) and **Shungopavi** (Shun-gó-pa-vee), other well-known, old villages on **Second Mesa**. You may either visit or see them from a distance. Continue toward Oraibi. Soon you'll see the Hopi Cultural Center, a cluster of pseudo-pueblos, on your right. You'll find a restaurant, gift shop, small museum, and overnight accommodations here.

Oraibi, Third Mesa. From the cultural center, continue west on AZ 264 to Oraibi. You may want to take a quick trip to Old Oraibi. Like Walpi, this community hovers on a high, narrow, rocky ledge. The road to Old Oraibi heads off to your left (south) shortly after you pass Oraibi (sometimes called "New Oraibi"). Although parts of the settlement are in ruins, the village is very much a part of modern Hopi life. When you're finished visiting here, drive west on AZ 264 toward Hotevilla to see that village.

McGee's Indian Art Gallery. AZ 264, Keams Canyon; (928) 738-2295; www.hopiart.com. This art-and-craft gallery and gift shop was originally a trading post started in 1874 by Thomas Keam. Keam sold it to Lorenzo Hubbell in 1902, and the McGee family has owned it since 1938. Open daily.

where to eat and stay

The Hopi Cultural Center. On AZ 264, 5 miles west of the junction with AZ 87; (928) 734-2401; www.hopiculturalcenter.com. This property is "tired" and could use a facelift, but it still has the feel of a Hopi village, and there is not a lot to choose from in this area. The dining room is big, and you'll be served by Hopi women in native dress. Order the Hopi specialties: Hopi stew made with chunks of lamb, and anything made with blue corn, a special type of corn grown and used here. Open daily. $–$$.

If you plan to spend the night, call ahead for reservations and be prepared to rough it. You will not find the same quality of service and accommodations here as in the Moenkopi, the tribe's upscale property in Tuba City. But unless you are self-contained, pulling a camper, or driving an RV, this is your only choice for an overnight stay. $$.

east

day trip 01

east

>>> **windswept vistas of ancient events:**
meteor crater, painted desert,
petrified forest national park

meteor crater

Leaving Flagstaff, drive east on I-40 toward Winslow. Twenty miles before you reach Winslow, you'll see an exit for Meteor Crater. Head south on the well-marked, paved road to this fascinating natural site.

Meteor Crater was formed about 20,000 BC when a meteoric mass, traveling 33,000 miles per hour from interplanetary space, struck Earth. The impact, blasting nearly a half-billion tons of rock from the surface, destroyed all plant and animal life within 100 miles. In contemporary times, this perfectly preserved, huge hole in the ground has tantalized scientists, who use it as a living laboratory. Meteor Crater hit the news when the Apollo astronauts used it as a practice surface to train for their lunar walk. Discovered in 1871, the crater has impressive statistics. It measures 4,150 feet from rim to rim, is more than 3 miles in circumference, and is 470 feet deep. In addition to staring at the crater, you can visit the Meteor Crater Museum of Astrogeology, the Astronaut Hall of Fame, and well-appointed gift and lapidary shops. Open daily. Call for extended summer hours. Fee. (928) 289-5898; www.meteorcrater.com.

From Meteor Crater, continue to Winslow on I-40. The town is named for F. Edward Winslow, who was president of the St. Louis and San Francisco Railroad, and like its neighbor, Holbrook, is devoted to transportation. Situated 30 miles west of the Mogollon Rim, this community serves as a conduit for visits to more remote and scenic areas of the state.

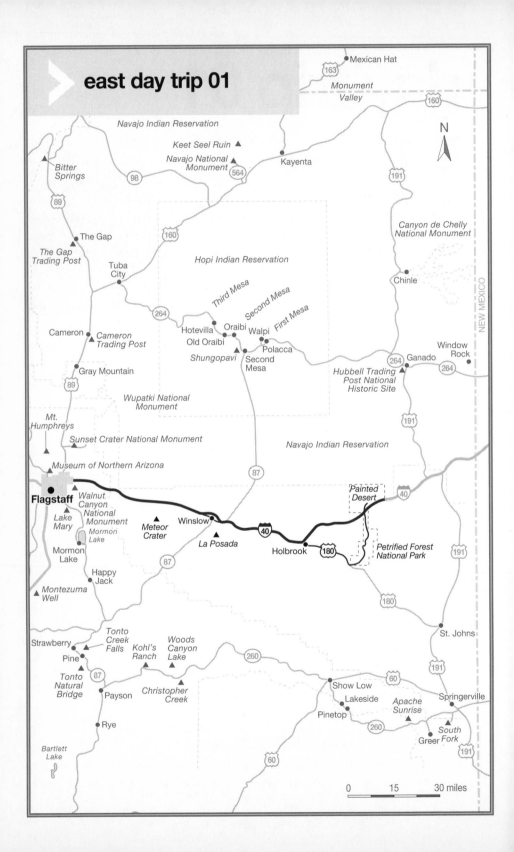

Mexican Hat

163

Monument
Valley

160

NEW MEXICO

Navajo Indian Reservation

Keet Seel Ruin ▲

Navajo National ▲
Monument

564

Kayenta

191

98

Bitter
Springs

89

Canyon de Chelly
National Monument

The Gap

The Gap
Trading Post

160

Hopi Indian Reservation

Chinle

Tuba
City

264

Cameron   Cameron
Trading Post

Third Mesa

Second Mesa

First Mesa

Hotevilla   Oraibi

Old Oraibi

Walpi

Polacca

Window
Rock

Gray Mountain

89

Shungopavi   Second
Mesa

264   Ganado

Hubbell Trading
Post National
Historic Site

264

Wupatki National
Monument

Navajo Indian Reservation

191

Mt.
Humphreys ▲

Sunset Crater National Monument

Museum of Northern Arizona

87

Painted
Desert

40

Flagstaff ●

▲ Walnut
Canyon
National
Monument

Winslow

40

Lake
Mary

Meteor
Crater

La Posada

Holbrook

180

Petrified Forest
National Park

191

Mormon
Lake

Mormon
Lake

87

Happy
Jack

180

Montezuma
Well

St. Johns

Tonto
Creek
Falls

Strawberry

Pine

Kohl's
Ranch

Woods
Canyon
Lake

260

191

Tonto
Natural
Bridge

87

Payson

Christopher
Creek

Show Low

Lakeside

60

Springerville

Apache
Sunrise

Pinetop

260

South
Greer Fork

Rye

Bartlett
Lake

60

191

0   15   30 miles

Known as "The Hub City" because of the transportation lines that intersect here, Holbrook also serves as the seat of Navajo County. It caters to tourists who are on their way to the Painted Desert and Petrified Forest National Park. It's a good place to stretch your legs, pick up a snack, or fill up the car with gas before going on.

where to stay

La Posada Hotel. 303 East 2nd St., Winslow; (928) 289-4366. www.laposada.org. At the intersection of US 66 and AZ 87, ¼ mile from I-40. One of the last great railroad hotels, this historic hotel was designed by Mary Colter, one of the most important architects in the Southwest, to serve railway guests for the Fred Harvey Company. Colter arrived in Winslow in 1929 and patterned the 70-room inn after a Spanish hacienda. When the era of the Harvey hotels passed, La Posada was abandoned until 1996, when Allan Affeldt and his artist wife bought the property, moved in, and began to painstakingly renovate it. Today, the hotel has 37 rooms available for guests, each one decorated individually. The Turquoise Room offers breakfast, lunch, and dinner and has a surprisingly large menu. Open daily. $$.

From Winslow, continue east on I-40 for 33 miles to Holbrook.

painted desert

From Holbrook, continue on I-40 approximately 19 miles to exit 311. As you approach the parks, the Painted Desert is the area due north of the highway; the Petrified Forest National Park lies south of it. Although the parks are referred to as separate entities, they are, in fact, contiguous. The Painted Desert offers a superb backdrop for travelers who enjoy the desert at its most delicately pastel, but the Petrified Forest is the better attraction.

Try to time your arrival during the early morning or late afternoon hours. At sunup or just before sunset, the fallen logs in the Petrified Forest seem most lifelike, and the colors of the Painted Desert appear most vibrant.

where to go

Painted Desert Inn. One mile north of I-40, at the entrance to the park; (928) 524-9753; www.nps.gov/pefo/historyculture/pdi.htm. This is your first stop. Inside you will learn how both the Painted Desert and the Petrified Forest were formed. Exhibits illustrate the evolution of the Painted Desert, and a short film describes how natural forces turn the forest to stone.

Wander around the displays and pick up information for a self-guided tour of both parks. Check for summer and winter hours. Fee.

petrified forest national park

The Petrified Forest National Park is the greatest and most colorful concentration of petrified wood ever discovered on Earth. The park, which consists of 93,431 acres of brilliantly colored stone logs, preserves the glassy remains of an ancient coniferous forest. About 200 million years ago, the trees grew in the highlands to the west and southwest. The area of the current forest was swampland, and as streams carried the dead logs down to this flat, depressed area, they were buried in sediment rich with volcanic ash.

Over eons, the chemical process worked its magic. The logs were slowly impregnated with silica until they turned to solid stone. Iron oxide and other minerals then stained the silica, producing the stone rainbows we see today. In the process, the logs became stony jewel boxes for quartz and other gemstones that developed in the wood during petrification.

Today, each chip and rock is carefully protected. No one is allowed to pick up even the tiniest souvenir. But in ancient times, the people who lived here carved on the petrified wood, chiseled messages on the rocks, and fashioned tools and weapons from the rainbow forest.

Take a slow drive through the area. If you've stopped at the Painted Desert Visitor Center, you've picked up a pamphlet that describes a self-guided drive. This brochure explains all the places you'll want to see. If you don't have a brochure, don't worry, because you'll find, as you approach each site, a written description clearly posted. Be sure to stop and get out of your car to see these unusual rock formations. You should hike to **Agate Bridge** in the First Forest. Here a petrified tree fell across a canyon, forming a stony bridge for eternity. Plan to climb down the 120 steps to **Newspaper Rock,** a large boulder covered with

the "magic hour" at petrified forest

The first time we drove through the Petrified Forest, we arrived late and were the last car allowed through before sunset. It was the "magic hour" just before the sun dipped into the horizon. It was a trick of light, but we saw the forest as it once was, millions of years ago, when enormous trees stood impossibly tall. I always advise friends and family to arrive as close as possible to closing time so they can have this experience. I also warn everyone that this drive goes through one of the more stark landscapes in Arizona, windswept and devoid of any running rivers. The towns of Winslow and Holbrook are not "charming" by traditional standards, but for those who want to explore an otherworldly environment, this day trip is filled with happy surprises.

ancient writing. No doubt this served as a kind of local bulletin board, announcing activities and goings-on to the Native Americans who lived in the area. If you follow all the side roads that are marked in this stony forest, you'll drive about 38 miles before you reach the south entrance, which is your exit point.

what to do

Rainbow Forest Museum. Near the south entrance; (928) 524-6228; www.nps.gov/pefo. This is your final stop before leaving the Petrified Forest. Inside you'll see geological exhibits. If you didn't stop at the north entrance, you can learn how the forests were formed here. Open daily except Christmas. Fee.

Return to Flagstaff by following US 180 northwest to Holbrook, where you'll pick up I-40 west to Flagstaff.

southeast

day trip 01

southeast

>>> **the high road to outdoor country:**
mormon lake, happy jack

mormon lake

Approximately 30 miles southeast of Flagstaff on Mormon Lake Road, Mormon Lake is an optimum destination for a quick, easy, scenic loop through some of Flagstaff's best outdoor country.

To get there from Flagstaff, follow I-17 south to the Lake Mary Road exit. Stay on Lake Mary Road until you reach the Mormon Lake area. As you drive, the road will wind through the Coconino National Forest and will take you near some great fishing lakes. Lake Mary is one of the favorites.

This area is long on scenery but short on facilities. Numerous campgrounds dot the countryside, but wise travelers will carry picnic hampers filled with lunch goodies. You won't find any fast food here, unless, of course, you are especially quick with hook and bait. What you will find, however, is serenity—ponderosa pines trimming lush meadows, backed up by a panorama of the San Francisco Peaks.

As you continue southeast, you'll see a dirt road off to your left (east), which leads to Ashurst Lake. Unless you have a four-wheel drive, avoid this. Dirt roads in this area can be hazardous to the health of your car. Unless you are driving a four-wheel-drive vehicle or a truck, it's advisable to stay on paved surfaces. During the rainy season you can get flooded out, and during the dry periods, these roads can be extremely rough.

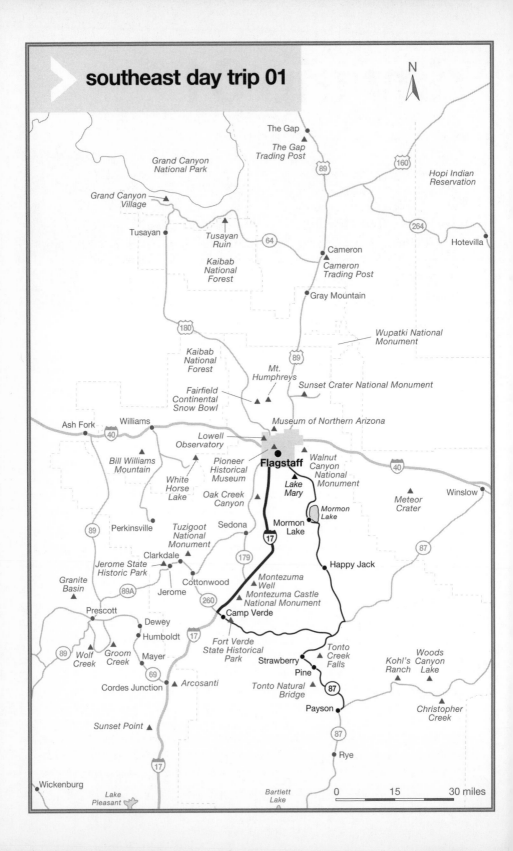

southeast day trip 01

easy access to high country

Arizona continues to surprise me. Within a few miles of the college town of Flagstaff, you can enjoy the rural serenity of Mormon Lake, unless it's a holiday when the place usually is jumping. The lake and the entire area have been a favorite destination of cyclists and cross-country skiers for years, and unlike some of the other trips described from Flagstaff, this day trip is a delightful and quick diversion. You can do it entirely from the comfort of your car or stop and include some hiking. I've always found it interesting that although this destination seems off the beaten track, the Mormon Lake Lodge dining room seats 300 people. So much for undiscovered beauty.

Continuing on Lake Mary Road, you'll come to Mormon Lake Road, a dirt byway that leads off to your right (west). Take this unpaved road, which will loop around Mormon Lake, the largest natural lake in Arizona. Cattle that roamed over the meadowland stamped down the earth, forming a natural dish that held the winter snowmelt. The Mormons, who remained in this vicinity for many years, ran a dairy and even built a cheese press here. It's not known why they left the area, but probably a drought forced them out.

Over the years, the snowmelt continually refilled the depressed area and formed a large natural lake surrounded by open range where cattle graze. The lake is also a haven for ducks and duck hunters.

Adjacent to the water is the village of Mormon Lake, which consists of Montezuma and Mormon Lake Lodges, a post office, a dance hall that seats 350 people, a steak house, and a general store. During big holiday weekends (including Fourth of July and Labor Day), the dance hall resounds with live entertainment.

what to do

Cross-country skiing. During the winter you'll find some of the best cross-country skiing in the state. You can drive up and ski for the day or make overnight arrangements at either of 2 lodges in the area. (See Where to Stay.)

where to eat

Mormon Lake Lodge. Mormon Lake; (928) 354-2227; www.mormonlakelodge.com. The menu features 7 kinds of steak, all reasonably priced. The restaurant is one of the few operating open-pit steak houses in the state. During the summer, the restaurant serves breakfast, lunch, and dinner daily. In winter, meals are available Fri, Sat, and Sun only. $$–$$$.

where to stay

Montezuma Lodge. Mormon Lake; (928) 354-2220; www.montezuma-lodge.com. At mile marker 324, turn right onto Mormon Lake Loop Road; take the dirt road 3½ miles to the lodge. Guests can stay in 16 freestanding cabins, with fully equipped kitchens, nestled in the woods against the Mormon Mountains. This is a favorite "ride-in" stop for bicyclists, who come, packs on their backs, to rest and then ride in the area. Closed Oct 15 to May 15. Meals by prior arrangement only. $–$$.

Mormon Lake Lodge. Mormon Lake; (928) 354-2227; www.mormonlakelodge.com. From Lake Mary Road, turn right onto Mormon Lake Road and continue 9 miles to the lodge. (You will pass Montezuma Lodge.) The property dates back to 1924, when it was built as Tumbler's Lodge. It was a place for men to bring their families and have a good meal. On July 4, 1924, the lodge burned to the ground while men were planning a big rodeo event. The local ranchers vowed to rebuild it on Labor Day weekend in time for the next rodeo. When they completed it, they burned their branding irons into the walls as a symbol of protection. The brands are still visible today.

The dining room of the Mormon Lake Lodge has seating for 300 and serves casual western-style dining. The 1880s-style saloon keeps its old-time charm.

The rustic resort features 53 bunkhouses and cabins, all nestled in the forest. Some have fireplaces and kitchenettes. Rentals are daily and weekly. Seventy-four RV sites with full hookups are available. Roping arena seats 1,200. Meeting rooms available for groups. $$.

happy jack

Another 12 miles southwest on Lake Mary Road is Happy Jack, a logging community. You'll see campgrounds and some private cabins tucked away on this not-so-beaten path. From Happy Jack you have a few options. You can continue to the junction with AZ 87 and follow AZ 87 northeast to Winslow. From Winslow, follow US 180 back to Flagstaff.

Or you may follow Lake Mary Road to the junction of AZ 87 and take AZ 87 to Strawberry and Pine, and then follow General Crook Highway west to Camp Verde. There you can pick up I-17 north and continue to Flagstaff. Along the way, you can stop at Montezuma Castle and Montezuma Well. (See Day Trip 02 North from Phoenix.)

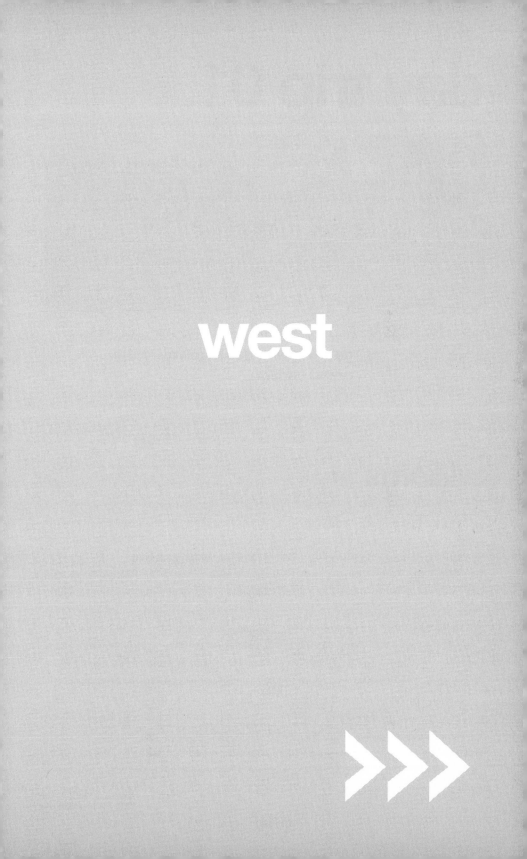

west >>>

day trip 01

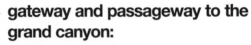

>>> **gateway and passageway to the grand canyon:**
williams, grand canyon caverns
worth more time: hualapai tribe,
grand canyon west and sky walk

williams

From Flagstaff, drive west 32 miles on I-40 across the golden meadowland known as Garland Prairie. During spring and summer, the meadow is a carpet of wildflowers. The fields shimmer with azure blues and dashing reds. As you continue toward Williams, you drive through the pine-scented, lush greenery of the **Kaibab National Forest**.

Called "The Gateway to the Grand Canyon," Williams is named for William S. (or "Old Bill") Williams, a master trapper and Native American scout who traveled on the Santa Fe Trail during the 1820s. A rugged eccentric, he was known to drink and gamble excessively. Called the "lone wolf" of trappers, Old Bill, like many of the mountain men of his day, spent most of his time working and sleeping in the wilderness. He emerged from the mountains only long enough to lose his money fast. Then he'd retreat to the wilds to trap and restock his supply of furs. Soon he'd reappear in town, get cash, and start the cycle again.

Although mountain men like Old Bill Williams are remembered primarily as trappers, they played a key role in Arizona history. True, they were an environmental disaster, wiping out the entire populations of grizzlies and beavers that once roamed through the forests and swam in the streams. But as explorers, mappers, and later guides for the military, these reclusive individuals provided invaluable services. Their knowledge of the wilderness made it possible to open the land for the settlers who followed.

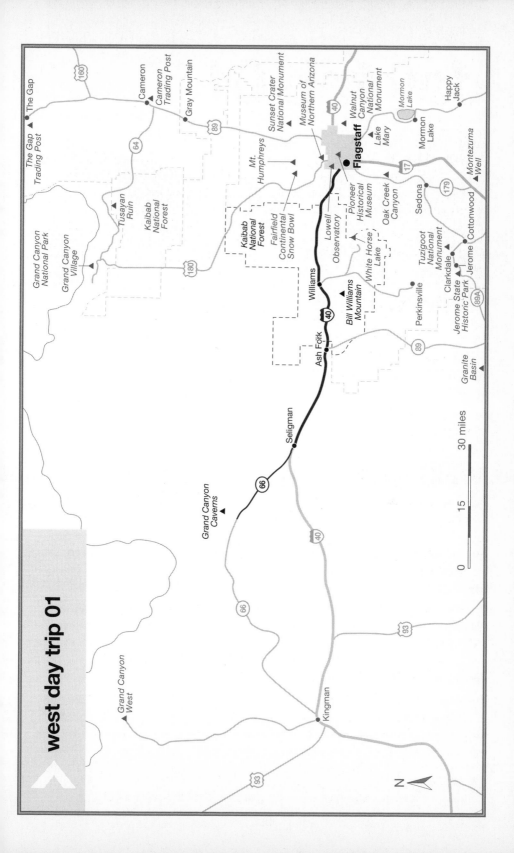

west day trip 01

history, nostalgia, and crazy fun

Williams has the historic distinction of being the last place in the country where the final piece of I-40 was completed. The new interstate meant that trucks and traffic no longer used Old Route 66, once the main drag through this part of the state. But Route 66 is alive and celebrated in Williams as it is in Seligman. In Williams you'll find funky Route 66 cafes and shops. Another reason to visit is the steam train, which runs from the Williams Depot to the South Rim of the Grand Canyon. The train is the vision of Max and Thelma Biegert, who reinstated passenger travel on this historic rail line and gave visitors more reasons to visit Williams and explore northern Arizona.

The spirit of Old Bill Williams is kept alive through the Bill Williams Mountain Men, who have their headquarters in Williams. If you are in town during any of the town's celebrations (see the Festivals and Celebrations section at the end of the book), you may have an opportunity to see them in full regalia, dressed in furs and leather. This group meets regularly to celebrate the spirit of Old Bill and reenact the mountain men's unique period of frontier history. They ride in parades, take part in rodeos, and whoop it up in festivities in Williams and elsewhere throughout the state.

Like many northern Arizona communities, Williams is a sportsman's paradise. The town sits in the shadow of Bill Williams Mountain, a 9,286-foot-high peak just south of this small community. Good walking trails scale both sides of the mountain. Seven fishing lakes, many with cabins and boating facilities, surround the town. During the winter, there's a small (450-foot vertical drop) downhill ski run. In addition to skiing, the **Benham Snow Play Area**, just south of town on County Road 173, echoes with "snow tubers," kids and adults careening down snowy slopes in inner tubes. For complete information on camping, fishing, and hiking in the vicinity, visit or write the Williams Grand Canyon Chamber of Commerce, 200 West Railroad Ave., Williams 86046; call (928) 635-1417 or (800) 863-0546; or visit www .williamschamber.com.

where to go

DeBerge Gallery of Fine Art and Western Wear. 213 West Rte. 66; (928) 635-2960. The owner not only makes saddles, he also is an artist. The store features a variety of leatherwork, including tack, belts, handbags, and boots. The gallery side includes prints, pottery, carvings, oils, watercolors, and bronzes. Closed Sun.

Grand Canyon Deer Farm. 6752 East Deer Farm Rd.; (928) 635-4073; www.deerfarm. com. As you drive toward Williams from Flagstaff, you'll see this unusual petting zoo that faces I-40. It is 8 miles east of Williams and some 24 miles west of Flagstaff. This is a fun stop for families with children. Adults who enjoy observing 8 varieties of these graceful animals will also like this farm. Some deer are common to other areas of the United States, but there are more unusual types, such as Japanese Sika deer and a herd of Spotted Fallow, a type found in the Mediterranean. Phone for specific hours. Fee.

The Little Grand Canyon (also called Sycamore Point). Twelve miles south of White Horse Lake on FR 110. This is a side trip for adventurous explorers. Locals call this "The Little Grand Canyon," and when you see it, you'll understand why. Follow the paved County Road 173 south of Williams (toward Perkinsville and Jerome) to the unpaved FR 110, which leads to White Horse Lake. Drive 12 miles south on FR 110, a rugged, bumpy road to Sycamore Point. When you arrive, feast your eyes on the steep limestone walls and pillars of sandstone that form this canyon.

Although Oak Creek Canyon offers a more dramatic vertical drop, and the Sedona area has more rocky sculptures, the Little Grand Canyon exudes a solitary beauty. With its rocky spires and stands of aspen, oak, and sycamore, it is largely undiscovered and appeals to those individuals who like the thrill of discovering a majestic, pristine jewel. Rugged adventurers can hike among the cliffs and rock formations. Since there are no established trails or facilities here, inexperienced hikers should not attempt to walk in this wilderness.

Planes of Fame. At Grand Canyon Valle Airport near the junction of AZ 64 and AZ 180; (928) 635-1000; www.planesoffame.org. Aviation enthusiasts will find this museum to their liking. The original museum is in Claremont, California, and was founded in 1957 by Edward T. Maloney. The collection has grown remarkably since then. This branch of the California museum houses 30 aircraft, most of which are flyable. Among those on display is the aircraft that Gen. Douglas MacArthur used as his personal transport plane. Called the *Bataan,* it is a Lockheed Constellation, and tours of the plane are available for an additional charge. They also have a German Messerschmitt BF 109G10 plane. This museum features the only gift shop in northern Arizona that specializes in aviation artifacts, gifts, books, etc. Open daily. Fee.

Steam Train from Williams to the Grand Canyon. 233 Grand Canyon Blvd. Take I-40 to exit 163, then follow Grand Canyon Boulevard for 1½ miles south to the depot. Steam engines opened the West, so what better way to see the territory than aboard one? The Grand Canyon Railway uses 1906 and 1926 Iron Horses to pull restored 1923 Harriman coach cars along original 1901 rails from Memorial Day through Labor Day, and a diesel engine year-round. Passengers are delivered to the threshold of the Grand Canyon. The train travels at a top speed of 35 miles per hour, so the trip takes about 2½ hours. Entertainment and refreshments add to the fun, and complimentary soft drinks and snacks are provided on upgrades. Box lunches may be purchased.

Spend about 3 hours at the canyon and come back, or stay the night. Summertime is a popular time to ride the rails to the Grand Canyon, but winter snows bring a unique beauty to the area. Ride the first-class glass-domed car, which gives a 360-degree view of the ever-changing landscape of northern Arizona.

The Grand Canyon Railway offers numerous value packages that combine the vintage train travel with a stay at the Grand Canyon Railway Hotel and other hotels in both Williams and the canyon. Round-trips operate daily year-round, leaving Williams at 10 a.m. $$. For information on fares, schedules, and special overnight packages at the canyon, call (800) THE-TRAIN (800-843-8724); www.thetrain.com.

where to eat

Grand Depot Café. Located adjacent to the Historic Williams Depot; (928) 635-8970. The restaurant features an all-you-can-eat buffet and menu entrees. $–$$.

Rod's Steak House. 301 East Rte. 66; (928) 635-2671; www.rods-steakhouse.com. Established in 1946, Rod's bills itself as "world famous," and since it has survived for more than 50 years, who can argue with that? The menu includes steaks, seafood, prime rib, ribs, and chicken. Lunch and dinner are served in this roadhouse-style restaurant. Closed Sun. $$.

where to stay

Grand Canyon Railway Hotel. 235 North Grand Canyon Blvd.; reservations: (928) 635-4010; www.thetrain.com. From I-40, take Williams exit 163 to Grand Canyon Boulevard. Go ½ mile south to the Grand Canyon Railway complex. This hotel offers 297 rooms and suites, all decorated in classic Southwest style. Spencer's Lounge features a beautifully carved wooden bar, which was bought in London and lovingly reassembled in Williams. It was originally carved in England by George O. Spencer, a London cabinetmaker. As part of his agreement, he had the privilege of drinking free at the bar. Indoor pool, spa, and exercise room. $$.

In recent years, Williams has started a new cottage industry—B&Bs. All are clean and comfortable. Here are a few favorites:

Red Garter Bed & Bakery. 137 Railroad Ave,; (928) 635-1484 or (800) 328-1484; www .redgarter.com. Stay upstairs in a restored 1897 saloon and bordello and enjoy the aroma of fresh-baked croissants and pastries being made in the bakery on the first floor. Timid souls need to know that there's a ghost reported to live on the premises. $$.

Sheridan House Inn. 460 East Sheridan; (888) 635-9345; www.grandcanyonbedand breakfast.com. This private-home-turned-inn offers 7 rooms (2 are suites), each with private bath. The owners serve a full gourmet breakfast. Located among the pines in a residential neighborhood, this inn features a flagstone patio with a seasonal hot tub, a pool room, and entertainment centers for guests to enjoy. Wireless Internet is available. $$.

Grand Living Bed & Breakfast. 701 Quarterhorse Rd.; (800) 210-5908; www.grandliving bnb.com. The owners have furnished their log home with antiques and offer 4 guest suites, each with private bath and king-size bed. Rooms have fireplaces and verandas. A full gourmet breakfast is served. $$.

grand canyon caverns

Continue west approximately 44 miles on I-40 through Ash Fork, which calls itself the "Flagstone Capital of the World," and go on to Seligman. Exit the interstate and pick up AZ 66, or "Old 66." Follow AZ 66 about 25 miles to the Grand Canyon Caverns.

Here is one of the world's largest completely dry cave systems. Meandering 21 stories beneath the earth, Grand Canyon Caverns are known to be closely related geologically to the Grand Canyon. Yet because of the off-the-beaten-path location, tourists often ignore them. Professional cave explorers are well acquainted with the caverns, and excavation goes on continuously because experts are certain that more rocky rooms wait to be discovered.

You'll enter through a commercial center, which has a coffee shop, motel, gift shop, and airstrip for private planes. A 45-minute guided tour leads you through the expanse of vaulted rooms, filled with colorful rock formations. You'll wander through mysterious passageways and hear an intriguing commentary about the history of the caves. For all its wild beauty, this is a comfortable experience for explorers of all ages; the paths are paved, and the formations are well lit.

The caverns became well known in 1927 when a heavy rain widened the natural funnel-shaped opening to the upper level. However, the Hualapai (Wal-pee) Indians, a tribe that lived here centuries ago, were familiar with that level of the caverns. Even today, elders caution young people that the original entrance is a sacred place and should be observed as such.

From fossils embedded in the redwall limestone, scientists have determined that many prehistoric sea and land dwellers once lived in these caves. Fossils of a giant ground sloth, estimated to have lived here more than 20,000 years ago, were also discovered in the caverns. Call for hours. Fee. (928) 422-3223; www.grandcanyoncaverns.com.

To return to Flagstaff, follow old AZ 66 east to Seligman. Pick up I-40 east through Williams to Flagstaff.

worth more time:

hualapai tribe, grand canyon west and sky walk

The Hualapai tribe offers visitors a trifecta of adventure tourism fun. You can raft the Colorado River at Diamond Point, experience the beauty of a lesser-known part of the Grand

Canyon at Grand Canyon West, and take a daring walk onto the glass Sky Walk that extends 4,000 feet above the Colorado River at Eagle Point. *NOTE:* This can also be taken as part of Day Trip 01 North from Phoenix.

what to do

Hualapai River Runners. (928) 769-2636; www.grandcanyonwest.com/rafting. Take a one-day rafting trip on the Colorado River. Seasonal. Fee.

Grand Canyon West and Grand Canyon Sky Walk at Eagle Point. (888) 868-9378 or (928) 769-2636; www.grandcanyonwest.com, www.grandcanyonskywalk.com. From Flagstaff, follow I-40 west.,Take I-40 to Kingman exit. Drive north 2 miles on Stockton Hill Road. Turn right to Pierce Ferry Road 7 miles. Turn right to Diamond Bar Road for 21 miles, which ends at Grand Canyon West.

Grand Canyon West was opened to the public by the Hualapai Tribe in 1988 as a tourism destination to make this more remote section of the Grand Canyon accessible to the public. The word, *Hualapai,* translates as "People of the Tall Pines". Before reservations were established, their ancestral land stretched across more than 5 million acres of forested northern Arizona and included much of the Grand Canyon. Today the Hualapai reservation spans almost 1 million acres, and 108 miles of the Colorado River and the Grand Canyon lie within the tribal boundary. The **Grand Canyon Sky Walk** at Eagle Point is an engineering marvel that opened in 2007. The glass observation deck is suspended 4,000 feet above the Colorado River and cantilevered out over the edge of the Grand Canyon. Visitors walk out onto the glass deck and get a bird's-eye view down to the Grand Canyon and Colorado River far below. Open daily. Fee.

where to stay

Hualapai Lodge. 900 Rte. 66; (888) 868-9378 or (928) 769-2636; www.grandcanyonwest .com/lodge. From Williams, go west on I-40 to Seligman and west on US 66. This lodge is owned by the Hualapai Tribe. Visitors can see and purchase authentic artwork and enjoy scheduled Native dance and music performances. More in the style of Old Route 66 motels, the lodge is not fancy, but the Hualapai people are very hospitable. There's a full service dining room. $$.

northwest

day trip 01

northwest

>>> **the grandest canyon and grandest views:**
the south rim of the grand canyon

the south rim of the grand canyon

From Flagstaff, drive north on US 180 approximately 60 miles to Grand Canyon Village, headquarters for this most spectacular national park. All visitors to Arizona put the Grand Canyon at the top of their "must-see" list, but few realize that the Grand Canyon is actually two parks: the North Rim and the South Rim. The South Rim is closer to Phoenix, located 223 miles north of that city, and is open to tourists all year. The more rugged and remote North Rim is a 230-mile drive from the southern park. Although it is possible to "do" the South Rim of the Grand Canyon in a long day's trip starting and ending in Phoenix, the experience is exhausting. It is far better to use Flagstaff as your headquarters if you plan to see the canyon in 1 day. Better yet, stay overnight in the Grand Canyon park area.

Should you decide to see both rims, you'll be in for two distinctly different experiences. The North Rim, more than 1,000 feet higher than the South Rim, is the more remote and rugged park. It is closed from late fall to mid-spring because the roads are snowed in from about late October through mid-May. Facilities at the North Rim exist on a smaller, more rustic scale. In contrast, although the facilities at the South Rim are superb, it's often crowded during the summer.

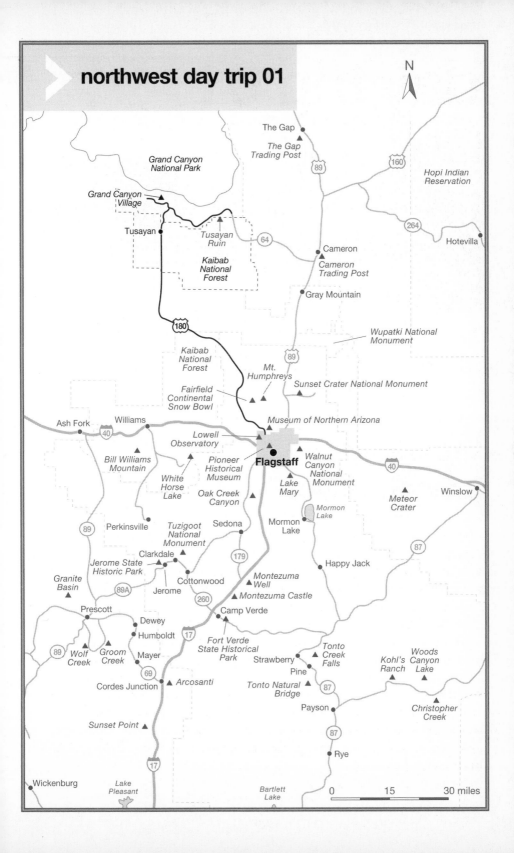

northwest day trip 01

N

The Gap
The Gap
Trading Post
89
160
Hopi Indian
Reservation

Grand Canyon
National Park
264
Hotevilla

Grand Canyon
Village
Tusayan
Tusayan
Ruin
64
Cameron
Cameron
Trading Post
Kaibab
National
Forest
Gray Mountain

Wupatki National
Monument

180
89
Kaibab
National
Forest
Mt.
Humphreys
Sunset Crater National Monument

Fairfield
Continental
Snow Bowl

Museum of Northern Arizona

Ash Fork
Williams
40
Lowell
Observatory
Walnut
Canyon
National
Monument
40
Bill Williams
Mountain
Pioneer
Historical
Museum
Flagstaff
Winslow

White
Horse
Lake
Oak Creek
Canyon
Lake
Mary
Meteor
Crater

Perkinsville
Tuzigoot
National
Monument
Sedona
Mormon
Lake
Mormon
Lake
87

Clarkdale
Happy Jack

Jerome State
Historic Park
179

Granite
Basin
89A
Cottonwood
Jerome
Montezuma
Well
Montezuma Castle
260

Prescott
Camp Verde

Dewey
Humboldt
Fort Verde
State Historical
Park
Tonto
Creek
Falls
Woods
Canyon
Lake

89
Wolf
Creek
Groom
Creek
Mayer
Strawberry
Pine
Kohl's
Ranch
69

Cordes Junction
Arcosanti
Tonto Natural
Bridge
87

Payson
Christopher
Creek

Sunset Point
87

17
Rye

Wickenburg
Lake
Pleasant
Bartlett
Lake
0   15   30 miles

a glorious and powerful place

The fascination with the Grand Canyon spans every age, nationality, and experience. The view into the chasm appears to be pure illusion, for it seems that nothing can be that deep, that mysterious, that endless. While volumes have been written about its majesty, no words or pictures can do justice to the happy shock of coming upon it. One writer notes that people who stare across and into the magnificent abyss, no matter how many pictures they've seen of it, find themselves instinctively looking back to check that the earth they're standing on is solid.

The first time I saw the Grand Canyon, our daughter was a baby. As my husband and I walked along the rim, the wind came up and her bassinet started swinging. I remember grabbing at the swinging basket to steady it, suddenly aware of the power in that chasm. Years later, we did our first trip down the Colorado River, putting in at Lee's Ferry. As the wall rose around us, I imagined how John Wesley Powell's crew must have felt as they rafted the unknown river, wondering if they would ever get out again. More recently I did women-only rim-to-rim hikes with friends, hiking down from the North Rim and up the South Rim on Bright Angel Trail. At Phantom Ranch, at the bottom of the canyon, a furry creature with a bushy tail and a taste for Power Bars decided it liked my bed. I realized once more that the canyon is a wild place.

In addition to hiking, we love to ride the rapids. My husband and I did an oar trip not long ago, camping on sandy beach beside the river and awakening in the mornings to the sound of the river rushing over rocks and the sight of towering cliffs still in shadow. On the long hike up and out, I charted our progress by noting the changing colors of the rocks on the canyon walls. When we saw the golden beige rock emerge, we knew we were getting closer to the top. I never tire of this grand and glorious place.

There are many ways to see the South Rim. You can travel on foot, on horseback, or cling to a mule. You can view the Grand Canyon from the top down—flying over it in a small plane or helicopter—or from the bottom up—riding the torrents of the Colorado River rapids. For more information on the South Rim, call the National Park Service at (928) 638-7888. During the busy tourist season (spring, summer, and early fall), you'll need reservations for either camping or lodging facilities. You must also make prior arrangements if you plan to journey into the canyon for an overnight hike or pack trip, because overnight hikers and campers must have permits. As with all national parks, there is an entrance fee. www.nps.gov/grca.

where to go

Grand Canyon IMAX Theater. Seven miles south of the South Rim on AZ 64/US 180 in Tusayan (Too-see-an); (928) 638-2468; www.explorethecanyon.com. If you haven't experienced an IMAX film, you're in for a treat. An IMAX film puts you into the action. You sit surrounded by a six-track soundtrack, looking up at a 70-foot-high screen. Even if you've seen any of the other IMAX films (they cover many subjects, from time to outer space), see this one especially if this is your first trip to the Grand Canyon. The IMAX Theater is a superb introduction to the history and geology of the Kaibab Plateau and the Grand Canyon, and it is a film that children and adults of all ages will greatly enjoy. *The Grand Canyon—The Hidden Secrets* is the most popular IMAX production shown in this country. In 34 minutes you get a crash course on the Grand Canyon and the Colorado River, and their geography, geology, history, and anthropology.

Thanks to the wonders of photographic magic, you even experience a wild river ride down the rapids of the Colorado River. The film is shown daily. Fee.

Visitor Center. In the Grand Canyon National Park, 1 mile east of Grand Canyon Village on Village Loop Drive; (928) 638-7888. This should be your first stop once you enter the park. No matter how you choose to experience the canyon, you'll get more out of it if you have an understanding of how grand it really is.

Spend some time studying the exhibits and dioramas that describe the formation of the canyon and the flora and fauna in the area. You'll find brochures and information on several self-guided walking tours that traverse the rim. Here you can also pick up trail maps for hiking into the canyon and get information on driving tours along the East Rim and West Rim drives.

East Rim Drive. A paved road leads from the visitor center past the **Yavapai Museum**, a delightful and informative geological facility, to Mather, Yaki, and Grand View Points. The road continues to Desert View, a spectacular lookout 25 miles east of Grand Canyon Village. Along the way, you may stop at any of the turnoffs to experience the panorama of the canyon. This is an especially impressive drive in the early morning hours or just before sunset, when the colors of the canyon are their richest.

West Rim Drive. This takes you past Powell Memorial and Hopi, Mohave, and Pima Points—equally outstanding places from which to observe the majesty of the canyon. This drive ends at Hermit's Rest. From April through September, the West Rim road is limited to tour buses to relieve traffic congestion and help preserve the ecological integrity of the canyon. For information about the bus tours, inquire at the visitor center.

Don't leave the visitor center without browsing through the selection of scientific and illustrated books for sale. The more you can learn about the canyon, the more you'll enjoy your visit. Even nonscientific types should know that this region encompasses five of the Northern Hemisphere's 7 ecological zones, and that no other place in the world so clearly illustrates such a vast panorama of time. Free.

El Tovar Hotel. On Village Loop Drive; (928) 638-2631; www.grandcanyonlodges.com. From the visitor center, follow Village Loop Drive west about ½ mile to the first right turn. This road takes you to the parking lot for El Tovar. Even if you do not intend to stay or eat at this hotel (see Where to Eat and Where to Stay sections), make it a point to visit this historic place. El Tovar is a rambling, wooden hotel that has long served as headquarters for activity at the South Rim. On any day, as you stand in the spacious, high-ceilinged lobby, you may hear a dozen different languages, see sunburned hikers who have just emerged from the canyon floor, listen to river rafters still riding high on their exhilaration, and see celebrities and dignitaries who have come to relax in the stately splendor afforded by this charming setting.

Bright Angel Trail. As you leave El Tovar, turn left and follow the Rim Walk toward Bright Angel Lodge. There's a sign pointing to the Bright Angel Trail, a well-maintained hiking path that twists and turns 20⁶/₁₀ miles round-trip to Phantom Ranch on the canyon floor.

For the first ½ mile, Bright Angel is gentle enough for even nonhikers to negotiate without any special equipment other than good walking shoes. However, as you peer down the trail from the rim, you'll see a splash of deep green in the distance. The green glistens against the sun-bleached yellows, oranges, and peach tones of the Grand Canyon. This is Indian Gardens, a 4⁴/₁₀-mile hike from the top. The trek to Indian Gardens takes you through manufactured tunnels and down a series of steep switchbacks. You can rest and picnic at this remarkable natural oasis, which is shaded by tall cottonwood trees. The hike to Indian Gardens is an excellent round-trip day experience that gives you a good workout and a sense of the serenity of the inner canyon.

The less ambitious may prefer a 15-minute walk down Bright Angel Trail. Go at least as far as the first tunnel or hole-in-the-rock. Remember, it will take you twice as long, or a half hour, to walk back up. Even this short excursion will give you a feeling for the grandeur of the canyon, an understanding that you can never get from standing at the rim and looking down into it.

where to eat

El Tovar Hotel. In the park on Village Loop Drive; (928) 638-2631 or (888) 297-2757; www.grandcanyonlodges.com. Count on hearty breakfasts and superb views from the dining room window. Pancakes are light and fluffy, and the syrup is hot. Lunches and dinners are more elegant. The food and the service rival those of any fine restaurant in the Phoenix or Tucson areas. During the spring, summer, and early fall, reservations are recommended for dinner. $$.

where to stay

El Tovar Hotel. In the park on Village Loop Drive; (928) 638-2631 or (888) 297-2757; www.grandcanyonlodges.com. Because this is a historic hotel, each room is different—some large and airy, others smaller—but the accommodations are uniformly charming. If you are looking for atmosphere and convenience, El Tovar, with its spacious lobby, is the optimum choice. $$.

The Grand Hotel. About 1½ miles south of the entrance to the Grand Canyon National Park on US 180/AZ 64 in Tusayan; (888) 634-7263; www.grandcanyongrandhotel.com. This newer hotel enjoys architecture reminiscent of the historic, grand hotels of the Old West. In addition to 120 fine rooms, some with balconies, the property includes an indoor pool and spa, shopping, and dining in the Canyon Star restaurant. The most unique feature, however, is the emphasis on educating visitors about the Native Americans who lived in and around the Grand Canyon before Europeans "discovered" this area. Workshops are scheduled, along with Native American dance groups, singers and drummers, storytellers, and arts and crafts demonstrations. $$.

what else to do

Colorado River trips. Motor-powered raft and rowing trips are regularly scheduled down the Colorado River during the summer months. Various kinds of boats and trips are geared to different types of travelers. You can choose anything from a rugged few weeks of boating and hiking to an exciting but still relaxing experience.

If you plan only one "outdoorsy" experience in your lifetime, this should be it. Nothing beats it. The Colorado River not only has the most rapids, but the most exciting rapids of any river, and there is only one Grand Canyon in the entire world to provide such a glorious backdrop for the thrills. If you're worried about roughing it, don't be. There are plenty of luxuries, including excellent food and even cakes baked fresh on the beach. For thrills in an incomparable setting, this trip cannot be equaled.

Would-be river rats (the local terminology for those who've run the river) should be in good physical condition. Each rafting company has its own list of requirements. Fee. For a complete listing of companies, write or call the National Park Service at the Grand Canyon. Address inquiries to the Superintendent, Grand Canyon National Park, Grand Canyon 86023, or call (928) 638-7888; www.nps.gov/grca.

Hiking and backpacking. Day hiking, whether for 1 hour or from sunrise to sunset, requires no permit. Day hikers are entirely on their own in the canyon—this means that if you plan to hike any of the trails, you are responsible for bringing your own water and allotting one-third of your time to hike down and ⅔ of your time to hike back up.

There are no loop trails for day hikers. Your hike will take you on the same trail in both directions. Great trails beckon. These include the West Rim and South Rim Trails, which are moderate-to-easy hikes, and the hike down to Indian Gardens and back, which is more strenuous. The South Kaibab Trail and Grandview Trail are both quite difficult. The Grandview Trail is unmaintained, steep, and is recommended only for experienced hikers. The Hermit Trail, like the Grandview Trail, is very strenuous, steep, and not maintained. Casual hikers should avoid both of these.

If you plan to hike into the canyon, a day hike beyond Three-Mile Resthouse is not recommended, as hikers who continue beyond this point have a much greater probability of heat-related illness. Under no circumstances should hikers attempt to hike from the rim to the river and back in 1 day. It is important, when hiking into the canyon, never to hike in the heat of the day, especially in the warmer months, and to be equipped with good hiking shoes and a hat. The Grand Canyon is a vast and wonderful natural landscape, but you must respect it. Permits and fees are required to camp below the rim; call (928)) 638-7875.

Muleback trips. Mules descend the Bright Angel Trail at the South Rim on full-day, half-day, and overnight trips. This is a strenuous trip—good physical condition is a must. A weight restriction for riders is enforced. Reservations are mandatory from May through October. Fee. For information about these excursions, call Grand Canyon National Park Lodges at (928) 638-2401.

appendix a: festivals and celebrations

january

phoenix area

Fiesta Bowl, University of Phoenix Stadium, Glendale; (800) 279-4444. This is becoming one of the major college bowls in the country, and each year attracts top university football talent.

Barrett-Jackson Classic Car Auction, Scottsdale; (480) 421-6694; www.barrett-jack son.com. Rare, historic cars—worth $100,000 and more—for sale.

FBR Open Golf Tournament, Tournament Players Course, Scottsdale; (602) 870-4431. One of the PGA Tour's top golf events, this draws the largest crowds on the tour.

february

phoenix area

Lost Dutchman Days, Apache Junction; (480) 982-3141; www.lostdutchmandays.org. A 3-day rodeo, parade, arts-and-crafts exhibit, antique car show, and carnival.

Parada del Sol, Scottsdale; (480) 945-8481. See top professional rodeo, an elaborate horse-drawn parade, and Wild West fun.

Yuma Crossing Day, Yuma; (928) 783-0071. This festival celebrates the "Crossing of the Fathers."

Quartzsite Annual Gem and Mineral Show, Quartzsite; (928) 927-5600. One of the world's largest gem and mineral shows.

tucson area

La Fiesta de Los Vaqueros, Tucson; (520) 792-1212. See the longest nonmechanized parade in the world.

Tubac Arts Festival, Tubac; (520) 398-2704. A nine-day outdoor festival featuring international craftspeople.

flagstaff area

Winterfest, Flagstaff; (928) 774-4505 or (800) 842-7293. Events include sled-dog races, llama games, cross-country and downhill skiing.

march

phoenix area

Phoenix Rodeo of Rodeos, Phoenix; (602) 254-6500. Professional cowboys compete in a national indoor rodeo.

Old Town Tempe Spring Festival of the Arts, Tempe; (480) 967-4877. Features work from national artists and craftspeople.

O'odham Day Celebration, Organ Pipe Cactus National Monument, near Ajo; (520) 387-6849. Exhibits and demonstrations illustrate traditional arts, crafts, and farming. Free.

Scottsdale Center for the Arts Annual Arts Festival, Center for the Arts, Scottsdale; (480) 994-ARTS. Rated among the top in the country, this juried fair brings 185 artists, performances, artist demonstrations, and presentations to 8 stages.

tucson area

Annual Civil War battle reenactment at Picacho Peak State Park; (520) 466-3183 or (602) 542-4174.

Tombstone Territorial Days, Tombstone; (520) 457-2211. Shoot-outs, the Arizona Firehose Cart Championship, and a pet parade make this fun.

april

phoenix area

Arid Land Plant Show, Superior; (520) 689-2811. Held at the Boyce Thompson Southwestern Arboretum, this show features drought-resistant trees, shrubs, cacti, and succulents.

Heard Museum Indian Fair, Phoenix; (602) 252-8848. Stroll around the museum grounds and see dances, arts, crafts, and exhibits from many Arizona Native American tribes.

tucson area

San Xavier (Ha-veer) Pageant and Fiesta, San Xavier Mission; (520) 792-1212 or (520) 294-2624. This event is held the Friday after Easter and features more than 100 Native American dancers celebrating the history of the mission. The Tohono O'odham Indians host a food and crafts market.

Fiesta de la Placita, Tucson; (520) 792-1212 or (800) 638-8350. Enjoy a full-fledged Mexican fiesta.

may

phoenix area

George Phippen Memorial Invitational Western Art Show and Sale, Prescott; (928) 778-1385. This show, held over Memorial Day weekend, attracts western artists from all over the country.

Annual Square Dance Festival, Prescott; (928) 445-2000.

flagstaff area

Bill Williams Rendezvous Days, Williams; (928) 635-0273. This festival is held on Memorial Day weekend and includes an authentic Mountain Men Rendezvous.

june

phoenix area

June Bug Blues Festival, Payson; (928) 474-4515. All kinds of bands, including bluegrass, country, and buck-dancing, compete in this nationally recognized music festival.

International Innertube Race, Parker; (928) 669-2174. People in outlandish costumes converge on the Colorado River to compete in a 7-mile race.

july

phoenix area

Prescott Frontier Days and Rodeo, Prescott; (928) 445-2000 or (928) 455-3103. See a glittering parade and rugged professional rodeo on Fourth of July weekend.

august

phoenix area

Payson Annual Continuous Rodeo, Payson; (928) 474-4515. The world's oldest continuously held professional rodeo.

flagstaff area

Arizona Cowpunchers' Reunion and Old Timers' Rodeo, Williams; (928) 635-0273. Real, working cowboys compete in all events.

september

phoenix area

Annual State Championship Old Time Fiddlers Contest, Payson; (928) 474-4515. Fiddlers from all over the state compete with their fanciest fingerwork.

National Indian Day, Parker; (928) 669-2174. Area tribes converge for traditional games, singing, dances, and other activities in Manataba Park the last Friday of September and the following Saturday.

october

tucson area

Helldorado Days, Tombstone; (520) 457-2211. Shoot-outs, a fast-draw contest, and a parade add to the general Wild West craziness.

november

phoenix area

Fountain Festival of the Arts, Fountain Hills; (480) 837-1654; www.fountainhillschamber .com. Enjoy this 3-day juried show and sale.

Annual Swiss Village Christmas Lighting, Payson; (928) 474-4515.

december

Here is a sampling of what happens during the holiday season. For a more complete listing, consult the city chamber of commerce or call the Arizona Office of Tourism at (602) 364-3700 or visit the website, www.arizonaguide.com.

phoenix area

Old Town Tempe Fall Festival of the Arts, Tempe; (480) 967-7891 or (480) 967-4877. A bazaar of arts, crafts, and unusual collectibles.

Pueblo Grande Indian Market, Phoenix; (602) 495-0901. Held at South Mountain Park Activity Center, this market attracts more than 450 Native American artists.

Victorian Christmas at Heritage Square, Phoenix; (602) 262-5071.

Wickenburg Annual Cowboy Christmas Cowboy Poets Gathering, Wickenburg; (928) 684-5479. Held at the Community Center and Desert Caballeros Western Museum.

Christmas Parade and Courthouse Lighting, Prescott; (520) 445-2000. The entire town turns out for the parade and comes to the square to see the courthouse blaze with colorful lights.

tucson area

Annual 4th Avenue Winter Street Fair, Tucson; (520) 624-5004 or (800) 933-2477. This arts-and-crafts and performance fair is held downtown.

Luminaria Night, Tucson; (520) 624-1817. Mariachis, bands, Yaqui Indian dancers, and other musicians add to the festivities at the Tucson Botanical Garden.

Tumacacori Fiesta, Tumacacori; (520) 398-2341. Enjoy folk dancing, music, food, and crafts from many of Santa Cruz County's cultural groups.

flagstaff area

Christmas Boat Parade of Lights, Lake Havasu; (520) 855-2178. Gaily decorated house-boats glide across Lake Havasu.
Holiday boat parades also are held on Lake Powell, Lake Mead, and Lake Mohave. For dates and times, check with the local chambers of commerce at Page, (520) 645-2741; Bullhead City, (520) 754-4121; and Parker, (520) 669-2174.

Sedona Annual Festival of Lights, Sedona; (520) 282-4838 or (877) 386-8687. Entertainment and 6,000 luminarias light up Tlaquepaque.

Annual Christmas Arts and Crafts Fair, Window Rock; (928) 871-7303 or (928) 871-6376. Sponsored by the Navajo Nation Library.

appendix b:
native american
reservations

Arizona is home to 21 Native American tribes that represent more than 160,000 people. A total of 20 reservations cover more than nineteen million acres. Visitors who wish to travel on Native American reservations may do so without prior permission. If, however, you want to know where to go to buy arts or crafts or observe dances, celebrations, or rodeos, call ahead or contact the tribal office for dates, times, and locations. Because tribes are known for their traditional crafts, these are noted below. However, many tribes have invested in a variety of other businesses, making traditional crafts less available to tourists. Today, tribes and Indian nations own shopping malls, manufacturing facilities, casinos, hotels, and golf courses.

Ak-Chin Reservation, 56 miles south of Phoenix in Pinal County; (520) 568-2227; www .itcaonline.com. The Ak-Chin tribe is noted for basketry.

Camp Verde Reservation, 94 miles north of Phoenix in Yavapai County; (928) 567-3649; www.yavapai-apache.org. This reservation includes Montezuma Castle National Monument and Montezuma Well. Basketry is the major art form for the people of the Yavapai-Apache nation.

Cocopah East and West Reservation, 12 miles southwest of Yuma in Yuma County; (928) 627-2102; www.cocopah.com. This tribe is well known for its intricate beadwork.

Colorado River Reservation, 189 miles west of Phoenix in Yuma County; (928) 669-9211; www.itcaonline.com/tribes_colriver.html. Collectors may want to buy baskets, beadwork, and Native American motif wall clocks made by these tribes.

Fort Apache Reservation, 194 miles northeast of Phoenix in Apache, Gila, and Navajo Counties; (928) 338-4346; www.wmat.nsn.us. The White Mountain Apache Tribe owns and operates Apache Sunrise Resort, a ski lodge and resort facility. The people create excellent beadwork and the highly prized "Burden Baskets," wonderfully woven baskets that are trimmed with leather thongs and silver metal "bells."

Fort McDowell Reservation, 36 miles northeast of Phoenix in Maricopa County; (480) 837-5121; www.ftmcdowell.org. Like other urban tribes, the Fort McDowell Yavapai Tribe has a diversified economy that includes tourism, agriculture, and industry. Basketry is a specialty.

Fort Mojave Reservation, 236 miles northwest of Phoenix in Mohave County; (760) 629-4591; www.itcaonline.com/tribes_mojave.html. This reservation borders Arizona, Nevada, and California; tribal headquarters are located in California. The Fort Mojave Indians are noted for their beadwork.

Fort Yuma-Quenchan, 185 miles southwest of Phoenix in Yuma County; (760) 572-1242; www.itcaonline.com. This reservation borders Arizona and California. Collectors may buy beadwork and other artifacts.

Gila (Hee-la) River Reservation, 40 miles south of Phoenix in Maricopa and Pinal Counties; (520) 562-3311; www.gric.nsn.us. Pima basketry and Maricopa pottery are prized traditional crafts of the Gila River Indians. The tribe is also a diversified community that includes a fine museum and resort.

Havasupai (Have-a-sue-pie) Reservation, at the bottom of the Grand Canyon via an 8-mile trail from Hilltop to Supai; (928) 448-2961 or (928) 448-2731; www.havasupaitribe .com. The Havasupais produce basketry and beadwork.

Hopi (Hoe-pee) Reservation, 323 miles northeast of Phoenix in Coconino and Navajo Counties; (928) 448-2731; www.hopi.nsn.us. The Hopi produce an assortment of art and collectibles. Hopi are best known for hand-carved and painted kachina dolls, which are spirits of the gods worshipped by this tribe, and are leaders in silver and gold jewelry, crafts, and pottery.

Hualapai (Wall-pie) Reservation, 252 miles northwest of Phoenix in Coconino, Yavapai, and Mohave Counties; (520) 769-2216; www.itcaonline.com. Dolls and basketry are the primary art forms of this tribe.

Kaibab-Paiute (Kigh-bab–Pie-ute) Reservation, 398 miles north of Phoenix in Mohave County; (928) 643-7245; www.itcaonline.com. This tribe specializes in coiled, shallow baskets known as "wedding baskets."

Navajo Reservation, 356 miles northeast of Phoenix in Apache, Coconino, and Navajo Counties; (928) 871-4941 or (928) 871-6352; www.navajonationparks.org. Best known for their museum-quality, hand-woven rugs and blankets, the Navajo also create magnificent silver crafts and some basketry.

Pascua-Yaqui Reservation, 135 miles southwest of Phoenix (adjacent to the city of Tucson) in Pima County; (520) 883-5000; www.pascuayaquitribe.org. Collectors appreciate the "Deer Dance" statues and cultural paintings created by the children of the tribe.

Salt River Pima-Maricopa Indian Community Reservation, 15 miles northeast of Phoenix adjacent to the city of Scottsdale; (480) 850-8000; www.saltriver.pima-maricopa .nsn.us. The Salt River Pima and Maricopa craftspeople are known for their basketry and pottery.

San Carlos Reservation, 115 miles northeast of Phoenix in Gila and Graham Counties; (928) 475-2331; www.itcaonline.com. Along with basketry and pottery, the San Carlos Apache Tribe craftspeople create unusual jewelry set with peridots, pale green semiprecious gemstones found in that area.

Tohono O'odham Reservation, 136 miles south of Phoenix (adjacent to the city of Tucson); (520) 383-2221; www.itcaonline.com. This reservation stretches across Maricopa, Pinal, and Pima Counties. Best known for its distinctive and valuable basketry, the tribe also produces fine pottery.

Tonto-Apache Reservation, 94 miles northeast of Phoenix in Gila County; (928) 474-5000; www.itcaonline.com/tribes_tonto.html. Native crafts of basketry and beadwork are emphasized.

Yavapai-Prescott Reservation, 103 miles northwest of Phoenix in Yavapai County; (928) 445-8790; www.ypit.com. Native baskets may be purchased.

NOTE: The San Juan Southern Paiute Tribe and the Zuni are both recognized as Arizona tribes. Zuni have some ancestral land in Arizona. Neither tribe has a reservation.

appendix c: arizona climate

Arizona is a land of dramatic contrasts, as varied in its climate as in its beauty. Temperatures and rainfall vary tremendously throughout the three main topographical areas within the state, for extremes in elevation are matched by extremes in temperatures. These three topographical areas can roughly be divided as follows: the desert mountains and valleys, elevations of 1,500 to 2,500 feet; the high mountain plateau, with average elevations of 5,000 to 7,000 feet; and the mountains, with peaks from 9,000 to 12,000 feet.

Temperatures can range as much as 60 degrees in a single day due to the dry air, but generally average temperatures are governed by elevation. As a rule of thumb, figure on a 3½-degree Fahrenheit difference for every 1,000-foot change in altitude.

Sunshine in Phoenix averages 86 percent of the possible amount, ranging from a minimum monthly average of 77 percent in January and December to a maximum of 94 percent in June.

Elevation and season also affect the amount of rain and snow that Arizona receives. These amounts vary dramatically. On the average, some desert areas have only 3 to 4 inches of rain a year, while certain mountain areas receive up to 30 inches. Pacific storms cause most of the rainfall from November through March, with winter snowfall totals sometimes reaching 100 inches on the highest mountains. Summer rainfall begins in July and extends through mid-September, when moisture-bearing winds from the southeast and south cause the Arizona monsoon. The thunderstorms that result can cause strong winds, blinding dust storms, and heavy rainfall. Heavy thunderstorms can cause flash flooding, and while major flooding is rare, it can—and does—happen.

Dry spells can last for many months, but count on April through June to be the driest part of the year. However, when thunderstorms occur, they can be wild. The damaging winds accompanying these storms are usually straight-line winds that can move in at speeds upward of 75 miles per hour.

index